PEOPLE'S SELF-DEVELOPMENT

MD ANISUR RAHMAN studied at the University of Dhaka before proceeding to Harvard University, where he completed his doctorate in Economics in 1962. His subsequent distinguished academic career has included holding the chair of Economics at the University of Islamabad (1967–70) and subsequently at the University of Dhaka (1970–75), as well as Visiting Fellowships at the East West Centre of the University of Hawaii, at Yale University, and at the Institute of Development Studies, Sussex University. From 1972 to 1974, he served as a member of the Bangladesh Planning Commission. In 1977, he was appointed as a Senior Research Officer at the ILO where he coordinated its Programme on Participatory Organisations of the Rural Poor (PORP) until his retirement in 1991.

He is the author of numerous publications in both Economics and Participatory Development. In addition to articles which have appeared in a wide range of scholarly economic journals, including *Oxford Economic Papers*, the *Quarterly Journal of Economics* and the *Review of Economics and Statistics*, he has also contributed to many development journals such as *Development Dialogue*, *IFDA Dossier* and the *Community Development Journal*. He is co-editor, with Orlando Fals Borda, of *Action and Knowledge: Breaking the Monopoly with Participatory Action Research* (New York, New Horizons Press, 1990).

MD ANISUR RAHMAN

People's Self-Development

Perspectives on Participatory Action Research

A Journey Through Experience

ZED BOOKS

London & New Jersey

UNIVERSITY PRESS LIMITED

Dhaka

People's Self-Development was first published in Bangladesh
by Mohiuddin Ahmed, The University Press Limited,
Red Crescent Building, 114 Motijheel Commercial Area,
P O Box 2611, Dhaka 1000, Bangladesh, and in the rest of the world
by Zed Books Ltd, 7 Cynthia Street, London N1 9JF, UK, and
165 First Avenue, Atlantic Highlands, New Jersey 07716, USA,
in 1993.

Cover designed by Andrew Corbett.
Typeset by EMS Photosetters, Thorpe Bay, Essex.
Printed and bound in the United Kingdom
by Biddles Ltd, Guildford and King's Lynn.

A catalogue record for this book
is available at the British Library

US CIP data is available from
the Library of Congress

ISBN 1 85649 079 3 Hb
ISBN 1 85649 080 7 Pb

In Bangladesh
ISBN 984 05 1207 2

Contents

In development, a new paradigm is taking shape. The main actors are the people. They are becoming the subjects of development – their own development. This is having an impact on the whole society. We 'outsiders' appreciate their potential, their power, their initiative and experiences. We can only be their assistants, for we will never be able to fully comprehend their real situation. The best we could hope to do is to choose to stand on their side in order to achieve an appreciation of their perspective, to complement their struggle; sharing with them what we have and what we are.

Source Seri Phongphit, 'Development Paradigm – Strategy, activities and reflection', *RUDOC News*, Vol. 4, No. 3–4, July–December 1989.

Acknowledgements and Credits

The author would like to thank the following for generous permission to reproduce various papers in this book:

Chapter 1: *The Weekly Wave*, Dhaka, 3 November 1974.

Chapter 2: First published in J. Galtung et al, (eds), *Self-Reliance: A Strategy for Development* (London: Bogle, l'Ouverture Publications, 1980). Copyright held by the IEUD, 24 Rue Rothschild, 1202 Geneva, Switzerland.

Chapter 3: *Rural Development Participation Review*, Vol. III, No. 1, Fall 1981.

Chapter 4: *Rural Development Communications Bulletin*, March 1987.

Chapter 5: This appeared in two parts: in *Praxis*, Vol. I, No. 4. March 1987; and *IFDA Dossier*, No. 50, November–December 1985.

Chapter 6: 'The theory and practice of participatory action research' (WEP 10/WP.29). Copyright 1983, International Labour Organisation, Geneva.

Chapter 8: 'Glimpses of the "Other Africa"' (WEP 10/WP.48). Copyright 1988, International Labour Organisation, Geneva.

Chapter 9: Paper presented at the ILO Workshop on the Inter-relationship between Macro-economic Policies and Rural Development, Geneva, December 1989 under the title 'Participation of the Rural Poor in Development.' Copyright 1989, International Labour Organisation, Geneva.

Chapter 10: *Journal of the Asiatic Society of Bangladesh* (Humanities), Vol. XXXIV, No. 2, December 1989.

Chapter 12: Bangladesh Economics Association, in preparation.

Introduction

Personal context of the journey

This volume presents the essence of my experience and philosophical–methodological thinking on 'participatory development' or, as my conceptualisation developed, on 'people's self-development', over the last seventeen–eighteen years, starting with my service in the first Bangladesh Planning Commission (1972–4) and ending with my last months in the International Labour Office (ILO) in Geneva. The publication of this volume coincides with the conclusion of a major phase of my explorations in this field, where I was in close contact with activist and intellectual trends worldwide, as the Coordinator of the ILO's Programme on Participatory Organisations of the Rural Poor (popularly known as PORP) which I started in 1977.

Work of this nature is stimulated by personal urges as well as by intellectual challenges. Both are stimulated in their turn through dialectical interaction with real life's initiatives, in this case at the grassroots level. The purpose of this Introduction is to acquaint the reader with this personal and intellectual context of my explorations.

Like many other of my compatriots, I had been inspired by popular mobilisations for social reconstruction and development in my country after its independence in 1971. I saw a breakthrough in the development status of the country to be possible only through a national mobilisation for popular initiatives; on a smaller scale, such initiatives were demonstrating their potential for solving people's problems and creating a spirit of personal sacrifice for collective objectives, challenging the premises of received economics and development thinking which were pushing us towards humiliating dependence on external 'assistance' rather than indicating a viable path for social progress.

As a teacher, I had been stimulated by demands from sections of the nation's student community for radical reform to integrate educational processes with processes of life. I launched in 1973, in collaboration with the then Secretary of Agriculture who was a passionate believer in self-reliant rural development,[1] a nationwide programme for students to go to the villages, live with peasants and farmers, work with them in the field and discuss their problems with them. In connection with my field visits in this programme in which about 1,400 students from 16 institutions participated, I had the opportunity to know and study many ongoing popular and youth initiatives aiming at community mobilisation for reconstruction and development.

I struggled unsuccessfully to use my new learning in my work in the Planning Commission where we were hopeless captives of teachings irrelevant to the support and stimulation of the constructive potential of society. I resigned from the Planning Commission in October 1974.

Most of the popular initiatives in the country faded, died or were repressed as reactionary forces gradually consolidated their hold on society's commanding structures. Personal circumstances caused my exit from the country in mid-1975, but I was able to continue pursuing my interest in popular mobilisation. For brief periods in 1975 and 1976 I worked for the United Nations Asian Development Institute (ADI) in Bangkok, collaborating on a joint publication 'Towards a theory of rural development' (Haque *et al.*, 1977) – a rejection of conventional rural development approaches and a vision, with some methodological approaches, of participatory rural development; I worked for one year (1975–6) at the United Nations Conference on Trade and Development (UNCTAD) in Geneva where I was able to develop further my analysis of self-reliant development; I spent another year at the University of Sussex from where I visited the Bhoomi Sena movement in Maharastra, India, along with three other South Asian colleagues in a continuation of our ADI work.

Joining the ILO in 1977, I have had the great good fortune to be able to pursue the same interest, linking up with significant trends in the grassroots movement in several countries; assisting such movements in linking with each other within and across countries and jointly reflecting on their approaches, experiences and visions; initiating methodological experiments in field animation work and in the sensitisation of animators; linking with intellectual trends working with popular movements; and in synthesising and conceptualising from the ongoing experiences. Thanks to an admirable gesture on the part of the ILO in response to my request, I was also able for a number of years since 1984 to obtain unpaid time to visit some projects in the new grassroots work in my own country in the programmes of so-called non-governmental organisations (NGOs).

Intellectual concerns, influences and collaboration

Socialism was the official ideology of newly independent Bangladesh. Many literate elements from among the freedom fighters coming from many walks of life – teachers, students, journalists, government officials, police and the army – publicly expressed aspirations to social equality and social mobilisation in a framework of austerity within a vision of socialism. By my own calling as both a teacher and a planner I was challenged to respond: to promote our own understanding of socialism we initiated seminar programmes on the subject for the faculty and for the students in the Economics Department in the University of Dhaka.

In my own contribution to the faculty seminars I raised as a basic problem for a transition to socialism the question of a 'consciousness gap' between revolutionary intellectuals, who usually provide leadership in socialist transition, and the 'masses' (Rahman, 1985). I suggested that socialism would be alienating if this consciousness gap could not be closed. This problem has remained one of my central concerns throughout my explorations of participatory or people's self-development.

As a planner, I saw the impossibility of solving the problem of mass poverty in the 'short run'; hence I initially conceptualised the social problem as that of taking society through a long and hard journey to the realisation of its aspirations within the framework of a stable social order. (This conceptualisation has changed its character in recent years into a creativist view of development, as noted subsequently.) My prescription at that time of 'shared austerity' and social mobilisation went unheeded at the government level. But I received confirmation of my convictions in an extraordinary popular movement in the northern part of Bangladesh.

Nur Muhammad Momtajuddin, a government agricultural officer and former freedom fighter, initiated a 'self-reliance' movement in 1973 in the district of Rangpur which spread to sixty villages in a year and a half. Under this initiative, villagers met in mass meetings to take an oath to reject any form of grant or relief from outside, and mobilised themselves to launch collective economic and social programmes. The rejection of relief was unshaken even in the devastating flood and famine of 1974 in which Rangpur was one of the hardest-hit districts: these sixty self-reliant villages announced a famine resistance programme that emphasised resistance to all forms of *relief*. The villagers pooled the surpluses of the well-to-do to provide the most acutely distressed families with one meal a day in return for dignified labour (Rahman, 1977). I visited this movement frequently, taking inspiration and pride from its demonstration of the highest in the human spirit, and spent long hours with Momtajuddin discussing our views of how to reverse the 'basket case' image of the nation.

While participating in the collaborative work for the Asian Development

Institute I benefited from the refreshing attitude of Niranjan Mehta of India, with his constant questioning of received doctrines. Then director of the National Institute of Bank Management in Bombay, Mehta was directing a programme of sending 'spearhead teams' to villages to promote collective initiatives by the underprivileged classes. The question of sensitising such cadres emerged in our dialogues as critical. At this stage I also met G. V. S. de Silva of Sri Lanka, a lone radical intellectual–activist with whom we struck a philosophical and intellectual chord. Through contact with Mehta we went to see the Bhoomi Sena movement in India.

The validity of self-reliance as a primary human urge, a concept first suggested to me by the Rangpur self-reliance movement, was further confirmed by Bhoomi Sena, whose leaders told us that 'no outsider will tell us what we should do'. I was enlightened and profoundly influenced by the experience of seeing the proud *and relaxed* assertion of self-determination of the mobilised *adivasis* (so-called tribals), in spite of their extreme material poverty, when I stayed with them in their homes, and went without food when they did. The immediate question was: can outsiders be of any help at all to such people and such movements?

Bhoomi Sena answered this question. They had needed a pedagogy to promote collective thinking and action by the adivasis, and a few social activists led by Dutta Savle, an educationist–activist, had helped them find it. The essence of this pedagogy is presented in discussions and references to Bhoomi Sena in this volume. This suggested to us that there was a role for *carefully conceptualised methodological work*, whether by outsiders or insiders, designed to stimulate people's collective self-inquiry without teaching them: such work would be highly sensitive and culture-dependent, hence not 'trainable' by any blueprint. However, individual workers could improve their methods by having the opportunity of engaging in appropriate dialogue and interacting during field work. We also recognised that our question reflected a sharp contrast to the orthodox left (Leninist) conception of revolutionary intellectuals 'indoctrinating' the working class and training 'cadres' for this purpose with a doctrinaire approach. This conception and tradition of attempting to promote socialism disturbed us deeply.

Another crucial question of political theory arose out of our dialogue with Bhoomi Sena. When asked about their attitude towards a leading macropolitical party of the orthodox left tradition, the Bhoomi Sena leaders replied that they considered it to be an 'ally' because it was also on the side of the oppressed classes, but that they would not join it themselves as it imposed its ideas on the people. The question of the 'consciousness gap' again, but possibly in reverse this time: whose consciousness was more 'advanced'?

We spent long hours with Dutta Savle, the self-liquidating 'guru' of

Bhoomi Sena who was progressively reducing his involvement with the movement now that its own leadership was becoming able to handle the pedagogical tasks. Savle's key word for the people was 'assertion'; and in his conception this act started with assertion by the people of their own 'truth', i.e. their own 'reality' as they perceived it. This was a major challenge to received epistemological beliefs.

Savle's pedagogy, although independently developed, had the same conceptual basis as Paulo Freire's conscientisation. Reading the Freirian literature, I found in it questions and statements on conventional approaches to education and training which struck a chord with my own thoughts as they were now evolving, and which naturally influenced my subsequent intellectual and methodological explorations and conceptualisations. The participatory development movement as a whole has, of course, been profoundly influenced by the Freirian concept of conscientisation – self-reflected learning as opposed to 'teaching' – although methodological approaches to conscientisation vary, as does the philosophical–ideological basis of conscientisation work in which Freire's own position has also been evolving.

After starting my work in the ILO I linked up with another trend in the participatory development movement – the so-called 'participatory (action) research' (PR or PAR) movement. The International Council for Adult Education (ICAE, Toronto) led by Budd Hall played a key role in promoting its conceptualisation and global networking. The movement also drew inspiration from Freirian work, and naturally had much in common with my own emerging concerns and ideas. With PORP I became a part of this movement. I collaborated with members of ICAE's network to promote some pioneering PR processes which convinced me of the ability of 'uneducated' or 'semi-educated' people to develop systematically scientific collective knowledge. One of these PR experimentations was a project Orlando Fals Borda and his colleagues were involved in, in Colombia, Nicaragua and Mexico (Fals Borda, 1985). I entered into a continuing intellectual collaboration and dialogue with Fals Borda, and at his invitation attempted a systematic theoretical–epistemological conceptualisation of PAR for the World Congress of Sociology in 1982.

On the basis of my growing convictions I persuaded PAR itself to transcend some of its assumptions and seek to promote as its primary aim not a research *partnership* with the people but *people's own research and own praxis*. In this way, we sought to unify the priorities of PAR with those of the Bhoomi Sena type for helping people to develop their intellectual capabilities and collective self-knowledge and to assert themselves as equals with any other intellectual trend. From this arose the concept of 'animation' work and of the 'animator' which were defined for PORP in two works by Susanta Tilakaratna (1985 and 1987). We started seeing animation work as aimed at changing the *relations of knowledge* and as a fundamentally important task in promoting what I started calling *people's self-development*.

My collaboration with Tilakaratna, who is coordinating the outstanding animation programme of the Participatory Institute for Development Alternatives (PIDA) in Sri Lanka, has been close and continuing. PIDA's work grew out of the 'Change Agents Programme' in Sri Lanka which was conceived and initiated in 1977 by G. V. S. de Silva in close collaboration with Niranjan Mehta on the basis of inspiration from Bhoomi Sena. In this, animators were trained successfully by dialogical methods without teaching. The experiment was repeated subsequently and just as successfully by Tilakaratna in Tanzania for PORP. Encouraged, we now sought to conceptualise an approach to the training of animators and their trainers through processes of collective search and self-discovery, leading them to become 'animated' themselves by experiencing a fulfilment which, rather than any knowledge gained from such processes, they would want to pass on to those whom they are in turn to animate.

Meanwhile, visiting grassroots work in Bangladesh I was worried by the negative, external-delivery orientation of some popular struggles, and I had started thinking of the increasing urgency of a creativist development philosophy. As a corollary, I had also started to question the 'ideology' of identifying people primarily by their economic status, recognising my own careless uses of the word 'poor'. I told a gathering of about 2,000 villagers in a review seminar in 1987 of the Organisation of Associations for Progress (ORAP) in Matabeleland, Zimbabwe, that the villagers in the ORAP movement were not poor as they were showing the wealth of human creativity (Rahman, 1987). I was deeply moved thereafter as villagers came to me privately to thank me for saying that they were not poor, as if I had helped to lift a deeply pressing burden from their backs.

Tracing the creativist view of development to Marx, and therefore to the philosophical roots of socialism, and recognising Mao Tse-tung's effort in China as its best application this century, we are challenged to understand why orthodox approaches to socialism cannot realise or sustain this vision of a self-mobilised society. This makes us review some of the standard premises of Marxism, and also calls for a theory of organic vanguards (an extension of Gramsci's concept of the organic intellectual) to represent the people's deeply held wish to transform society, as opposed to Lenin's theory of revolutionary intellectuals as the vanguards of social change not necessarily rooted in the people's lives or in popular initiatives.

It is sadly revealing that some of the great experiments in socialism are swinging away from 'socialist fundamentalism' towards 'market fundamentalism' rather than questioning how socialism was misunderstood; also that the leaders who are dismantling 'socialism' seem incapable of inviting the people to participate for once in an intellectual search for an answer, and to articulate their own vision of the kind of society they want beyond a mere ballot-box democracy. Such is the strength of hierarchical thinking and institutions which are at the root of the 'consciousness gap'. This calls for a paradigm shift in development thinking and the philosophy of human relations rather than variations in experiments in social engineering within essentially the same development paradigm.

In recent years we have been collaborating more with grassroots work in Africa. The traditions of cooperation are still alive in many African societies where attempts at modernisation have not penetrated so deeply as to destroy them, and where community structures are less polarised. The task of animation in such societies has thus been more to strengthen and dynamise the already existing spirit of *solidarity* by encouraging the people to look into their own traditions, rather than to regenerate this spirit. The assertion of people's indigenous culture and the use of its positive elements as a developmental force are salient features of African grassroots mobilisation, and this has been repeatedly asserted in many forums and conversations by Sithembiso Nyoni, the coordinator of ORAP in Zimbabwe. From this we learn that development need not mean sacrificing the best of popular values in order to embrace those through which some other societies have advanced from a material point of view. Our work has entered into the realisation that culture is in a sense the central tool for domination and must be resisted with an *alternative culture*, concerning not only people but also nature (in response to the ecological crisis). Much more work needs to be done to illuminate this aspect of people's self-development.

We are also left with the challenge of articulating a macropolitical theory of social change with organic vanguards. But we cannot respond to this challenge except by matching our own steps as social researchers *organically* with the grassroots movement which is still far from solving this question in its own context. One therefore has to wait, aware that humankind will only survive, and preserve the spirit which distinguishes it from other species, if the attempt of the grassroots movement to assert this spirit is successful.

The papers in this volume

The above is but a brief account of how I came to question the conventional orthodoxies in economics and development thinking and practice of both the 'right' and 'left' varieties and discovered new intellectual challenges in walking with grassroots movements. The papers in this volume will take the reader through my praxis in greater detail, including the field experiences which have been critical in providing the stimulus for my theoretical thinking. The papers have been presented in the order in which they were written, naturally the most logical way to trace the evolution of my praxis.

However, each paper is self-contained (accounts of field experiences in two papers have been deleted to avoid major duplication), and they can be read independently of each other in any order. Representing as they do an evolution rather than constituting a 'treatise', the papers overlap in some respects, as well as presenting their own individual features which may not necessarily relate to each other with precise consistency.

Chapter 1 reconstructs my farewell address to the Bangladesh Planning Commission in which in an informal invocation I rejected the conventional approach to planning. Chapter 2 represents an attempt to understand some conceptual questions on self-reliant development at an early stage of my journey. Chapter 3 reflects on some dimensions of people's participation in the Bhoomi Sena movement. Chapter 4 is an account of an experiment under PORP in initial animation work in four *barangays* in the Philippines which has subsequently become independent of PORP in a significant nationwide programme. Chapter 5 presents field observations, and reflections on them, of some organising work with the rural landless in Bangladesh.

Chapter 6 presents my first formal theoretical reflection on the standpoint of participatory action research, on the question of social transformation and the epistemology of knowledge generation, based on practical experiences in PORP and intellectual interactions with the wider PAR movement. Chapter 7 presents further field observations from Bangladesh, and in Chapter 8 we travel to Africa to see some of its grassroots work and present some reflections on them.

The last four chapters are attempts to look at the whole experience of this journey and beyond it. Chapter 9 is a comprehensive review of PORP's work and experience until the end of 1989. Chapter 10 presents a creativist view of development in opposition to the consumerist view, and reflects upon the experience and premises of socialism. Chapter 11 brings together the qualitative dimensions of social development embodied in a vision of a participatory society. The final chapter draws the contours of the alternative development paradigm that are emerging from the practice and thinking in people's self-development.

Further acknowledgements

While I must take formal responsibility for whatever is presented in these chapters, it should be clear from the foregoing that my experience, understanding, philosophy and conceptualisation have evolved in close intellectual (and sometimes emotional) contact with many, many persons, groups, organisations and trends all over the world, from the grassroots up to higher-level intellectual and bureaucratic groups and structures. I am not able to separate my personal contribution from the contributions of a wider collective search on a global scale for a way to conceive and promote the fundamental human right of today's underprivileged people to mobilise themselves for a collective assertion of their humanity.

Besides the influences and collaborations mentioned above, I am indebted to many other colleagues and friends for intellectual stimulation, and material and moral support for a pursuit which has naturally encountered resistances. Dharam Ghai as the Chief of the ILO's Rural Employment Policies Branch (EMP/RU) in the Employment and Development Department (EMPLOI) was instrumental in bringing me to the ILO and letting me singlemindedly pursue my own interests. My constant intellectual association with him has challenged me to keep trying to clarify my philosophical standpoint amidst so many trends which claim to be promoting people's participation. Zubeida Ahmad, to whom I directly reported in EMP/RU in the initial years, was a great source of moral support and shielded me from awkward bureaucratic questioning of my pursuits. Surendra K. Jain, as the Deputy Director-General of the ILO for technical matters for the first ten years after I joined, gave me strategic support when I got into more serious problems. Peggy Rada in EMPLOI was a staunch ally of PORP and helped to smooth many procedural frictions. And the warm encouragement and support I always received from Jack Martin as the Director of EMPLOI from 1981 to 1987 are never to be forgotten. Altogether, I worked with an amazing 'hierarchy' in my first decade at the ILO without ever feeling that I was in a hierarchy – implying that our vision of a hierarchy-free alternative development paradigm may not be an altogether impractical one!

Among other colleagues in EMP/RU, Philippe Egger started assisting PORP in 1983 and progressively 'asserted' himself and seized many of its initiatives, and gave me a comradeship from which I have been much enriched. In particular, it was through his work for PORP with grassroots trends in so-called Francophone Africa that I learnt so much about these trends. Jean Majeres, Ajit Ghose, Peter Peek and Hamid Tabatabai, though working in the conventional paradigm, were always ready to read PORP's works and my writings and offer constructive comments.

Outside EMP/RU in the ILO, Dennis Hodsdon of the Workers' Education Unit gave my work solid support even as a tough trade unionist, and I had the privilege of working closely with him in efforts to move ILO policy in the direction of participatory development. Zafar Shaheed of the Industrial Relations Department provided me with the intellectual stimulus to check my thoughts, and also gave great personal release for my stresses. And Josephine Karavasil, now Chief of the ILO's editorial branch, went out of her way to encourage my writing even though their sensitive nature precluded much of them from her official jurisdiction.

While working in the ILO I was fortunate to have two secretaries, Lynda Pond and Evelyn Ralph, who provided me with more than first-rate secretarial services: they personally identified with PORP.

All the chapters in this book except the first two were written while I was employed by the ILO, and Chapters 6, 8 and 9 were originally printed by the ILO. I am grateful to the ILO for allowing their publication in this volume.

Outside the ILO, Jan Bertelling and Willem Veenstra of the Netherlands Ministry of Development Cooperation supported a number of PORP's field experiments, offering genuine solidarity over and above the customary donor–recipient relations. Marc Nerfin of the International Foundation for Development Alternatives gave my work and writing constant encouragement.

Finally, the present volume owes its life to the insistence of another stimulating colleague, Peter Oakley of the University of Reading, who insisted that I bring out a collection of my writings.

And to my wife Dora, and daughters Lita and Rubina, for forgiving my failings at home when I became engrossed, excited or frustrated in my work, my debt is of a different order.

Note

1. Mahboob Alam Chashi, who had become a social worker with the slogan 'transform the beggar's hands into a worker's tools'.

References

Fals Borda, Orlando (1985) *Knowledge and People's Power, Lessons with Peasants in Nicaragua, Mexico and Colombia*, New Delhi: Indian Social Institute.

Haque, Wahidul *et al.* (1977) 'Towards a theory of rural development', *Development Dialogue*, No. 2.

Rahman, Md. Anisur (1977) 'Goodbye to gruel kitchens', *The New Internationalist*, No. 49, March 1977.

Rahman, Md. Anisur (1985) *The Meaning of Marxism*, Department of Economics, University of Dhaka (mimeo).

Rahman, Md. Anisur (1987) 'The concept of community participation through family units to break the "vicious circle of hunger and poverty"', Paper presented at the biennial Seminar in Rural Development of the Organisation of Rural Associations for Progress, Matandele, Nswazi, Zimbabwe, 7–9 April 1987.

Tilakaratna, S. (1985) *The Animator in Participatory Rural Development: Some Experiences from Sri Lanka*, Geneva: ILO, World Employment Programme Research working Paper WEP 10/WP 37.

Tilakaratna, S. (1987) *The Animator in Participatory Rural Development Concept and Practice)*, Geneva: ILO.

1. Planners and society

The threat of professional intellectuals invading the government of liberated Bangladesh was always there. I was personally against this, and told my colleagues so on different occasions before liberation. My reasons were at that time purely selfish. I knew that in a parliamentary democracy the people's elected representatives would determine the fate of the nation. The ideas of these representatives on the national interest would not necessarily coincide with those of intellectuals who by and large come from a very different background and tradition. I also knew that, while there never are many to advise a political party as long as it is on the wrong side of the court, there would be many, very many, to advise it once it crossed over. The intellectuals' position would then tend to be compromised, and it would be prudent to stay out and advise, if advice were to be sought, from an independent forum. But circumstances, including heat-of-the-moment impulses, pushed the intellectuals in.

The framework in which the intellectuals had to operate was peculiar and perhaps unique. The Planning Commission, virtually monopolised by them, was to work in a compartment of its own, isolated both from the regular civil service and from the ruling party. This was absurd, and inherently self-contradictory and self-defeating. First, a development plan must be administrable, and good administrators are logically the best judges of this quality. Second, a plan cannot be written in a political vacuum, and a systematic machinery must exist for a continuous dialogue between specialists and politicians in the course of the planning process. Finally, a Planning Commission isolated from both the above groups, as it has been in Bangladesh, must naturally generate hostilities in them, and it should also be natural that the aggrieved parties operate jointly to resist encroachment by outsiders on their respective jurisdictions. Without the support of either, a plan, however good it may be, will not be implemented.

Reconstructed from an extempore farewell speech to the Planning Commission, 4 October 1974, this chapter originally appeared in the *Wave Weekly*, Dhaka, 3 November 1974.

The Planning Commission was doomed to fail, then, because of the very way it was conceived – fail, in the sense of its ability to steer the nation through a process of disciplined planned development. For this the fault lies with the conception and not so much with individual specialists in the Commission. It is in fact an irony that while in effect the Planning Commission has been made an isolated advisory body it has not enjoyed an autonomous status from which to make its recommendations public without subjecting them to the Censor's scrutiny. It has thus been a loser on both fronts. The nation has not been the gainer, not because the Commission would have delivered the goods otherwise, but because a more intimate dialogue between the intellectuals, the civil service and the politicians might have produced a greater realisation on the part of each of these groups about its own shortcomings and this might have made all of us somewhat more humble.

The civil servants, trained and experienced in the colonial traditions through no fault of their own, have seen and administered society from the point of view of colonial rulers. The field experience they claim to have *vis-à-vis* the professional intellectuals is not relevant to the administration of a free society with democratic and egalitarian aspirations. I have toured the country with civil servants, some among the most illustrious of our sons. They have hoped to find another Dhaka in the villages. Not finding it, they for the most part stay in the circuit house and do not go to the village. Such 'circuit house' administration and the field experience it gives was good enough for the colonial rulers, but is worthless for a people's government and for the people. On the other hand the politicians, who claim to have the correct sense of the pulse of the people, are themselves alien to their own constituencies, have visited most of the villages in their areas once only before the election, and are now wondering how to visit them again for the next election. However, none of these two groups comes anywhere near the intellectuals in terms of false vanity.

The intellectuals of Bangladesh, like its educated class generally, have also been trained in a colonial environment with colonial attitudes and aspirations. The entire philosophy of education with which we have learnt what we have learnt is summed up in the well-known Bengali proverb: 'He who studies will ride the car and the horse'; in other words, will be alienated from his society which has neither the car nor the horse to give except to a very few, and is not even accessible physically or symbolically, by these lofty means of transport. With such a philosophy we intellectuals have been educated only to form and to join a class of our own, aspiring for recognition by the international brotherhood of intellectuals, but alien from our own society and, in particular, ignorant of the social life and conditions in the countryside and of the mind, the spirit and the potentials of the man in rural Bangladesh.

For intellectuals engaged in development planning this lapse, admittedly of historical origin and no direct fault of their own, leaves very few credentials in their bag for the task they have undertaken. For development will not be brought about by statistics or with machines – it will be brought about by the men, the millions of men (and women) of Bangladesh, the great bulk of whom live in the villages and will continue to do so, the bulk of whom we intellectuals living in the cities have not seen and hardly know of. Even more fundamentally, the economic and social development of Bangladesh will be brought about by the mind, the living spirit, of these millions of men (and women), the mind which is almost totally unknown to the planners of the country. It is the mind alone which steers human action, and it is the quality of this mind in all its complexity, its dynamism, its response to examples and stimuli, good and bad, individually and collectively, that will determine the course and character of social change.

Sitting in Dhaka very little can be known of this mind. The newspaper reports, conventional statistics mechanically collected or cooked up from the field and sent up through indifferent channels, evening parleys and the television in which the viewers mostly see their own images, hardly reveal anything. What they reveal is generally dismal – there is suffering all around, lawlessness, the inability of the government to administer almost any policy, erosion of youth morals, a sense of drift and despair, violence without any social purpose. This alone makes it imperative that a very close examination be made of the Bengali mind, in order to discover if there is any positive element left in it, and if so how it can be nourished and brought to blossom. If there is none the seed must be implanted somewhere early, or else what are we planning for?

Let us, therefore, take a tour of the countryside. Go to Comilla, the world-famous Academy,[1] where experimentation with rural development has been going on for a decade. There has been a noticeable increase in production, but there has hardly been any development in the wider sociological sense, and the twin objectives of self-help and wide sharing of the fruits of the efforts have both been frustrated. What is worse, Akhtar Hameed Khan's[2] own admission of a dream thus shattered, in his *Tour of Twenty Thanas*,[3] is not as a rule shown to visitors to the Academy. In Rangunia[4] there is a different colour. The institutional framework is not very different from Comilla's but the men are. The experiment is wide open for any one to visit, there is a lot of very intense and frank discussion going on in forums where farmers, students (both boys and a large number of girls) and officers all participate without inhibition, and a lot of voluntary youth work. The ideas and the methods are gradually spreading in other *thanas* of Chittagong and are generating a process of dialectics of their own, with vested interests resisting and progressive elements pressing for change.

There is the Ganamillan in Gurudaspur[5] where the local youth are experimenting in various areas of social development with cooperatives, mass education, the development of cottage industries; their fundamental objective is still unarticulated, at least explicitly, but they have become the natural leaders of the society in the area, adding much to the discomposure of traditional vested interests and elements in the bureaucracy all the way up to Dhaka. Come to the village of Katchubari-Krishtapur in Thakurgaon, where the local high school and college boys have totally eradicated any need for the thumb impression (as a substitute for a signature), with every villager above the age of seven now familiar with the alphabets and able to sign his or her name;[6] the achievement has set a new standard in youth activity which the youth of several other villages in Thakurgaon and elsewhere in the country have accepted as a challenge. On the way to other villages you may stop at Azizul Huq College in Bogra, where the students of Titumir Hostel are cultivating rice, fish and banana and are weaving and making shirts, *lungis*, sarees and bedsheets in a bid to relieve their guardians of the burden of financing their education. Other hostels in the college, both boys' and girls', are hurrying to catch up with this pioneering venture. Go to the village of Kunjipukur in Rangpur, where a local officer has reportedly initiated economic and social development on the basis of self-help. This village has also eliminated the thumb impression, has repaid all outstanding external debt previously incurred through its cooperative society, eliminated beggary and unemployment, provided shelter to everyone in the village, raised the sharecropper's share to 60 per cent of the produce from the previous 50 per cent, and formed workers' brigades to supervise work in the village, to devise work for all, to meet periodically to discuss socialism and to send teams to neighbouring villages to tell what they are doing and invite and help others to follow. Finally, get on the IR-20 train[7] to see what the students are doing – some 1,400 students from eleven institutions are working with their hands, in the fields beside the peasants. These volunteers from a student body alleged by many to consist mostly of hijackers and other misguided youth had no inhibitions about enlisting in a pilot project.

There must be others, many other efforts like this, which are going unnoticed. Some efforts have perhaps died premature deaths. Some others, maybe even from among those mentioned above, will perhaps end in the same abortive way. Some will possibly take wrong turns, falling, as they all must be prone to fall, into reactionary hands. The total size of such efforts in relation to the breadth of the society is perhaps very small in any case. But all this is nevertheless evidence of the tenacity of the Bengali mind, its efforts to live through disasters which come one after another, its imaginativeness; evidence, in other words, that this mind still lives and thinks and takes positive steps, evidence that is not available to the planners in the conventional statistics on which conventional plans are built but is nevertheless vital, very vital, to the task of development planning.

With all our impressive academic training we have not been exposed to a really creative definition of development and development planning. The sterile economists of the Anglo-Saxon world have tried very hard to keep us limited to growth of GNP. This is rubbish and should be treated as such. Development is the liberation of the creative energy of man, and development planning is planning how to do this. How many railway wagons to be imported, how many miles of road to be constructed, and how much land to be shifted from Desi to high-yielding variety rice, all this is development *accounting* and the task of skilled accountants. The planners' task is to plan how to open the door on which the spirit of man is knocking. Make a tour of the countryside of Bangladesh, and you will hear these knocks. Maybe they are few and not fully articulate, but open the door and let the spirit burst in, lift it high so it can see its perspective, and then let it surge forward. Thus alone can Bangladesh reach its full height.

A draft Five-Year Plan has been prepared in a short time through very hard work by our planners. These are dedicated persons, and brilliant analytically, technically. In their respective spheres they compare with the best in the world. In the entire government of Bangladesh there is no other ministry where such honest, dedicated and hard teamwork has been demonstrated over the last year and a half against a general environment in the nation's capital that has been so totally demoralising. The nation should appreciate this dedication and take note of the potential of these intellectuals. But they must go to the village to complete their study and to collect the relevant statistics, the statistics of man and his mind. Split yourselves in groups of eight to ten, select three villages at random, and live in each for a month. Live in the village, not in the nearest circuit house. A mat on the floor of the village primary school, with at most a mosquito coil if you cannot stand the mosquitoes, should be enough. There in the village you should live the life of the villagers, work with them in the field a few hours every day, talking to them while you work and at other times, individually and in groups. Stay outdoors as long as you can after dusk, and as the night thickens the totality of the social psychology of the village will gradually reveal itself to you while you recall the day's events. You will then, and only then, see the possibilities of the Bengali peasantry. Live thus in three villages, and spend another month in an industrial area, with workers. It is the worker, not the factory or the machine, and more precisely the mind of the worker, which will make our industrial history. Study this mind, the energy and the imagination hidden therein, by living with him, walking with him to the factory in the morning and listening to his casual talk, giving him a hand in the factory as he works and listening to him talk again, and look for what is constraining him from making his history.

After these four months come back and look at the draft plan again. You will want to change it, and the extent of change you want will be a measure of your shortcomings today.

Notes

1. The Rural Development Academy, Kotbari, Comilla, Bangladesh.
2. The founder of the Comilla Rural Development Academy.
3. Akhtar Hameed Khan wrote this personal reflection which was published by the Comilla Academy shortly before the independence of Bangladesh.
4. A cooperative-based rural development effort in Rangunia Thana, Chittagong District.
5. Another cooperative-based rural development programme in Gurudaspur which was initiated after independence by a group of freedom-fighting youth.
6. A literacy movement led by the freedom-fighting village youth.
7. A programme which I initiated in 1973 for students to go to the villages to live and work in the field, transplanting IRRI-20 rice.

2. Mobilisation without tears: a conceptual discussion of self-reliant development

Broadly speaking, the term mobilisation will be taken to mean the simultaneous engagement of large masses of people in activities that have a predominantly social or collective objective. As a strategy for social and economic development this phenomenon is a historical reality today, being practised as an official policy in a number of societies ideologically inspired by socialism. The demonstration of its possibilities as well as its ideological appeal are generating social forces in many other countries to press for mobilisation as the central thrust in development, and 'liberation' struggles aimed at the necessary structural changes as well as autonomous experiments in mobilisation even under unfavourable structural conditions are both under way.[1]

The case for mobilisation as a development strategy, and as a matter of fact as a very way of life, has arisen historically from the failure of the individualist (pursuit of private gains) ethic to alleviate human misery and bring fulfilment to man in large parts of the globe. Even in the economically advanced societies considerable human misery has not only characterised the process of economic development but also, in a different form, exists today because of a sense of 'isolation' and purposelessness that is increasingly becoming manifest.[2] This only shows that man's needs, or rather urges, are both 'material' and 'emotional' (for example, the urge to have a sense of purpose for one's existence, a place of respect and affection in society, a sense of sharing life with others and working for common social

This chapter was originally published in Galtung, J. *et al* (ed.) *Self-reliance: A Strategy for Development*, London: Bogle-L'ouverture Publications.

The author is indebted to Edward Dommen of the Research Division, UNCTAD, whose comments on an earlier sketch of this chapter resulted in some conceptual revision. Useful comments have also been received personally from Johan Galtung, Jagadish Saigal, Biplab Dasgupta and Wahidal Haque, and from participants in the self-reliance colloquium at the Institute of Development Studies where some of the ideas in this chapter were presented. All of them deserve my gratitude without sharing any responsibility whatsoever for my ideas.

objectives). As regards the economically backward societies of today, oppressive social relations (for example, feudal) make liberation from them as important for the emotional fulfilment of the masses of the oppressed as a rise in their material condition *per se*, and mobilisation of these masses for liberation struggles is increasingly being seen as a necessary means for attaining this objective.

To this may be added a new historical compulsion: any realistic rate of increase in the level of *economic* well-being of the masses in most of these societies will be too slow in terms of modern standards of economic need, so that compensatory fulfilment in emotional terms may be needed for the economically poor societies that are exposed to such standards. The individualist ethic, by its appeal to individual acquisition, typically aggravates rather than eases this fulfilment problem as far as the masses (as distinct from the few who win the competition for acquisition) are concerned. On the other hand, men are known to have lived a full life even if materially poor, dedicated to higher (social or collective) ideals. If the problem of human fulfilment is now seen at the mass level, it is in the direction of mass mobilisation – stimulating people in collective creative activity for collective achievements, in the very process of which men may be fulfilled emotionally while economic progress is also being made – that the solution may lie.

But this requires *emotional stimulation* of communities as 'collectives', whereas mobilisation may, instead, be *coercive* and emotionally repressive. The purpose of this chapter is to discuss at the conceptual and analytical level the requirements of mobilisation that is emotionally stimulating, in the sense of generating, and relying on, appropriate *inner urges* in the people for collective activity, an inner urge being defined as an urge that arises from one's own consciousness, the satisfaction of which gives one direct emotional fulfilment. Such mobilisation should be distinguished both from the (Keynesian) concept of employment, which means working not out of an inner urge but for direct material reward in an alienated labour-capital framework, and also from forced labour. It is, indeed, the failure to generate an inner urge for work that necessitates either direct material reward as a *quid pro quo* for work, or coercion, in order to engage labour in productive activity.

As will be argued, mobilisation viewed as an expression of inner urges in a society is integrally connected with *self-reliance*, which in its turn implies de-alienation of man from his economic and social environment. Such de-alienation may also be understood as the fundamental aim of socialism, as a humanist ideology. The analytical journey to socialism via the requirements of non-coercive mobilisation brings out some of the dynamic interrelationships between the development of people's consciousness, on the one hand, and the necessary allocation of control over the society's resources and hence the social, economic and political institutions, on the other.

Mobilisation and self-reliance

If mobilisation is to rest on the inner urges of the people and not be externally imposed, it requires the following:

1. Subjective *internalisation* of factors of creativity objectively external to individuals (for example, means of production) through institutions, knowledge and culture, social interactions and so on. Specifically, this varies with: (i) a sense of owning the means of production, and (ii) a sense of being the subject of decision-making. This in an ultimate sense must be the essence of *ownership*, but may be stated separately in view of the complex combinations of the distribution of formal ownership and decision-making power that obtain in reality.
2. A sense of (positive) *purpose* in the exercise of ownership and decision-making.
3. Above all, *self-reliance*, for it is from reliance on one's own resources, including those objectively external but subjectively internalised, that an inner urge for creative work may be generated. However, the concept of self-reliance is used in a variety of senses, so that a discussion of its meaning in the context of mobilisation is necessary.

In its fundamental sense self-reliance is defined as a state of mind that regards one's own mental and material resources as the primary stock to draw on in the pursuit of one's objectives, and finds emotional fulfilment not only in achieving the objectives as such but also in the very fact of having achieved them primarily by using one's own resources. This does not reject the use of external resources (to which a sense of ownership does not extend), but these, if used, are considered secondary and their use does not directly bring any emotional fulfilment. It does, however, reject the use of external resources at the cost of the following:

1. One's self-respect, thus ruling out: (i) external help, except when it is either mutual or in times of extreme and abnormal calamity immediately threatening survival (for example, danger of drowning, being hit by a cyclone) when, by accepting external help, one may also help preserve self-respect of the helper (so that help becomes, after all, mutual!); and (ii) appropriating others' resources without a mutually honourable *quid pro quo*.[3]
2. One's autonomy of choice and action, current and future, which one considers significant. As a corollary, self-reliance is against the use or

commitment of one's own resources in a way that endangers one's future autonomy (for example, overdependence on specific markets, vulnerable statistically, politically, and so on).

Self-reliance conceived in these terms has operational implications that are both creatively positive as well as resistance-oriented and hence defensive. For oppressed people to be mobilised for purposeful economic and social development they have to be mobilised, at least initially, for resistance against exploitation that thrives essentially on dominance–dependence relations, that is, on the exploited depending on the resources and goodwill of the exploiter for their livelihood: self-reliance in this context has first to be seen as an act of negating such relations obtaining historically, and may increase material hardship initially. To be self-reliant in such a context and sustain the struggle, one needs an appropriate combination of *material and mental staying power*.

Material staying power is defined as the capacity to produce goods for *direct use*, or for *self-reliant exchange* (exchange without risk of getting into a state of dependence, vulnerable to market availability or pressure on autonomy) of resources at one's own command; resources for this purpose need to be measured in what may be termed 'self-reliant units': of two alternative resource bundles each assumed to be put to the most preferred use, the one that yields a final goods bundle that is the more preferred in a self-reliant context (that is, barring non-self-reliant options) by the subjects concerned is defined to be the higher in such units.[4]

Mental staying power is defined as the mental strength to reject non-self-reliant options at any given level of material staying power. Obviously, the lower the level of material staying power of the subject concerned, the higher the mental staying power needed to remain self-reliant. Historically, oppressed masses in a society may with the level of their material staying power initially lack the requisite amount of mental staying power to throw off exploitative dominance–dependence relations, and this power then needs to be increased. This may be done by one of the following or a combination of the two:

1. *Cultivation*: cultural or political education, practice (experience) of self-reliance in specific tasks, exposure to examples of self-reliance under difficult conditions by other groups, communities and so on.
2. *Energisation*: generating an impulse of self-reliance through inspiring leadership, examples, invocations and, perhaps most effectively, through *liberation struggles*. The relation between self-reliance and liberation struggles may be seen as a dialectical one. Self-reliance, indeed, must be one of the qualities that a liberation struggle seeks to liberate, and for this the quality must be present in the consciousness (active); for it is not logically possible to liberate something that either does not exist, or exists

only in the unconscious (dormant). Liberation struggles start therefore after the quality (qualities) to be liberated has (have) become 'conscientised',[5] so to say, by cultivation and other means, and seeks an expression in conscious life. Once conscientised, however, the character of self-reliance asserts, enriches and strengthens itself in response to the challenge of the liberation struggle through the hardship it necessitates, and the experience in building up the material basis of self-reliance in the process of the struggle which must include organisation of the oppressed as productive forces for its sustenance. Obviously, the more intensive and longer the struggle is, the more lasting the impact of the impulse of self-reliance may be on the character of the people concerned.

In a more positive sense, self-reliance as a driving force for creative activity requires an awareness of one's creative assets, arising again out of a combination of material resources under one's control, and such mental resources as confidence in one's ability to solve original problems of life, the courage to take on challenging tasks and the stamina to make sustained efforts to accomplish them, and so on. Once more, the necessary mental resources are cultivable and conscientisable. Furthermore, the resistance-oriented needs of self-reliance overlap with its creative needs in so far as resistance requires creative responses to challenges, so that resistance itself generates and promotes the constructive potentials of self-reliance.

The collective

As defined, mobilisation implies serving a collective purpose. For inner-urge-oriented (self-reliant, non-coercive, non-alienating) mobilisation it is obviously necessary that such an objective is not imposed on the people concerned but is an expression of an 'organic unity of consciousness' of these people who may to this extent be said to have formed, and belong to, a *collective*. A collective is thus defined as an association of individuals who possess a sense of identity with the association, so that the collective interest (as defined collectively by an agreed procedure) registers emotionally in the consciousness of its members as part of their 'individual' interest, that is, realisation of the collective objective gives direct fulfilment to the individual members.

The collective interest may be 'material' or 'non-material', or a combination of both. It may be emphasised that collectivism as we view it does not deny, nor does it necessarily advocate, the pursuit of material interests, and it is not on the basis of material versus non-material motivation that it is distinguished from individualism, as is often the case. In reality all collectivist societies do seem to have a high content of material motivation for their collective pursuits: the Chinese and the Vietnamese, for example, seem to aim at high standards of material development, whose benefits are naturally to be enjoyed by individual members of these societies. The distinction between individualism and collectivism is seen, instead, in that while individualism consists of the pursuit of individual 'objective functions' (for example, maximisation of individual acquisition) separate from collective objectives, collectivism as we are viewing it conceives of an integration of individual and collective objectives through a process that is *emotionally organic* rather than *quantitatively aggregative*.

A simple example of such organic unity (integration) of consciousness is the sense of nationalism. That national independence is to be preserved is an expression not of quantitative aggregation of individual interests but of an emotional bond between individuals. To this extent every nation is, indeed, a collective and would be mobilised by an inner urge if national independence were threatened. However, collectivist societies are distinguished from individualist societies in that the former are thus mobilised as a way of normal daily life, motivated by an organic sense of identity that embraces a very significant area of everyday consciousness so as to become the dominant element therein, so much so that individuals are fulfilled most by serving the collective interests rather than individual interests perceived independently of the former.

Through such organic integration, subjective internalisation of individual consciousnesses, objectively external to each other, takes place. This makes self-reliance a collective state of mind which, however, *extends from* and *does not replace* individual self-reliance, as the sense of the individual itself is extended to embrace the collective. It is then and to this extent that social alienation is eliminated. *Collective self-reliance* thus viewed, with a collective sense of 'ownership' over the material environment and a sense of collective identity and reliance on the mental and material resources of the collective as a whole in the sense defined in the previous section, is the interpretation the author gives to Marx's vision of de-alienated man (from his physical and social environment): an alienated man cannot be self-reliant, and vice versa. Furthermore, it is the above conceptual extension from individual to collective self-reliance without negating self-reliance at the individual level, that constitutes the synthesis between collectivism and individualism which otherwise could exist as antitheses of one another. The synthesis moreover reinforces self-reliance both in the individual and the collective (or in two collectives of different 'orders' linked by organic integration of consciousness): by expanding the material and social base of one's identity, greater amounts of objectively external mental and material resources become subjectively internalised for each individual, thereby augmenting the staying power, both mental and material, needed for self-reliance; this in turn stimulates and strengthens the collective resolve for self-reliance with further feedback on the individual and so on, and material development itself (growth of material staying power) can be expedited by concomitant mobilisation and more efficient resource allocation (see below); in turn, this would advance further self-reliance, both individual and collective.

In accordance with the theory of unity of opposites which is finding empirical psychoanalytical verification as far as human consciousness is concerned,[6] the collective sense must be present in man either in his conscious mind or (if the latter is dominated by individualism of a native, that is opposed to the collective, sense) in his 'unconscious'. Some of the factors that seem to contribute generally to collective consciousness in different degrees are the sharing of everyday lives, a common heritage and culture, the sharing of common problems, involvement in common-purpose activities and so on. Depending on the nature and degree of collective consciousness already present, more may have to be done by way of conscientisation for a society to collectively mobilise itself for resistance against specific forms of exploitation and for sustained social and economic development in a collectivist framework wherein serving the collective action in areas where the state of development of collective purpose itself could yield direct fulfilment. Among other means, this may be attained through the very exercise of collective consciousness and the specific circumstances of the time permit this. Two factors that may be of considerable importance in such action, promoting collective consciousness further, are: (a) the sharing of power in common, in other words, participation in the decision-making of the collective, whereby one may feel that one has been the subject in the process so that the decision has been one's own (along with others); and (b) critical comprehension, through an interaction of collective deliberation and individual reflection, that the collective is serving the member individuals' interests equitably. It may be noted that in the process of such comprehension one's notion of interest itself may transcend narrow individualistic objectives and embrace more the ideal of serving the collective as the latter appears more and more to be the fairest social organisation, and creative urges of individuals may then increasingly seek more conscious fulfilment in contributing to this ideal.

What seems to be very pertinent is that collective consciousness of individuals is not as a rule identified with one single collective, but is spread over a range of collectives (the family, the local community, the 'commune', the nation) in various degrees of emotional intensity, and often in the context of different specific social or economic functions. Thus a society may be mobilised spontaneously to defend the national flag while a village or urban community may not be so mobilised in this way to resist a natural disaster (for example, a flood) that could have been tackled by collective action. On the other hand 'collectivisation' of decision-making or even of property may be spontaneously practised at the local community (or family) level while an attempt at such collectivisation at higher levels may be resisted.

Analytically, such a 'spread' of collective consciousness necessitates: (a) characterisation of collectives according to such factors as size, function, intensity of emotional identification of their individual members, the method of operation as regards the process of involvement of the members in their decision-making and implementation thereof, the interrelationship between collectives, and so on (thus, for example, one may classify collectives according to whether their size and spatial characteristics make direct physical participation by all their members in any decision-making possible – for instance, a family or village – in which case they may be called *primary* collectives; or whether representative institutions become necessary by these very characteristics of what may be called *secondary*, or 'higher-order', collectives [the 'commune', the nation]); (b) for the purpose of organised social and economic development, the identification of a *set* of collectives to act as the formal driving forces in such development; and, very importantly, (c) relating the distribution of the control over a society's resources (decision-making) with the distribution of emotional identity of the people over these different collectives, and seeing this relation in a dynamic framework where the collective consciousness of the people and the socio-economic institutions interact in a simultaneous process of evolution.

The first two points, (a) and (b), are relatively self-evident. The third one is the main analytical question raised in this chapter, and is discussed in the following sections.

The centre(s) of gravity in the development effort

In so far as mobilisation, even if inner-urge-oriented, may not be spontaneous and may require an organisational medium for its stimulation and direction, a collective as we have defined it naturally suggests itself as such a medium. Since there may be multiple collectives in the same society to which the same set of people may belong (the family, the village community, the 'commune', the nation), a choice of collectives for specific tasks of mobilisation has to be made.[7] Self-reliant mobilisation requires, moreover, that (a) there should be sufficient emotional identification of the people concerned with a collective chosen for such purpose, and (b) the requisite resource control be vested in the chosen collective in order to provide the material basis of self-reliance as conceptualised above.

Point (a) above indicates that the level of mobilisation – that is, the collective through which, operationally, an act of mobilisation is generated. and directed and hence also the *unit* of self-reliance – may be too high, meaning that people's sense of identity with the chosen collective may not be strong enough for them to be mobilised *non-alienatingly* at this level. Point (b) cautions, on the other hand, that the chosen level of mobilisation may be too low, in the sense that the desired mobilisation could have been achieved at a higher level, gaining at the same time a wider choice of resource allocation, as a higher-level mobilisation could allow resources to be put under the control of a correspondingly higher (larger) collective, permitting more efficient resource use to the extent that such possibilities (economies of scale) exist. Thus, for example, mobilisation at the level of the *family*, by requiring private plots wherein each family might want to produce some staple foodgrains (material staying power) might be inefficient in the aggregate if (a) the state of collective consciousness also permitted mobilisation at a higher (for example, village) level, and (b) land ownership by the village community as a whole rather than by individual families would have enabled more efficient planning of crops, irrigation and so on.

The above calls for careful consideration of two questions: the efficient balancing of the distribution of a society's *economic resources* among its different collectives, and the state of its collective consciousness as viewed in terms of distribution of its *emotional resources* among these collectives. The nature of an efficiently balanced distribution of mobilisational responsibility and corresponding control over resources may not be suggested *a priori*. But one may conjecture that the interdependence of many economic and social functions and the economies of concentrating (up to a point) responsibilities in specific organisations may indicate an efficient distribution of such responsibility and control at any state (distribution) of collective consciousness of the society, to be not too spread out; it may instead give a few, even a single, concentration points or point in the space of collectives for such a purpose.

Such concentration points – to be called henceforth the *centres of gravity* in a society's development effort – may be identified for communication purposes by qualitative reasoning or operationally measured for quantitative purposes by possible approximate indicators such as, for example, the relative amounts of resources (per capita) under the control of the various collectives. Needless to say, the existence of a small number of such centres of gravity would make analytical discussion of the above choice and resource allocation questions simpler, and this may itself be an additional reason for the relevant decision-makers in the society concerned actually to choose for formal action a few centres of gravity instead of a less manageable large number of collectives for mobilised development.

The dynamics of mobilised development

Seen in a dynamic context, the centre(s) of gravity as conceived above should not as a rule remain unchanged until, if at all, equilibrium positions exist and can be reached. There are at least three good reasons why temporal shifts in the centre(s) of gravity may occur or may be desired:

1. Growth of collective consciousness: the experience of collective effort in the framework of any given distribution of centres of gravity may raise collective consciousness further and create inner urges for forming, and working through, 'higher-order' collectives. Negative experience, however, may not be ruled out, and will be touched upon subsequently.
2. Ideological commitment: commitment to 'socialism'[8] may generate more systematic motivation to move the centre(s) of gravity upwards. The Marxist objective of attaining full communism is usually taken to include as a necessary condition complete socialisation of all essential means of production, which means having *the* centre of gravity at the very highest level; the other condition of non-alienation, so as to exclude both direct material reward and coercion for work, makes this by itself an insufficient condition, and requires the centre(s) of gravity to correspond also to the state of development of the collective consciousness of the people ('emotional socialisation'). Whether the second condition may ever permit the resting of the centre of gravity at the very apex, a historically open question, will also be discussed subsequently.
3. The role of economies of scale in defining efficient centres of gravity: this has already been touched upon. Economically poor societies desiring a rapid rate of economic development would want upward shifts of centres of gravity to gain from further economies of scale if they exist or, with technological and organisational development, may be generated. As with reason (2), this also requires conscious social efforts towards raising collective consciousness so that people may identify themselves more strongly than before with higher (larger) collectives.

Some of the factors that may contribute to the generation of collective consciousness in general have already been touched upon. The specific process of *development* of collective consciousness in the sense of progressively embracing higher and higher collectives should be an important research area by itself. The methods of cultivation and energisation (impulse-generation) mentioned in the context of generating self-reliance apply here also; but the fact that, beyond a point, representative institutions have to replace direct physical participation in collective decision-making and collective actions, and higher-order collectives are in this sense less tangible in terms of one's physical perceptions, introduces special dimensions in the question of developing collective consciousness to embrace such higher-order collectives.

These dimensions seem to require: (a) identification with representative institutions, and the representatives themselves, who may be alienating unless they are rooted in the constituency in the sense of an integration of lives; (b) critical comprehension that the process of representation is equitable and serves the purpose of the collective; (c) critical comprehension of the 'higher-order' (macro, inter-sectorial and inter-collective, global) issues, and their relevance for individual and social lives, that are delegated to be in the jurisdiction of the higher-order collective wherein one may not physically participate; and (d) critical realisation of the need to delegate jurisdiction for these issues to the latter.

Such requirements are by no means easy to realise, and need appropriate levels of general and social education, cultural and social interaction between groups and communities in the society, and concrete positive experience in collective deliberation and action in limited areas at the higher levels while mobilisation is still weighted in favour of lower collectives. Obviously, such development of collective consciousness and hence advancement of the centre(s) of gravity should depend on the overall rate of socio-economic development and cannot be too much out of pace with the latter. But the centre of gravity is itself conceived as the major instrument for such development.

Such a dialectical relation holds even more directly between the centre(s) of gravity and collective consciousness: the former serves to protect or 'encapsulate'[9] communities sufficiently from alienating influences arising beyond its boundaries, while at the same time providing opportunity for constructive/progressive interaction with the 'outside' and hence development of consciousness and comprehension (of issues of larger and more complex dimensions). After a stage communities may thus 'mature' for a higher-order collective and corresponding upward shift in the centre of gravity for the mobilisational tasks in question, as though the membrane of the smaller 'capsule' melts to bring a larger one into a fuller role. The process has a parallel with a family providing an encapsulating role to a child who finds in it security, an emotional 'home' and at the same time a base for interaction with the wider society, until he or she outgrows this base and identifies himself or herself more directly with a wider community.

The above is not a theory of balanced development, nor have the various questions been raised in order to find neat answers to them. It merely presents a conceptual perspective in the light of which mobilisational efforts and their results may perhaps be better understood. Actual mobilisational efforts proceed necessarily by the dialectical interaction of forces in the society. Specifically, forces representing mobilisational development have to follow innovative policies in response to circumstances and challenges presented by specific historic moments. These will often consist of galvanising thrusts indifferent to finer considerations of balance or efficiency, often of sheer experimental probing, and often of calculated risks.[10] The results will often fall short of, and often be beyond, expectations. They will generate new social, political, economic and emotional forces which will guide subsequent policy.

However, while any well-intentioned policy taken in response to concrete historical circumstances may be rationalised, policies grossly out of tune with the state of society's consciousness will obviously have their costs in terms of alienation which should be seriously considered.

It may be mentioned also that the question whether a sustained monotonic rise in a society's collective consciousness is possible, and to what temporal and spatial extent, is very much an open one. While the experience of collective life itself may generate forces in favour of the development of such life (a forward shift in the centre(s) of gravity), negative forces may also be generated or strengthened in this very process. For one thing, little is known psychoanalytically as to how stable a synthesis between individualism and collectivism can be in which, as conceptualised above, the latter absorbs rather than opposes the former. For another, the increase in the representative character of decision-making as the centre(s) of gravity is moved forward generates its own dynamics wherein a tendency towards divergence between representatives (and representative institutions) and their constituencies in terms of the required sense of identity may not be ruled out: in particular, representative functions develop by their own dynamic logic and may generate a diverging 'comprehension gap' in the system, for even with the best of intentions communication between the representatives and their constituencies may not be as close and as often as may be needed to avoid such a tendency, and the tendency of power to 'corrupt' is also there.

Such developments may easily have alienating effects on the people's consciousness, with adverse implications for their continued emotional identification with the collective in question and their urges to move towards even higher collectives. To resist the above 'comprehension gap' and hence stop the corresponding 'class' cleavage in the society from widening is one aspect of the 'class struggle' under socialism, which as the Chinese variant of Marxism asserts may be a continuous one. Obviously, the bigger the society, the bigger the question, for the larger a collective is, the deeper and more dominant will be its representative institutions.

Finally, it may be noted that the systematic generation and development of self-reliant collective consciousness is a task to be pursued under organised leadership whose commitment to the values concerned is a crucial variable in the process. In particular, self-reliance by definition is a value that cannot be *imposed* and has to be *conscientised*. This sets standards for leadership behaviour in which respect also there may be failures. The resulting alienation, the tensions between the leader and the led, and the 'two-line struggles' within the leadership itself, will also contribute their own dynamics to the further development of the society.

Concluding comments

The central idea developed in this essay is that self-reliant mobilisation of people requires a delegation of control over resources parallel to the development of a society's collective consciousness. In a dynamic context this introduces the question of the method and limits of raising the level of self-reliant mobilisation. As regards the question of its desirability, a historical case is indicated for economically poor societies to embrace (non-coercive) collectivism as a more dominant way of life. How far this may be carried is left open, however, since it is partly an ideological question and partly to be dictated by the internal dynamics of collectivist development itself which may generate forces both for and against its further development.

The discussion does not deal with the question of a political framework for mobilised development with which development – and particularly socialist – literature is already well preoccupied. Obviously, no radical departure from a traditional development – or 'under-development' – framework can take place without a fundamental alteration in the political framework, and in bringing about this political change questions of concrete social relations within the country concerned and international interests and linkages are of crucial importance.

It is hoped that the discussion in this essay may contribute towards developing a conceptual basis for institution-building and the allocation of resources (power) to the various institutions in self-reliant development strategy, and also towards an understanding of the role of institutions in promoting self-reliant development in concrete historical cases. Thus, for example, the recent Soviet emphasis on greater direct material incentives, essentially a reflection of a growing alienation between labour and decision-making (control over material resources), may be traced to a pace of 'material socialisation' which put the centre of gravity in Soviet development right at the apex of the society at a relatively early stage, out of line with that of emotional socialisation or the development of collective consciousness in the society.

The Chinese experiment in the transition to socialism seems more cautious in bringing resource ownership under 'the whole people' (state): although this remains an ideological objective, the centre of gravity of China's development effort after nearly three decades of communist rule remains no higher than the commune for the great bulk of its economic (and social) activities, which may be rationalised in terms of a greater concern for building socialism on the consciousness of the people rather than on the material base alone, and thus for building socialism more on the basis of self-reliance as we have conceptualised it. This experiment for the same reason should be more revealing of the tensions between consciousness and the material basis of collectivism when both are intended to be dynamic actors in the scene to interact in a process of joint evolution.

The relevance of the discussion should not be confined to societies which are actually in the stage of experimenting with the process of transition to socialism, in other words where the initial 'liberation struggle' has been fought and won by forces representing socialism. To the extent that such forces have also emerged or are in the process of emerging in preliberated societies, there are two important reasons why the concrete experience of societies in transition to socialism, and the understanding of the conceptual issues involved, should be of great value. The first is that socialism, like self-reliance, has interpretations on which even socialist societies differ, and even such terms as 'dictatorship of the proletariat' and 'socialist democracy' are losing the communicability they may have had previously. An ideological underpinning of the emerging new forces challenging the status quo in the many countries of the Third World today, purportedly in favour of a 'socialist' order, therefore needs the application of concepts more discerning than the above, and these forces themselves may benefit from articulation of their ideology in such terms for conceptual clarity as well as for wider communicability. Second, as we have asserted already, a quality to be liberated must be conscientised; and historical materialism would have it that the more a society is endowed with positive qualities in the old order, the richer in constructive potentials will be the new order which inherits whatever there was of value in the former, and the very process of dialectical overthrow of the old order may be hastened by generating more of the positive qualities in it. From this point of view the cultivation of self-reliance may never be considered too early.

Postscript

See further reflections in Chapter 10 on the question of non-coercive ('organic') transition to socialism and on attempts to force the centre of gravity at the very apex, in the light of the collapse of East European socialism. The centre of gravity in China is also shifting, with the communes now being abandoned; but unlike in Eastern Europe the changes in China seem to owe more to the ideology of the country's new leaders than the pressure of popular will.

Notes

1. For examples of the latter see Wahidul Haque *et al.*, *Towards a Theory of Rural Development*, Asian Development Institute, 1975.

2. In a touching BBC programme on 'Isolation' in Britain, broadcast on 17 May 1976, it was suggested, among other things, that one positive contribution of the contemporary economic crisis in Britain might be to make people realise again how much they needed each other.

3. The bourgeois concept of 'self-*help*' that glorifies animalistic competition for maximising individual acquisition by fair means or foul, including conscious exploitation of others' resources through one's political and military powers, is to be sharply distinguished from the concept of self-*reliance* as used in this paper and as seen as an emerging force in the Third World.

4. For example, the material staying power represented by the resources at the disposal of an urban community which lacks a sense of collective identity (see the following section) with the countryside, may in self-reliant units be considerably lower than indicated by conventional measurement of their income or assets, since very few of an urban community's priority needs may be satisfied by production and exchange in a self-reliant framework. Specific ordering of resources in self-reliant units is the task of the community concerned whose objective measurement has to evolve from institutions chosen by the community to represent its collective performances.

5. The term is used in a different sense from that of 'conscientisation' by Paulo Freire (*Cultural Action for Freedom*, Harmondsworth: Penguin, 1972), referring to a 'process in which men, not as recipients, but as knowing subjects, achieve a deepening awareness both of the sociological reality which shapes their lives and of their capacity to transform that reality'.

6. See Carl G. Jung (ed.), *Man and His Symbols*, New York: Dell Publishing House, 1968.

7. By the 'society' concerned, meaning for such purposes the institutional complex through which various elements in the society interact to arrive at collective decisions.

8. In the sense of the desire to build a 'classless (non-alienated) society'. It may be held that class divisions in society are fundamentally the result and also the reflection of unequal and differentiated command over resources and as such can be fully eliminated only when all resources are owned by the 'whole people', not in the sense of formal state ownership but in the sense of ownership by the highest collective in the society with this collective itself representing a state of full organic unity of consciousness. The enormity of the task of building a fully classless society may be immediately apparent. For further discussion, see later in this section.

9. See R. De Nitish, *An Action Research Approach to Asian Development*, 1975, mimeograph.

10. Mobilisational thrusts at levels higher than the prevailing level of collective consciousness may sometimes be judged to contribute to raising the latter, and considered to be 'dialectically consonant', if not directly with the latter, in the sense that the expected synthesis of the contradiction thus generated would move the society forward in terms of collectivist development.

3. Dimensions of people's participation in the Bhoomi Sena movement

Introduction

Over recent years people's participation has been emerging as a major concern in development thinking. Its articulation has not yet evolved enough to ensure that by talking about 'participation', one is communicating any commonly understood meaning. Moreover, the work of formally defining 'participation' has thus far been carried out by educated elites, within the limits of their own perceptions.

Under such conditions, it may be worth while to observe the various ways in which people actually 'participate' in different situations, and to seek to understand their underlying perceptions and urges. This is one way of developing concepts – i.e. by building first their empirical base. As a contribution in this direction the present paper explores some of the dimensions of participation in the Bhoomi Sena (Land Army) movement of the *adivasis* in Junglepatti, Thana District, in Maharastra, India.[1]

Despite the lack of an objective (communicable) definition of the idea of participation, few observers would deny that the Bhoomi Sena movement seems to be seeking to promote the adivasis' active participation in the social life that concerns them, and also that the movement is in itself highly *participatory*. There is thus a sense of participation in the movement which is, as it were, enunciating itself. This makes it legitimate to discuss the movement as an empirical expression of participation. There are two other reasons that favour a discussion of this movement: one is that it is largely a 'spontaneous' movement, generated by the initiative of the adivasis' own leaders, not by an external design of the government, a political party or any

Originally published as a Participation Occasional Paper by the United Nations Research Institute for Social Development, Geneva, in 1981, under the title 'Some dimensions of people's participation in the Bhoomi Sena movement, followed by a discussion on the issues'. Three Annexes and the Discussions are omitted.

other such organisation. Because of this, and also because it is terribly jealous of its autonomy, Bhoomi Sena represents a relatively 'pure' response of the people to their environment, and may thus serve as a reference point in discussing people's participation (in the type of historical and structural conditions in which the movement has emerged). The other reason is that the movement is now highly articulate. Its leadership, a Vanguard Group of ten members as of the end of 1978, with whom the author has had the opportunity to interact extensively, is engaged in continuous 'self-conscientisation' through systematic collective analysis of the unfolding movement. This may serve as a check against gross distortions in interpreting its motivation and urges.

The unfolding of Bhoomi Sena: a brief summary

Historical background
Once free men, the adivasis of Junglepatti lost their land and ultimately their freedom to ruthless outsiders called *sawkars* – a class of landlords, moneylenders, forest contractors and grass traders of mostly non-Maharastrian origin who had settled in the area over several decades before the First World War. The sawkars defrauded and cheated the adivasis of most of their lands, and in time turned the adivasis into virtual serfs. The adivasis rose in revolt in 1945–7 – a spontaneous outburst that was, however, controlled and guided by the Communist Party. For a time, this raised the adivasis' status from bonded labourers to tenants. A 'land to the tiller' movement led by middle-rank farmers, mostly non-adivasis, resulted in the abolition of tenancy in 1957 in the state of Maharastra. The adivasis, among others, became owners of the land they were cultivating. Special measures were also enacted to prevent the sale of adivasi land to non-adivasis. But most of the adivasis could not survive without heavy borrowing. By 1970 the adivasis had again lost the bulk of their land, mostly through unofficial and illegal transactions, to the moneylending sawkars. Many of them descended into bondage again.

In the meantime, there had been slow but substantial politico-economic changes in the broader world affecting Junglepatti. Capitalism was developing in western India, though at a modest pace. In Junglepatti, the landlord class had virtually disappeared, some of its members having made a successful transition to orchard-based capitalism on the outskirts of the area providing wage employment to seasonally migrating adivasis from Junglepatti. With the decline of the feudal sawkars, a non-producer mercantile class emerged – the moneylender–trader sawkar – which had also acquired some land as part of their investments. A class of rich farmers also emerged, composed almost entirely of producer middle castes like the *kunbis* who came and settled from outside. They were themselves engaged in production, but the richer among them refrained completely from physical labour and took increasingly to mercantile activities such as trading, moneylending and contracting, and this hindered their transformation into true capitalist farmers. The poorer among the kunbis and the richer among the adivasis comprised the class of middle peasants, the kunbis being the more efficient and enterprising. The adivasi middle peasants could save and reinvest little because of their communal tradition of sharing their fortunes. At the bottom of the hierarchy were the poor peasants and the landless labouring class, almost exclusively adivasis, with no social status, exploited by the sawkars and by the rich peasants through usurious moneylending, through wage labour at one taka a day, despite the legal minimum wage of three-and-a-half taka, and through illegal tenancy at exorbitant rents for cultivating their own land which had been illegally usurped by the masters.

Although the rule of the exploiting classes was total, the state political power operated through them locally. The broader commitments of a populist regime, however, compelled the state to pass legislation dealing with tenancy, minimum wages, employment guarantees, etc., which were inimical to the sawkars' interests and provided a legal basis for the demands of the adivasis. The state, which was no longer willing to support serfdom and extra-legal economic oppression, did, however, back capitalist exploitation based on 'efficient' farming.

This was the economic and political scene in Junglepatti from which the Bhoomi Sena movement emerged.

The birth and eclipse of Bhoomi Sena

Acutely oppressed, a number of adivasis joined the 'land-grab' movement initiated by the left parties in India in 1970. The adivasi leaders participating in the movement from Junglepatti were soon disillusioned by what they saw as the 'symbolic' character of the movement which in their area ended with the temporary jailing of the participants. Seeing that leaders of the left had no plans to carry forward their movement for land rights, the adivasi leaders in jail realised that their rights could be achieved only by a sustained struggle of their own. Once out of jail and led by Kaluram, an adivasi leader and activist from a tenant family in Junglepatti, they initiated an investigation in several villages, with the active participation of the people, on the illegal usurpation of land by the sawkars. Small meetings of the adivasis were held in the area, village by village. The investigations revealed innumerable cases of illegal usurpation of adivasi land by the sawkars. The adivasis thus became collectively aware of the situation, and new bonds among them were forged through the exchange of common problems in the villages. Thus aroused, a group of young adivasis, led by Kaluram, founded their own organisation and called it Bhoomi Sena. Eight hundred 'soldiers' initially joined Bhoomi Sena.

By collective decision of the people (adivasis), Bhoomi Sena led a militant movement for crop seizure on land that belonged legally to the adivasis but had been usurped by the sawkars. Hundreds of adivasis went into the fields wielding their sickles. The sawkars, taken by surprise, offered no resistance initially. Later, they called in the police. The adivasis faced the police fearlessly and charged that it was the police, not they, who were acting against the law by siding with the sawkars. The police could not do very much, and the adivasis went on seizing crops from sawkar-usurped fields in village after village. A sociologist Member of the Legislative Assembly (MLA) raised the issue in the Maharastra State Assembly, and this brought the Sub-Divisional Officer (SDO) to Manor, the market centre of Junglepatti, to discuss the matter with Bhoomi Sena. At the insistence of Bhoomi Sena, the SDO brought the court to Manor to settle 800 pending cases of land rights; 799 of these cases were settled in favour of the adivasis within a matter of three days.

Beyond the crop seizure, however, Bhoomi Sena had no clear strategy to consolidate and sustain their gains and to move forward. A number of grain banks were created spontaneously to build collective reserves to provide working capital for cultivation in the next season; but these were mismanaged and in some cases abused by those to whose care they had been entrusted. When the next season came some of the adivasis who had recovered their land had to return it to the sawkars for lack of cultivation facilities, and some went to the latter once again for loans.

With the movement in this confused state, some urban social workers came in early 1972, at the request of Kaluram, with massive supplies of bank money and modern technology to improve quickly the economic situation of the adivasis. The adivasis, including Kaluram, succumbed to what was a very paternalist intervention in which people's cooperation was purchased with money and which did not seek or encourage their active involvement in the experiment.

Technocratic thrust

This technocratic thrust consisted initially of projects aimed at increasing production through the use of modern methods of agriculture – the familiar irrigation, seed and fertiliser technology. The leader of the experiment, however, in his overenthusiasm to help the adivasis, started manipulating bank loans which were taken in the name of specific adivasis but which he gave to any number of others under a 'mini-bank' operation of his own without regard to the repayability of these 'mini-loans'. As a result, the operation ended in financial disaster. An attempt was made to repay the debt to the bank through grass trade. This also failed miserably as grass stored in anticipation of a price increase decomposed while the price kept falling. In 1975, the adivasis were finally humiliated when they received bank notices for default in repayment of the loans for which they had signed but whose actual disbursement and utilisation had not been in their hands. An audit and inquiry revealed that the bank funds had been badly mismanaged and diverted to unauthorised and unsound projects although there had been no actual misappropriation of funds. Shocked at this humiliation, the adivasis of thirty villages now held their own meeting in which Kaluram admitted his mistake in submitting to outsiders, and the people voted for ending the programme.

Resurgence and development

This experience ushered in a new phase of the Bhoomi Sena movement, with the adivasis now committed to deciding their course of action themselves. A few outsiders who had come with the earlier team of social workers, but who were committed to the promotion of people's self-reliance, remained with the movement.

Bhoomi Sena's central leadership, or the Vanguard Group,[2] now encouraged the adivasis to take local action in their own villages according to their own priorities and collective deliberations. Not only were outsiders not allowed to dictate what should be done, Bhoomi Sena itself shunned centralism of any sort. The role of the centre – i.e. the Vanguard Group – that now developed consisted of catalytic, supportive, coordinating and synthesising tasks such as: learning from local, village-level struggle and disseminating their experiences and methods to other villages; coming to the assistance of local struggle when this was needed; organising mass demonstrations in support of local struggles and coordinating wider struggles on specific issues; representing local grievances in government offices, courts, etc.; conducting investigations for identifying the nature of cases of injustice and exploitation; developing selective external contacts for obtaining support and assistance for the movement; and organising conscientisation camps called *shibirs* for collective analysis by the adivasis of their experiences, from which the meaning of their struggle is being progressively conceptualised to give the movement an increasingly self-created direction.

The resulting resurgence of spontaneous people's action again took the form of confronting the sawkars to resist their oppressive actions – specifically, to reclaim adivasi land illegally held by the sawkars, and to fight for legal minimum wages. Atrocities by government officials were also resisted. The nature of adivasi action varied according to the nature of the atrocities, the response of the oppressors and the innovativeness of the people at the village level. For example, in one village a demonstration was organised against a government official who had beaten up an adivasi cultivator. In this demonstration each adivasi carried a sheet of paper containing his hand impression along with an impression of his sandals, and these were delivered to the official as a symbol of hundreds of 'slaps' intended for him. The official panicked and apologised to the aggrieved adivasi, and was later transferred.

In another village adivasi youths were mobilised to cut the crop on a plot of land belonging to an old lady – land which had been illegally usurped by a sawkar. The sawkar retaliated by sending a private army of 50–60 men. The adivasis fought them with stones and slingshots until the hirelings panicked and ran away. This experience of success in militant confrontation with the hitherto feared private armies of sawkars gave the adivasis a new self-confidence. In another village adivasi youth resisted the distribution of some 200 acres of land which had been taken over by the government from a sawkar under the land ceiling act, and was now being distributed among relatives of local political leaders. A letter was published by six Bhoomi Sena cadres in the *Maharastra Times* protesting against the betrayal of the actual cultivators. Under mounting pressure, the district collector finally came to the village, discussed the question with the adivasis and Bhoomi Sena cadres, and conceded fully to the demand of the people by annulling the previous distribution of the surplus land and redistributing it among the real cultivators. Other spontaneous forms of confrontation against injustices emerged in many other villages.

In the course of their struggles, the adivasis in a few villages spontaneously formed people's organisations at the village level called Tarun Mandals[3] which included all poor adivasi peasants of a village as members. As the news spread, Tarun Mandals began to spring up in many villages. Apart from conducting local struggles, the Tarun Mandals have created collective funds through monthly subscriptions from their members that are now being more responsibly managed. The funds are used according to collective decisions to advance consumption, other kinds of distress loans, marriage loans to members, and, in general, to provide an alternative to the sawkars' lending which had in the past resulted in loss of land or in bondage, or both.

One major issue taken up by many Tarun Mandals was the bonded labour system, by which poor adivasis were bonded to the moneylending sawkars to serve as virtual slave labour, in some cases for many generations. Typically, the Tarun Mandals first wrote to the local officials protesting against this illegal practice in their villages, and thereafter pressed the village headmen to declare publicly that the people concerned were free under the law. The headmen, in league with the sawkars, would not comply, whereupon the adivasis went on strike. Eventually, with the growing strength of the movement, the sawkars began to yield and bonded labourers started becoming free.

In a span of three years since its resurgence, the Bhoomi Sena movement spread to about 120 villages in and around Junglepatti, with Tarun Mandals in about 40 of them, functioning systematically and holding regular weekly meetings. Almost all bonded labourers in these villages have been freed. As a direct and indirect result of the movement, minimum wage is now an effective law not only in the Bhoomi Sena villages but in many other villages in the area. The Tarun Mandals are spontaneously creating people's institutions to respond in innovative ways to various social and economic needs of the people such as the settlement of people's disputes and people's education. Education, for example, is seen not as formal literacy but as conscientisation in the people's struggle, and learning the three Rs is a part of that integrated process.

In the February 1978 state assembly elections, Bhoomi Sena's candidate won by a large margin from Palghar (an electoral constituency reserved for the adivasis), and in the subsequent *panchayet* elections, candidates supported by the Tarun Mandals won in every panchayet that had a Tarun Mandal. Late in 1978 Bhoomi Sena initiated an agricultural workers' union in Thana District while itself continuing as an independent movement.

The emerging sense of participation

People's Power
The basic fist-raising slogan in Bhoomi Sena is the establishment of Lokanche Sarkar, literally meaning 'People's Government'. The Vanguard Group calls this People's Power. The aim of the movement, as articulated by the Vanguard Group, is to transform the social order in Junglepatti so that 'Sawkars' Power' ends and People's Power is established. The people, not the sawkars, will rule. The precise institutional form of this new order has not been elaborated because the movement is in the process of a search for a new order rather than the establishment of any preconceived social system. The real possibilities in this direction are at this stage uncertain.

The chief instrument of the movement is the exercise and assertion of People's Power itself. The Vanguard Group has a clear conception of this unity of ends and means, and recognises that People's Power can be established only by exercising it, in the process of which it will develop its own institutions. An example of this institution-building is the Tarun Mandal itself, created by the people in the process of exercising their power. Other institutions like people's courts are also emerging.

Political struggle
Three corollaries follow logically: first, in relation to the existing social structure in Junglepatti, participation in Bhoomi Sena has taken the form of mobilisation for political struggle, to achieve a transformation of social

relations through the exercise of power. As illustrated already, power is exercised by the adivasis through refusal to obey the sawkar, police or government officials when they appear to encroach upon their legal and basic human rights; through assertion of the people's will; and when other methods fail, by physically confronting what they see as oppression. In Bhoomi Sena's conceptualisation this political struggle has now become primary, and questions of economic and social development, at the time of writing, are secondary.[4]

This does not mean that economic and social tasks are neglected. Bhoomi Sena continues to seek ways of improving adivasi productivity in agriculture as well as adivasi education, health, etc., as means to sustain and promote the political struggle. But there is a clear concern that preoccupation with economics and social welfare may again disorient the movement away from their basic objective of replacing Sawkars' Power by People's Power.

Liberation and the development of spontaneity

Second, People's Power implies spontaneous (creative) collective action by the people as opposed to centrally directed people's action. This is also implied in the concept that institutions arise and evolve from the creative actions of people. One observes an almost religious commitment to spontaneity in Bhoomi Sena. (In their language, *swatasphurtata* literally means 'self-generation'.) A concrete illustration is the totally informal character of the centre, which does not conceive of itself as an organisation but only as a catalyst in the formation of people's organisations. The centre has no constitution or office holders (except its president, who represents Bhoomi Sena in its external relations). People's organisations are at this stage conceived as organs to be created by the people where the people are (i.e. in the village), where they are forming Tarun Mandals by their own voluntary decisions.

There are, however, different levels of collective spontaneity. It can be of a primordial character, or no more than an emotional outburst without a conscious sense of direction. It is likely that such spontaneity characterised the adivasis' revolt of 1945–7 which did not result in any fundamental gain for them. In the beginning of the Bhoomi Sena movement, adivasi spontaneity was deliberately stimulated and coordinated by Bhoomi Sena's Vanguard Group with a prior, collectively reflected consciousness of the need for people's assertion of their rights, somewhat more 'advanced' than the consciousness of the average adivasi. The Vanguard Group had acquired such consciousness through their leadership of the land-grab movement in 1970, and subsequently in jail where they had the opportunity to reflect together on the situation of the adivasis.

Since the resurgence of Bhoomi Sena, the Vanguard Group is systematically trying to conscientise the adivasis, by stimulating in the shibirs their collective self-reflection on the experience of their struggle. It is also seeking to stimulate self-conscientisation sessions in the village Tarun Mandal meetings. Through this, the adivasis can be expected to acquire, at different speeds, an increasing awareness of the direction of their struggle. Finally, the Vanguard Group is systematically propagating the idea of the need for forming organisations at the village level while leaving the actual decision to do so and its timing to the people. Once formed, such organisations are given full autonomy to conduct the local struggle according to locally determined priorities. Thus the Tarun Mandal is an expression of spontaneity, and its activities remain spontaneous *vis-à-vis* the centre. The concept of spontaneity in Bhoomi Sena, with its implicit sense of participation, thus has a developmental element: it (spontaneity) progressively becomes more conscious of its direction and, at least at the village level, it (spontaneity) organises itself.

Participation and organisation

In a basic sense, however, participation is opposed[5] to organisation. Organisations create formal power which needs to be conceptually distinguished from the power of those whose organisation it is or should be. While 'People's Power' needs organisation for purposeful action, the concept of People's Power transcends that of people's organisations which vest power in offices which can be abused, and creates rules of business which may inhibit spontaneity and may also become outmoded over time. There may be circumstances when a rigid adherence to organisational discipline becomes necessary and is perceived by the people to be so, for the attainment of specific objectives set by the people. Organisation or formal power then becomes the instrument through which People's Power is asserted in order to achieve the objective in question. Such situations may arise, for example, if the struggle confronts the organised might of a more powerful enemy at a level and scale greater than that which the adivasis have so far confronted. But there is a danger of degeneration if there is a continued domination of organisation over people even with the consent of the people, as this is liable to create vested interests in the organisation as such, and to consolidate the power and privilege of such interests. When an organisation thus fails to serve the basic purpose of liberating people's creativity, People's Power needs to be reasserted as a countervailing power within its own formal organisation.[6]

A basic requirement of such countervailing power is a consciousness of and vigilance against the possibility of internal authoritarianism. This may be sufficient if formal power is responsive to spontaneous expressions of the people's concern over misuse of authority or of their desire to seek newer institutional forms to express their unfolding creativity. But if such responsiveness and flexibility are lacking, then the people – i.e. the rank and file membership – need to have the capability to institutionalise quickly new forms of People's Power, in order to confront their own formal power. This capability itself develops through experience (practice). Hence it is desirable in the early stages that the organisation be not created mechanically, before there has been a process through which pre-organisational or informal people's institutions may develop which may later crystallise into more formal organisational structures. The act of transcendence – in this case, of formal power by People's Power – is an evolutionary act for which People's Power is created, so that it may absorb the latter while asserting its right to go beyond it to create newer formal power and may actually do so.

The following is an example of the countervailing nature of People's Power in the Bhoomi Sena movement, to prevent anti-people interests being vested in formal power. In one village a founding leader of the Tarun Mandal, who was also a cadre of Bhoomi Sena, collaborated with the sawkars to get himself elected a member of the panchayet and then, with the sawkars' assistance, to become the headman of the village. The membership of the Tarun Mandal learnt of this plot, put up its own candidates against the sawkars' and informed Bhoomi Sena. Kaluram came to the village on the night before the election and confronted the cadre with the facts. The cadre admitted his mistake, apologised to the Tarun Mandal and asked that he be allowed to run for election. Kaluram suggested that the cadre could be forgiven and elected, but the people remained unconvinced and defeated the cadre along with the candidate of the sawkars. This phenomenon was discussed in a positive light by the Vanguard Group who consider it healthy that People's Power remain such a living force, and that the pace of formation of either the Tarun Mandal or a formal central organisation should not be forced. The first essential task is the creation of People's Power through its assertion, conscientisation and spontaneous exercise, in order for it to know itself before it chooses a mode of formal expression. At the initial stage of the movement, participation in Bhoomi Sena is essentially this particular creative act.

Self-reliance

Finally, the assertion and exercise of People's Power as well as its two corollaries discussed above imply self-reliance. This is a value which Bhoomi Sena is asserting and seeking to enhance, again not merely as an end but also as a means in their struggle. They have seen their oppression as directly caused by their dependence on the sawkars and the various government organs – a dependence which is primarily economic, but which is compounded by their psychological and cultural dependence on those who have been perceived as superior.

A number of concrete activities of Bhoomi Sena are now consciously rationalised in terms of the adivasis' newly emerged will to become self-reliant. Land seizure was their first collective act, but the element of conscientisation in it was low. Systematic conscientisation started with the shibirs.

As conscientisation progressed, liberation from bonded labour became the prime issue. This was the beginning of self-reliance: the liberation of the being who is to assert and seek self-expression. The seizure of alienated land continued, now as a more conscious effort at self-reliance – to obtain the necessary access to economic assets. The struggle for the minimum wage was then added and given priority, not merely as a supplement to their earnings but also as a way to reduce dependence on the sawkars for their livelihood. This was a conscious objective, implemented tangibly through the development of collective saving funds in each Tarun Mandal and financed by the higher wages now received. The adivasis saw that the greater economic staying power they needed could be achieved only through a collective insurance system of this sort rather than individual control of higher wages.

In non-economic areas, the development of institutions such as people's courts may also be seen as dependency-reducing measures. In the social field, a new marriage convention has emerged in which the adivasis of a village decide collectively on the cost of the ceremony in order to save the families concerned from heavy borrowing that throws them into bondage. An interesting illustration of the emerging adivasi consciousness of their cultural dependence and the depth of their search for its subtle ways was obtained in one shabir: in a lengthy dialogue the participants discussed why they had accepted without question the humiliating distortion of their names by their oppressors – e.g. Babu would be changed to Babya by the sawkars as well as by the adivasis themselves, whereas the sawkar would be called Babu Seth and the government officer, Babu Saab. The adivasis now recognised this as a device used by their oppressors to strengthen their social power and to give the adivasis an inferior self-image. The cultural domination was such that not only did the oppressor not respect them, but they also did not respect themselves, or any of the others who were oppressed.[7] The adivasis in the shibir then experimented with distorting the sawkars' names in subsequent references to them – a method of 'extrojection' or 'casting out the introjected self-portrait which one's exploiters have a vested interest in perpetuating' (Goulet, 1979:2).

The dimensions of self-reliance

It is important to recognise that the emergence of self-reliance consciousness in the adivasis has not come naturally or easily. To begin with, they had clearly become a very dependent community economically, socially, culturally and psychologically. Self-reliance first manifested itself in the decision of the jailed adivasi activists in 1970 to launch their own movement for recovery of alienated land independently of the left parties. But this movement was distorted for two important reasons: first, the adivasis had as yet little experience in collective self-management, for lack of which their experiment with the collective grain banks failed. Second, at this stage, a very attractive non-self-reliant option was offered to them in the form of massive bank loans and modern technology. Although self-reliance had appeared in their consciousness it could not take root, and sank again into the unconscious.[8] It reappeared only *after the disastrous failure of the experiment in delivery of development from the outside*, and was asserted with a force equal to the disillusionment and humiliation they suffered from this intervention.

The following dialogue (by the authors of the basic study) with Bhoomi Sena cadres on the question of self-reliance illustrates their emerging concepts and attitudes:

Question (to Bhoomi Sena): Is this fierce self-reliance a matter of having no other concrete option, or a value also? A conscious ethical choice between alternatives that exist, or compulsion?

Answer: Self-reliance is an ideal for us, but it is also linked with our practical situation. Without this, our struggle will not develop.

Question: Refusing to pay bank loans could also be regarded as a kind of self-reliance. Have you considered this option? After all, it is your money that the sawkar puts in the bank.

Answer: It is better to rely on our own accumulation. If a loan is taken at all, it should be returned, or else corruption may come in the mind.

Question: What is your attitude to snatching bank money?

Answer: If we get money through concrete struggle then everyone becomes more responsible for its use. If money is just snatched away, then such money is misused – individuals snatch it also for themselves. . . . Such soft options will divert us from the hardship of the struggle which will be long and arduous.

Question: Your opponents also understand this, and offer soft options. Do you succeed in convincing people that these should be rejected?

Answer: When *individuals* want something, we ask them to make the demand *collectively*. Then we know the demand cannot be met, and the people will remain struggle-minded. This is the way to combat the tendency of individuals to fall into the trap of soft options.

Had the technocratic intervention been successful, we may speculate that the story of Bhoomi Sena might have been very different. Self-reliance is a very laudable value that friends of the rural poor talk about, but for those actually struggling for daily survival it may have little appeal if non-self-reliant options are available that give them hope of a better life. The history of Bhoomi Sena illustrates that such a value may not become a real and conscious urge for a poor community unless it actually undergoes a deep shock as a result of a dependent course. Until then, such a community may keep looking for whatever course of action would make its members' lives somewhat more bearable. Their participation in social action, and their very perception of participation, might then take on a different character from that manifested in the present Bhoomi Sena struggle.

Today, self-reliance in Bhoomi Sena is a conscious urge and a driving force. Its meaning, however, is complex and defies formal definition. There is no question, yet, of Bhoomi Sena settling down to an equilibrium relationship with outsiders and the outside world that could be defined as the concrete meaning of self-reliance. Currently, it is receiving critical assistance from outsiders at the same time that it is rejecting paternalistic external gestures. In this sense it is critically dependent on outsiders for promotion of its self-reliance. This dependence has been particularly noticeable in two vital areas – economic sustenance and the development of knowledge.

Staying power

Many adivasis in the Bhoomi Sena movement, particularly in the early phases of struggle in a village, are finding their economic sustenance even more difficult than when the sawkars were 'taking care of them'. It was in the interest of the sawkars to keep them alive in order to be able to exploit them. Now that this exploitation is being resisted, the sawkars are, in turn, withholding their moneylending operations even when the adivasis come back to them in desperation, often denying them even wage work. The adivasis are facing the resulting hardship heroically – in one village they have, as a substitute for wage work, for a month cut trees and taken headloads of wood to a market 15 miles away, at night to avoid the scorching sun. In another village, considered to be one of the most advanced in the struggle, they lived on roots for a couple of weeks and were on the point of abandoning the movement and submitting to the sawkars when the Vanguard Group succeeded in raising a loan for them from a Christian missionary. Obviously, a sense of identity with the movement and the sharing of hardships for their liberation is giving them some mental staying power with which they are able to survive a period of acute hardship, and to some extent this acts as a substitute for economic staying power.[9] But this substitution obviously has its limits, and alternative sources of economic sustenance, including occasional assistance from outside, remain necessary to keep the 'self-reliant' movement alive. At the centre, there is the expense of paying the full-time cadres (at Rs 100 a month each) who constitute the

Vanguard Group, and overhead costs, travel, etc. have also to be financed. For these, Bhoomi Sena is still critically dependent on voluntary contributions, mainly from its urban middle-class friends. In accepting such assistance Bhoomi Sena is highly selective, and accepts only unconditional contributions from quarters without apparent direct interest in the movement. Nevertheless, dependence on such assistance has its implicit costs and may very well limit the character of the movement, for example in terms of the legality of the adivasis' demands and actions as perceived by their urban middle-class friends.

Endogenous knowledge-building and the role of outsiders

No less important is the adivasis' need to develop their knowledge, in order to conduct their struggle with a growing sense of direction and to enhance their capacity for self-management of the political, institutional, social and economic tasks they are facing. While trial and error is a great educator in itself, there exists knowledge in the outside world which people can adapt to their needs and thereby accelerate their own endogenous process of learning.

Contrary to romantic notions about the people as the best repository of the knowledge they need to improve their lives, the adivasis are acutely conscious of their deficiencies in this regard. Bhoomi Sena seeks the assistance of outsiders who can help in the acceleration of their learning. At the same time they are aware from bitter experience that blind submission to external knowledge dehumanises them and, instead of raising their capability, makes them dependent.

Learning is a creative process that cannot be accomplished by a mechanical transfer of external knowledge. The latter has to be adapted by critical reflection and creative application in order to be internalised. Bhoomi Sena has itself learned through experience that knowledge cannot be transferred: in its second shibir (March 1976) the leadership concentrated on communicating to the participants what had been creatively learned through collective reflection by another set of participants in the first shibir held a month earlier; while the people listened and nodded, this had very little stimulating effect on them. Compared to the first shibir, where people had learned through a dynamic process, those in the second had only listened, but not learned. Since then, the effort of Bhoomi Sena has been to stimulate processes of collective reflection in which individuals are encouraged to articulate their own experiences, perceptions and thoughts, followed by collective discussion of what has been expressed, with a particular effort to understand the structural (universal) features in the experiences narrated that generate a commonality of individual perceptions. In this process, knowledge already generated elsewhere (e.g. in another shibir or Tarun Mandal meeting, or in some other people's movement) is presented only as an input to the discussion.

In the effort to develop an endogenous process of people's knowledge-building, Bhoomi Sena is receiving critical help from a few outside activists. Without this assistance, the adivasis' learning process might be considerably slower. The help of outsiders in this regard is explicitly recognised by the Bhoomi Sena leadership who explain:

> In the first shibir, we had not come out of dependence. We had no political understanding. We wanted to link the political issues with our problems and needed the help of outsiders in this respect. When we learned the linking, we can now do this analysis on our own. We now go to the Tarun Mandals and tell them the method by which we learned, and ask them to learn the method of learning how to link economic problems with politics. (de Silva *et al.*, 1979: 45–6)

From these and other experiences with outsiders in relation to their process of learning the Bhoomi Sena leaders have conceptualised in their own words the role of outsiders in promoting their movement and, for that matter, other self-reliant people's movements. This concept, in the view of the author, is worthy of repetition:

> We need outside help for analysis and understanding of our situation and experience, but not for telling us what we should do.
>
> Initially, we had genuinely thought that outsiders had our good at heart and knew better. We did not think much of ourselves and did not have ideas of our own.
>
> An outsider who comes with ready-made solutions and advice is worse than useless. He must first understand *from us* what our questions are, and help *us* to articulate the questions better, and then help *us* to find solutions. Outsiders also have to change. He alone is a friend who helps us to think about our problems *on our own*.
>
> The relation between outsiders and Bhoomi Sena should be similar to that between Bhoomi Sena and Tarun Mandal. The principle should be minimum intervention. The Bhoomi Sena cadres do not offer any solutions to Tarun Mandal. When Tarun Mandal faces some genuine problem, Bhoomi Sena tells them only how problems of this type have been solved in other villages. Then Tarun Mandal decides.

Redistribution of the 'means of thinking'

Bhoomi Sena is asserting that the people's right to think for themselves is basic to self-reliance. But it is seeking outside help to develop its 'means of thinking' – a dynamic dimension of self-reliance. In this duality there is unity as well as tension. Bhoomi Sena defines what may be considered one of the most important and delicate roles for outsiders in assisting participatory people's development.[10]

As the adivasis' earlier experiences suggest, participation with primordial consciousness in a modern world is hardly possible. The successful development of any participatory initiative requires on the part of the people an understanding of the complex social relations of which they are a part but which go much beyond their immediate experience. Moreover, what are known as modern science and technology have developed in the hands of educated elites who thereby have acquired tremendous social power. With this power they have monopolised not only the means of further development of science and technology – e.g. access to existing knowledge and means of research – but also the very power to determine what *is* scientific knowledge. This monopoly gives them the power to dominate the people, reducing them to pawns in scientific and social experiments. At the same time, the compulsion for rapid economic development is so great in the perception of the people themselves in many poor societies that they tend often to submit to such non-participatory paternalistic relations.

The re-establishment of people's participation requires not only a redistribution of the access to economic resources but also a redistribution of the means of thinking for which Bhoomi Sena is striving. This requires, among other things, people's access to existing knowledge (in the people's language); people's control over research resources; the development of people's own institutions of collective thinking for objective development of knowledge (e.g. the shibirs or 'people's seminars', 'people's school or university'). As knowledge cannot be transferred but has to be creatively generated or adapted, the above in a basic sense means the generation and assertion of an endogenous process of people's knowledge-building.

The assertion is as important as the process of learning, and is in fact essential for liberation of the learning process. In the Bhoomi Sena shibirs the adivasis are encouraged to assert that what one perceives and understands is the truth for oneself – what is specific to an individual is a subjective truth; what others share and can verify becomes objective (or 'scientific') truth for the concerned group of individuals. It does not matter if 'outsiders' do not believe in the 'ghost' that the people may all have seen – the 'ghost' is nevertheless a scientific truth for the people with reference to their own learning process.[11]

For promoting people's self-reliance and participation, it is vitally important to assert the validity of this process for every community, and to assert that self-reliant rational action by the people will not be determined by others' knowledge but by the people's own knowledge at whatever stage this happens to be. Only by reconsideration of 'truth' in the light of their own unfolding experience, will people's knowledge develop rather than be stultified, devalued and blocked, as has happened in so many societies.

Bhoomi Sena demonstrates that within this context, the role of outsiders – educated intellectuals – can still be critical in stimulating and assisting the people's endogenous learning process by bringing to it external knowledge and tools of analysis to be creatively absorbed, thereby enriching, strengthening and accelerating the process. At the same time, the delicacy of this role should be recognised, for there is always the danger that commitment may slacken and a dependent relation re-emerge, or, in the hands of inexperienced intellectuals, even those who are committed, the process may be pushed beyond its capacity at any one time to be absorbed and alienation may result rather than the desired self-reliance.[12]

Concluding observations

In Bhoomi Sena, people's participation is expressing itself in the form of the people's struggle against oppression and exploitation, the assertion of their right to self-determination, the search for institutional forms of releasing people's creativity, and interaction with outsiders to build their self-reliance capability. A concept of unity of ends and means is clearly implied in their approach which rejects mechanical or authoritarian methods and relies on creative acts by the people to achieve their objectives. The emerging sense of participation is closely identified with spontaneity, which is the primary source of human creativity, and with self-reliance. These concepts are viewed, however, dialectically, not rejecting their opposites – organisation and dependence – but seeking to unite with them in order to take whatever there is of value in them in a dynamic, developmental view. The task is delicate – to develop spontaneity and self-reliance in such necessary interaction with their opposites without being taken over by the latter may indeed be seen as a central internal problem in efforts like that of Bhoomi Sena to promote participation.

Relativity of participation–perception

Viewed from outside, the relativity of the notion of participation should be obvious. The specific way in which the urge for participation is expressing itself in the Bhoomi Sena movement today is rooted in the adivasis' concrete historical experience of their past efforts in promoting participation. If either the Communist Party or the social workers who came later could have brought sustained benefit to the adivasis with some institutional arrangement for their formal participation in the management of their affairs – e.g. through people's elected representatives – the adivasis might have been content with the feeling that they were participating quite well in the process of development. It might then have been considered presumptuous for outsiders to claim, on the basis of some abstract notion, that this was not 'true participation'. In view of such variety of expression that people's participation may take, it is not clear whether it would be at all useful to try to construct a general definition of participation which many, including the present author, have been prone to do.

A dilemma in macro action

A deeper problem arises in connection with macro action to promote people's participation (e.g. policy and effort to change institutions on a macro scale). Such action is taken by macro organisations such as governments, trade unions and political parties, who may have some measure of genuine commitment. The problem, nevertheless, is that macro action, in order to be successful, will often require adherence by local units to macro discipline imposed centrally, and the acceptance as a result of centrally conceived forms of participation (e.g. institutions). It may not be able to permit the luxury of the type of creative local search for participatory institutions in which Bhoomi Sena is engaged.

Often, in order to promote participation on a wide scale, macro action will involve struggles with opposing macro forces representing the status quo of the social structure and institutions, and the contingencies of such struggles may necessitate that the immediate issues and methods of action be determined centrally. The dilemma is that in thus seeking to 'liberate', the very thing to be liberated – i.e. people's creativity – may fail to be created, and what has not been created cannot be liberated. In such a situation the most likely outcome of a 'successful' macro action would seem to be the domination of the new institutions by one or another of the forces that already exist (e.g. party or government bureaucracy), to promote their power rather than people's power.

Armed with this awareness, Bhoomi Sena actually rejects the idea of belonging to any macro organisation. At most, it agrees to be an ally, and insists on retaining its autonomy, a relation that may not always be helpful to the operations of its would-be bigger partner. At the same time Bhoomi Sena itself recognises that at some stage, its struggle may come up against a more serious macro constraint than it has encountered so far,[13] and may then require macro effort to overcome it.

The dilemma is real, both for Bhoomi Sena and for those macro organisations which may have a commitment to its struggle and objectives but have their own strategy of action based on a multitude of complex considerations. It would be useless to speculate on how this dilemma might be resolved. It is suggested, however, that a first step in resolving it is to recognise it. The second step is to try to understand the ways and aspirations expressed in autonomous people's movements on the basis of which a constructive micro–macro dialogue may begin.

Postscript

The Bhoomi Sena movement, which I visited again in 1986, has by now achieved its primary aim of liberating the adivasis from bonded labour in much of Palghar Taluk, and is now acting as a political organisation of the adivasis, asserting adivasi self-determination and working as a pressure group for the adivasis' economic and social rights *vis-à-vis* state and other non-adivasi structures.

Notes

1. Junglepatti is in Palghar Taluk in Maharastra, with a land area of about 140,000 acres, of which forest accounts for 80,000 acres and 38,000 are under agriculture. It has a population of 90,000 spread over about 100 villages, of which the adivasis – a generic term loosely used to describe the aborigines of India – comprise over 65 per cent. The Bhoomi Sena (Land Army) movement was studied by a team of social researchers in collaboration with the activists and cadres of the movement over the period 1977–8 by the method of 'participatory research' (de Silva *et al.*, 1979). This study provides the empirical basis of the present paper.

2. The term Bhoomi Sena is used, as the adivasis use it, to describe both the movement and its Vanguard Group. The context will make clear which of these senses is being used in any instance.

3. The literal meaning is 'youth assembly'.

4. In a visit to Bombay late in 1979 the author was told by a senior activist of Bhoomi Sena that two other organisations of the rural poor had emerged in Maharastra – the Kranti Sena (Army of the Crossroads) and Kashtakari Shangathan (Organisation of Those who do Hard Labour) – which took inspiration and assistance from Bhoomi Sena but were independent organisations. Early in 1980 it was reported that the former had merged with Bhoomi Sena.

5. The term 'opposed to' is used here in the sense not of negating, but of a dialectical duality of opposites in which one requires the other for its own development at the same time that they may confront one another. (See the section 'Concluding observations'.)

6. This conceptualisation of People's Power as countervailing power came out of a dialogue held in August 1977 between Amit Bhaduri, G. V. S. de Silva, Niranjan Mehta, M. A. Rahman, Pouna Wignaraja and Datta Savale (the most senior activists in Bhoomi Sena). The argument has been reconstructed from the author's notes on the dialogue ('Collective reflections on People's Power arising out of Bhoomi Sena', Bombay, 26–28 August 1977), reproduced in a special issue on rural participation edited by the author in *Development: Seeds of Change*, Society for International Development, Rome, April–July 1981.

7. An account of this shibir, which the author also attended, is in Harsh Sethi, *Lok Chetna Jagaran* ('The awakening of people's awareness'), New Delhi, 1978 (mimeo).

8. See Carl Jung's works for a psychological theory of duality of human values, with the opposites of conscious values in the unconscious, liable to emerge into the consciousness under specific conditions. For a lucid exposition

see David Cox, *Analytical Psychology: An Introduction to the Work of C. G. Jung*, Chapter 7.

9. For elaboration of this idea, see Md. Anisur Rahman, *Self-reliant Mobilisation, a Conceptual Study in Development Strategy*, UNCTAD/RD/123, Geneva, November 1976, pp. 28–30.

10. Irrespective of production relations, i.e. whether they are feudal, capitalist or socialist. In fact, an increasingly emergent lesson of history is that a redistribution of the means of production in favour of the people in no way ensures a redistribution of the means of thinking, and through monopoly of control over the latter a minority is able to continue ruling over the majority without giving them a real voice and involvement in social affairs. For further discussion of this idea see Md. Anisur Rahman 'A policy-oriented note on the all-India Convention of people's science movements', in K. P. Kannan (ed.), *Towards a People's Science Movement, Papers and Proceedings of the all-Indian Convention of People's Science Movements Held in Trivandrum, India, during 10, 11, and 12 November 1978*, Kerala Sastrasahitya Parishad, Trivandrum, 1979. See also Orlando Fals Borda, 'Science and the common people', paper presented to the International Forum on Participatory Research, Ljubljana, Yugoslavia, 13–22 April 1980.

11. 'Scientists' have their own 'ghosts' – i.e. theories which are held to be true and objective knowledge until they are proved wrong and discarded.

12. A broad term increasingly being used to connote an organic interaction between intellectuals and people's movements is 'action' or 'participatory' research. It is significant that the study of Bhoomi Sena on which the present paper is based was participatory. It indeed had to be, for Bhoomi Sena with its commitment to self-reliance would not agree to outsiders merely coming to study them. They must themselves participate in the study and see its value in promoting their own movement. For a seminal contribution to the understanding of action research, see Orlando Fals Borda, 'Investigating reality in order to transform it: the Colombian experience', *Dialectical Anthropology*, 1979, pp. 33–55.

13. It appears that Bhoomi Sena has found a space to develop in the way it has because of contradictions between the 'semi-feudal' sawkars and emerging capitalist farmers in Junglepatti and the respective links of these two classes at the state level. Bhoomi Sena may have to confront a very different situation if eventually, and thanks to some extent to its own efforts, capitalism begins to emerge as the dominant production relation in Junglepatti agriculture with firm support from the state government. If Bhoomi Sena then chooses to confront this newly emerging power, it is conceivable that it may then have to encounter serious macro resistance. For a discussion of this and other possibilities, see de Silva *et al.*, 1979: Chapter 7.

References

de Silva, G. V. S. *et al.* (1979) 'Bhoomi Sena: a struggle for people's power', *Development Dialogue*, No. 2.
Goulet, Denis (1979) 'Development as liberation: policy lessons from case studies', *IFDA Dossier*, No. 3.

4. SARILAKAS means strength: initiating people's organisations in Philippine barangays

SARILAKAS – *sariling lakas* meaning 'own strength' – is the name given to an effort to promote people's participation in a recent initiative in a few Philippine villages. This effort took over from an earlier intervention by the Philippine government's Rural Workers' Office (now the Bureau of Rural Workers) in an ILO-sponsored project called Project AID (Action Identification for the Development of Landless Rural Workers) launched in July 1979. Under this project 'community facilitators' went to villages in four areas to initiate participatory research with poor rural workers, and to stimulate the formation of their organisations. Organisations were formed, to which projects were promised by the community facilitators, and the members kept waiting for resources and other deliveries to come from the government. Hardly anything came, and the people began to lose interest in their organisations. At this point an ILO-sponsored exchange (August–October 1980), with participatory initiatives in India, Bangladesh and Sri Lanka under a 'TCDC' project, stimulated a reorientation of the Philippine project towards a dedicated effort to promote participatory people's processes in two of the four areas (Tibiao and Balayan municipalities in Antique and Batangas provinces respectively). Most of the community facilitators were changed in view of the project's new orientation. SARILAKAS was thus born, supported until the end of 1982 by the ILO, the Netherlands government and the International Centre for Law in Development (New York).

The following accounts are taken mostly from the report of an evaluation of SARILAKAS conducted in July 1982 by the ILO and the Dutch government in collaboration with the Bureau of Rural Workers, with more recent information added from reports received from the project staff.

Originally published in *Reading Rural Development Communications (RRDC) Bulletin*, March 1987, under the title 'The Philippines: "Sarilakas" means strength'.

Barangay Amar: an authentic popular organisation emerges

Intervention in Tibiao municipality has been in three *barangays* (villages) – Amar, Malabor and Importante.

Barangay Amar has a population of about 800, whose principal occupations are rice cultivation as tenant farmers and working as *sacadas* (migrant labourers) on sugar plantations in other areas. Almost all inhabitants are poor, always unsure of a means of survival beyond a few months without borrowing.

Under Project AID, thirty-eight persons formed an organisation in March 1980 called the Barangay Amar Farmers' Association (BAFA). The organisation depended for initiative on the community facilitators, who promised projects and loans, but nothing actually materialised. Members, losing interest in the organisation, started dropping off, until the SARILAKAS facilitators came in February 1981.

The SARILAKAS facilitators developed a much closer social relation with the members, integrating with them in terms of daily lifestyle. They stimulated the members, now twenty-eight in number, to deliberate themselves on their immediate problems and to take initiatives of their own according to their own priorities. The members first decided to negotiate production loans for fertilisers and chemicals from the Land Bank in the name of BAFA, and these were in turn distributed by the organisation among the members. This was an improvement over borrowing from landlords and moneylenders. But collective deliberations were generating an attitude of critical inquiry among the members, and they soon discovered that the bank loan, with its 14 per cent interest rate and many other deductions and the procedural complexities, was also quite exploitative. The members then decided to initiate their own collective savings fund to replace the Land Bank as a source of production loans. Each member agreed to contribute P50 (P9 = $1 approximately) or one sack of rice after the cropping season (twice a year). The fund grew to the size of about P2,000 by June 1982 when the members began taking production loans from it at a 10 per cent interest rate, the interest augmenting their own fund.

About the same time the organisation also purchased a hand-tractor which the members decided they needed, as many of them did not have a bullock and plough which they had to rent at a high cost. The community facilitators helped by negotiating a loan in the amount of P20,000 from the Canadian government through its embassy, with the stipulation that this would be utilised as a revolving fund in supporting other worthwhile socio-economic projects in other communities as well. The services of the tractor were offered both to members and non-members, against rental, and all the members learnt to operate it so as to take turns in assisting the chief hand-tractor operator, also a member, who had been professionally trained in its operation.

In less than a month (by the third week of July 1982) a gross amount of P3,000 had been realised from this operation, and BAFA targeted repayment of the loan for the tractor in three years instead of a formally stipulated six years.

Late in 1982 the organisation purchased a rice mill, there being none nearby and the members having to go for rice milling to a very distant barangay and pay a lot for the service. They planned to use the engine of the hand-tractor to operate the rice mill when the tractor was not in use, and to use the profits from the mill towards amortisation of the tractor. They also constructed a warehouse with the help of collective free labour and voluntary contributions from all members, where they keep their rice mill, tractor and rice grains.

It was reported that, seeing the development of BAFA, field staff of the Ministry of Agrarian Reform and the Ministry of Agriculture, who were supposed to organise the tenants to implement certain land reform legislation but who had not made much progress in this regard, now became active to develop another organisation in the barangay for land reform purposes. The Land Bank is already charging the tenant farmers a deduction for the land reform programme. BAFA is resisting what its members see as an attempt to weaken their authentic organisation by creating others. A letter has been sent to the Land Bank, asking for the transfer to BAFA of the collections the bank is making for the land reform programme.

BAFA has a formal meeting of its General Assembly once every month. But by now collective meetings and deliberations have become part of the daily life of the members, who gather almost every day informally (whoever is able to come), and the formal monthly meetings in many cases only synthesise ongoing deliberations and take formal decisions. The attendance in formal meetings is reported to be almost full.

Barangay Malabor: struggles for economic rights

All the inhabitants of this barangay, with a population a little over 1,600, are poor. They are engaged in combinations of owner and tenant farming, farming and fishing, and farming or fishing and working as sacadas on sugar-cane plantations or as house workers.

Under Project AID, two separate organisations were formed in Malabor in April 1980 – one farmers' organisation and one fishermen's organisation. These were merged into one in July 1980 at the suggestion of the Rural Workers' Office, in view of the dual (farmer–fisherman) status of many of the members. Membership at that time totalled fifty-two.

The community facilitators of Project AID emphasised the undertaking of income-generating projects with bank loans. Feasibility studies on a number of projects (e.g. ice plant, fishing gear) were undertaken with the help of the facilitators, and submitted to the Rural Workers' Office. Nothing happened; the members lost interest and the organisation became defunct, with only nine members by the end of 1980.

Stimulation to collective activity came from another source. The ILO's TCDC exchange project brought a leader from Bangladesh's Proshika and one from India's PIDT, two NGOs who talked of self-reliant people's initiatives in their respective countries and challenged the workers in Malabor to take collective initiatives of their own without waiting for government projects (see chapter 6). The visitors left, but the nine members had been inspired.

An irrigation project had been undertaken in the area under the government's National Irrigation Scheme. The work had been incomplete with poor supervision and water was not flowing. The nine members of the *kasamma* (the term used in the local dialect for an association of progressive workers) now initiated a mobilisation of the villagers to repair and rehabilitate the scheme. The villagers contributed free labour and materials and worked for fifteen days to repair and complete the project. Water began to flow in December 1980, from then on making two crops instead of one crop possible.

There was still the problem of water distribution to be resolved. The irrigation scheme was formally under the responsibility of the Tibiao Irrigation Services Association (TISA) which was reportedly in a mess, and a number of farmers who had contributed to the rehabilitation of the irrigation scheme were being denied a fair share of water. At this stage (February 1981) the SARILAKAS facilitators came to the area, and the TISA asked them to help resolve the water distribution problem. The facilitators consulted the farmers, attended meetings of the TISA Board, and helped resolve organisational problems of the TISA, including those of collection of fees, water management, etc.

This experience, and the motivational work of the SARILAKAS facilitators to stimulate self-deliberated collective action, rekindled interest in the kasamma. Membership began to rise again, reaching almost seventy by July 1982.

This kasamma also negotiated a production loan from the Land Bank. Then it put pressure on the Ministry of Agrarian Reform for the issue of tenancy certificates with which tenant farmers could obtain National Food Authority (NFA) passbooks which would entitle them to sell their produce to the NFA for a higher price than they could get in the market. Most members now obtained the passbooks, a privilege which they had so long been unable to procure.

Another question the kasamma took up was the change in the farmers' status from sharecropping tenancy to fixed-rent leaseholding. Tenancy had already been abolished by a presidential decree, but this had hardly been put into effect in this area. The farmers were either unaware of the decree, or ignorant of the procedure to secure this right, or afraid of reprisals by the landowner if they pressed for its implementation. Now they learnt about the decree and the procedures from educational seminars sponsored by the kasamma, and gained courage from their organisation to ask for its implementation. One after another the members began to acquire the status of leaseholders.

Among other activities, the kasamma sponsored a meeting with the Bureau of Fisheries and Aquatic Resources (BFAR) to discuss the threat fishermen of the barangay faced from the operation of commercial fishing boats, which could come to a depth of seven fathoms of water in all coastal areas. In Malabor the depth of seven fathoms is much closer to the shore than normal, and after discussing this matter the kasamma sent a petition to the President of the country requesting that the limit for commercial fishing boats in Malabor and adjacent waters be made seven kilometres instead. The petition, sent in May 1982, was signed by small fishermen in Malabor as well as in other areas, and was supported by other small fishermen's organisations and the mayor's League of Antique through separate resolutions. Apparently some steps have been taken by the BFAR on the petition. Action by top officials is still awaited.

The organisation has also raised with the mayor of Tibiao the issue of a 10 per cent 'concessioner's fee' the fishermen have to pay to the municipality on their catches, which upon study of the relevant laws they discovered to be illegal. The mayor has promised that the fee will be dropped, although a new tax of some kind may have to be levied to cover municipal expenses.

The kasamma is currently engaged in developing a collective fishing project with Japanese equipment for which it is negotiating for credit from the National Livelihood Programme of the Ministry of Human Settlement.

Barangay Importante: spirit in the face of setback

This is a forest area, with a population of nearly 800. The occupations are different combinations of farming, migrant labour and housekeeping.

A kasamma was formed here in March 1980, with twenty-three members. Project AID facilitators promised loans, together with a rice mill. Nothing was delivered and the members lost interest. By the end of the year membership was down to eleven. No meetings were held, except when outsiders visited the project in that area.

The SARILAKAS facilitators came in February 1981 and did house-to-house motivational work for revival of the organisation with emphasis on people's initiatives and people's issues. The people were stimulated and the kasamma was reborn.

The first issue the people now took up was the abuse of their forestry rights by forest guards. Under the government's Communal Tree Farming Programme the people are entitled to an allotment of two hectares of forest land each. But they hardly knew of these rights, and the forest guards denied them access to forest land and themselves appropriated its fruit.

The people had learnt of their forest rights from the Project AID facilitators, but the promise of loans and projects had disoriented their attention. Stimulated now to take their own initiatives, they confronted the forest guards and asserted their forest rights. The latter yielded and land started being allotted to the people according to law.

Next, with the help of the SARILAKAS facilitators, the kasamma negotiated production loans from the Land Bank. Many members availed themselves of these loans, but as in Amar the people here also found this to be not very much better than borrowing from the moneylender. In order to become independent of outside borrowing the members decided early in 1982 to launch a project of collective mango care, with the idea of building their own collective savings fund from out of the profits from this project.

The project consisted of taking care of forty-nine trees mostly owned by landlords. To provide the capital to start the project the members made ad hoc contributions of about P740 and, using this as a counterpart fund, they raised a bank loan of P5,000 through the Rural Workers' Office.

Unfortunately, the municipality was hit that year by the worst typhoon in sixteen years, and in addition a new kind of pest attacked the trees both before and after it. In place of an expected profit in the order of P30,000 planned both to repay the bank loan and to purchase transportation to market the mangoes, the bank loan itself could not be repaid in full. This did not dampen the spirit of the members, totalling thirty-four by July 1982, who met, analysed their experience, and decided to reduce the number of trees to take care of and to take more intensive care of them. The problems, however, continue: the mango project is now suffering from widespread drought in addition to severe attacks from pests. But the spirit of the organisation remains undampened, and the members see their experience with the mango project as a continuous learning process.

Barangay Taludtod: farmers fight the landlords

Barangay Taludtod in Balayan, with a population of nearly 600, belongs to a sugar-producing area where most land is owned by big landowners and worked by tenants and landless labourers. For the past few years the tenants have had trouble in obtaining their customary 50 per cent of the proceeds. The crop is taken to the mills, from where the proceeds are given to the landowners who are responsible for determining and distributing their tenants' share. A deduction is made for transporting the cane to the mills in trucks usually owned by the landlords. Everything taken together, the landlords' hold over the tenants was tight, made only tighter by the tenants surviving with debts incurred to the very same landowners.

In 1975 the landlords in *sitio* Taludtod (one of the three hamlets in Barangay Taludtod) raised the trucking fee from P15 to P28 per ton for carrying sugar cane to a mill. The tenants refused to pay the higher fee, and the landlords retaliated by withholding their 50 per cent share of the proceeds. The tenants filed a case with the Court of Agrarian Relations in 1976, requesting the court to designate court personnel to supervise the harvesting and milling of the cane, and order that all mill proceeds be deposited with the court. The court complied. But this failed to improve matters for the tenants, as court hearings were repeatedly postponed, resulting in great delays in the release of tenants' shares of the proceeds. The court personnel were also deducting travel expenses, and the tenants' own lawyer was making withdrawals, both without their prior knowledge and consent.

Under Project AID a number of tenants in Taludtod formed an organisation in 1980. But Project AID did not address the issue which was agitating them, and the organisation as a result remained inactive.

Two SARILAKAS facilitators came early in 1981 and sought to revive interest in the organisation. Nineteen tenants from sitio Taludtod began to meet, with the trucking fee case as the usual agenda. In December 1981 the majority of the fifteen members decided on a militant strategy; they sent an open letter to the President of the country protesting against what they perceived as anomalies in the court's handling of the case and began attending the court hearings in a body, often creating a sensation in the court. They also filed a case through a legal facilitator provided by SARILAKAS in the Supreme Court for speedy disposal of the case and for showing them all the accounts that came to the court from the mills. The Supreme Court, in response, ordered the Commission for Audit to examine the accounts of the court.

Resolution of the court case nevertheless continued to be procrastinated, with hearings being postponed repeatedly. Finally, the landlords struck again by refusing to send trucks to their farms, willing to let the canes dry up. At this point (February 1983) the director of the Bureau of Rural Workers (as the former Rural Workers' Office is now called) intervened personally, and persuaded the landlords to come to an amicable settlement with the tenants: the trucking fee was considerably reduced, and a number of other obligations on both sides were agreed upon.

The Taludtod organisation also started in September 1982 a rice distribution project, to buy the monthly rice needs of the members at one time, enabling it to be bought at a cheaper price as well as providing a ready supply and thereby reducing the members' dependence on the landowner. However, the members observed that owing to this project their consumption of rice also increased considerably, and hence they have to assess their capacity to pay for the additional rice consumed. This assessment they plan to do after the current crop-year.

Conclusion: no bypassing economic justice

Although a recent and small project, SARILAKAS already illustrates sharply, in contrast to Project AID, how under specific structural conditions the rural poor, when they are given the necessary stimulation, opportunity and assistance, actually *participate* in collective efforts to improve their lives.

Under Project AID the promises of the project staff kept the people alienated from their own capabilities and strength to tackle their own issues and achieve their rights. The SARILAKAS facilitators behaved differently. They integrated with the people, and stimulated them to deliberate upon what they could do themselves. The educational seminars raised the people's awareness of their rights. Armed with this knowledge and stimulated to take initiatives themselves, the people deliberated and took action which ranged from the purely economic to full 'pressure-group' activities to assert and achieve their rights as rural workers.

It is significant that in Amar and Importante, people's collective self-deliberation has looked at borrowing from the Land Bank critically, and is taking them towards efforts to achieve greater financial self-reliance by building their own collective savings fund. The economic efforts have not all been successful, but failure is seen as a learning experience in continuing collective effort; it is a more fulfilling life in itself than the static and apathetic state of being which they had previously experienced.

It is also significant that the people did not in all cases go for new economic activities right away, but decided first to settle questions of economic rights by way of access to resources, better distribution of production, fair price for services received, etc. Some of these questions they chose to tackle after becoming aware of their rights through the educational seminars sponsored by their organisations; others they had already been preoccupied with.

For achieving such rights the people confronted at least the local-level status quo, and were supported by 'legal facilitators' provided by the project. Such action, while fully 'legitimate', invites reflection on the way conventional rural development projects are designed (externally) to promote incomes and employment or to provide basic amenities, but typically bypassing outstanding questions of economic justice and rights. If successful, such projects might even distract the people's attention from such questions and thus keep basic wrongs unrighted. In SARILAKAS the people show that when their spirit of independence is roused and they are stimulated to think and choose for themselves, they do not wish to bypass these questions and go for incremental income- and employment-generating activities only. To face basic questions is participation for them; indeed, this is, to them, *development*.

It is not easy, however, to imagine many official development agencies, including donor agencies, undertaking or supporting projects which would seek to stimulate people's legitimate participation of the kind described above.

Postscript (1983)

After two years of pilot experimentation SARILAKAS was poised to expand its activity. Requests were coming from poor communities in other areas for assistance in initiating similar organisational development, training and legal assistance activities for them. The SARILAKAS staff, however, felt constrained by an increasing bureaucratisation of the Bureau of Rural Workers and questioning of the unconventional procedures they had to adopt in implementing the project, and they set up in 1983 a non-government agency by the name of PROCESS – Participatory Research, Organisation of Communities and Education Towards Struggle for Self-reliance – to continue and expand their work. SARILAKAS remained the spirit of the movement. Today, PROCESS is active in about thirty municipalities in three provinces – Antique, Bohol and Batangas – working in more than 300 villages and 50 towns in what is perhaps the largest non-church-based participatory rural development movement in the country. In each province the village-level people's organisations, while engaged in solving immediate local problems, have linked up, through formal federations or otherwise, to initiate wider mass mobilisation and workshops on problems of common concern such as fishing rights of small fishermen and land rights of sugar-cane growers. A new dimension of PROCESS's work is the systematic involvement of students of law schools in the relevant provinces to provide legal support to the people's organisations. These mobilisations have produced impressive results, particularly with respect to fishing rights for the small fishermen over wide areas in the coastal belt of Antique province.

The animators ('facilitators') in PROCESS are making themselves progressively dispensable to the organisations whose self-reliant development they are helping. There were, for example, two SARILAKAS facilitators working in the three pilot villages in Tibiao in 1980–1; today two PROCESS facilitators are covering some forty villages in the same municipality, intensively working in new areas where work has started more recently, and only as occasional 'consultants' in the older villages where 'folk catalysts' or people's own leaders have taken over.

5. News from 'nowhere': Bangladesh field notes and reflections

Field notes

This is a brief personal diary to share with friends involved with grassroots organising work with the rural poor. I spent some time during the period I was on special leave (September–December 1984) interacting with such work in Bangladesh. Some highlights of my experience are given below.

The number of agencies, mostly private, working with the rural poor in Bangladesh has increased phenomenally, now totalling from 500 to 600, claiming a total coverage of about 8,000 to 10,000 villages. The nature of the work varies widely, from purely technocratic projects to consciousness-raising and organisation development efforts for economic as well as pressure-group action.

I had the opportunity to interact with samples of leaderships and members of organisations of the rural poor created through the intervention of two of the larger NGOs. The samples were chosen ad hoc and are not necessarily representative. But they did generate some important questions and issues of wide relevance.

Conscientisation
One NGO is using the Paulo Freirian pedagogy of literacy to develop self-reflected awareness ('conscientisation') of the landless. A three-month course is the starting point of external intervention to give literacy through words chosen from the people's daily vocabulary, around which discussions on social reality and ways of transforming it are generated. Through the course the landless develop organisation consciousness and form their own organisation at the village level, start a savings programme, and in collaboration with the NGO launch a succession of economic and social activities.

Originally published in *PRAXIS*, Vol. 1, No. 4, March 1987, under the title 'Participation of the rural poor in development (Bangladesh field notes)'.

It was a treat to dialogue for nearly three hours with about a hundred leaders of about thirty landless organisations (male) in as many adjacent villages under this programme in one area. (Professor Tilakaratna of PIDA, Sri Lanka, and Ms Angelita Gregorio-Medel of the Center for Community Services in the Philippines were also present.) Work in this area had started about five years back, and the organisations of the landless were engaged in various economic enterprises, both individual and collective, with their own funds and with loans from the intervening NGO. They showed a self-reliance consciousness not commonly seen: they wanted to become independent of credit from the NGO, and one of their policies aiming at this objective was to charge themselves at a rate of interest of 50 per cent; from out of this they gave the 18 per cent which the NGO charged, and put the remaining 32 per cent in their own collective fund to have it grow fast. When asked what advice they had for the NGO, they came out with the unexpected answer that the NGO should leave them in two to three years by which time they expected to become fully self-reliant; the NGO should then go and work in other areas for organising landless people like themselves.

Stimulated by the quality of their responses we asked progressively deeper questions. Did they have a position on the land question? Yes, they replied. They had been discussing this question for the last five years, and had concluded that land must be collectively owned and tilled. Were they themselves practising this? Yes, wherever they were able to lease land they held and tilled it collectively, without a single exception, and they had worked out their own system of collective management, distribution of labour and reward, etc.

What was their position on the existing political parties? There was absolutely no political party which represented their interests and only when there would be organisations of the landless like theirs throughout the country would there emerge the relevant political party – 'our own organisation will itself be the party'. Quite a challenge even to left parties led by 'vanguards' with 'advanced consciousness'.[1]

From pressure-group action to dependent economism

Work of another NGO had come to a crossroads. Its earlier work had emphasised conscientisation, not by the Freirian method but by stimulating direct social analysis by the landless. In many places this had led to intense and sustained pressure-group action to confront social injustice and oppression by rural elites and touts. The landless were successful in some of these confrontations and failed in others; but in general they dissipated their energy and in some places their funds in pursuits that did not bring much material gain. As a result in many places a sense of fatigue and frustration ensued. This led to rethinking among the NGO staff, and many started de-emphasising conscientisation work and concentrating on deliveries to raise incomes and employment of the rural poor. Simultaneously, a move was taken to include small farmers in the village organisations.

The result: in one village organisation of the poor we saw a horrifying absolute dependence on external deliveries. The leaders stated that their organisation existed only to get external credit and would collapse without it. They wanted more credit until their fund reached 1 million Takas; they could not dream of ever doing without the NGO workers who were always correct in guiding them and had never said anything with which they could disagree.

Question of alliance with small farmers

In another area which I visited, some landless groups were resisting the new policy of opening their organisations to small farmers while other groups accepted it. In a session where members from four adjacent village-level organisations were present, I initiated a debate among them as to the merits of this proposal. Among the more clearly articulated points of view which emerged were the following two: leaders of one village organisation where small farmers had been admitted said that theirs was a small village with a small number of landless, so that they neither could develop collective funds of any meaningful size, nor could get enough member time to run their organisation as each member was busy with his daily work for subsistence. With the inclusion of small farmers they now had a fund of meaningful size and were able to devise a workable division of labour among the members to run the organisation.

From out of this arose the question as to whether inclusion of small farmers was desirable irrespective of the number of landless in a village. From the debate that followed, the following statement from a landless leader of one village was the most penetrating. This village earlier had a joint organisation of landless and small farmers in which the leadership was dominated by small farmers. The result was that the interests of the landless were neglected, and there were also cases of misappropriation of funds controlled by the small farmers. As a consequence the organisation broke up. Later the landless formed their own separate organisation in the NGO's programme. Now that the question of inclusion of small farmers was being raised, they were in principle in favour of opening membership to those who were really very poor, and there were some who were poorer than many landless. But the management of the organisation should remain in the hands of the landless. Poor small farmers were welcome to join the organisation, contribute to its fund and enjoy the benefits from it, but not to run it.

The debate was ad hoc, but demonstrated the capability of the landless to analyse critically the question of alliance with small and marginal farmers. The NGO concerned can demonstrate its own commitment to people's participation by encouraging the people to deliberate on such questions systematically – their resolution should come from the people rather than from the interveners. I left the landless groups with the suggestion that they seek to develop their own collective position on such important questions by debating their different points of view systematically in village as well as intervillage meetings of their organisations.

Some weeks later I was told that the weekly meetings of the organisations in that area had livened up. Apart from debating questions such as the above, the people had started challenging the NGO workers for making major policy decisions without consulting them. 'I was perspiring all over in fear as they challenged me,' one of the NGO workers told me, 'and yet I was happy, for this is what we should encourage, and they said that they loved me even though they were criticising me.'

Should the painful past be forgotten?

In another area confrontational activity to resist social oppression by rural elites had been particularly intense for several years and had led to many forms of harassment, both of the landless leaders and of the NGO workers involving police, jail, etc. Although in the end most of their positions were vindicated, the cost in terms of resources, energy and alternatives forgone was high. After several years of such activity the landless organisations were dismantled, and 'village development associations' were formed in about twenty villages, now to take care of the 'empty bellies' with economic programmes, with membership open both to the landless and small farmers.

While visiting these villages I was told only of the activities of the last year or so, since the birth of the village development organisations. The same was repeated in a meeting of leaders from a number of villages which I attended. They had started work about a year before, had accumulated some savings, were engaged in some small economic activities with their own funds and/or with credit from the NGO or from the bank, and had plans to launch some more economic projects if they got more credit.

I decided to drag them out of whatever was causing them to withhold their past. I told them that I had come to them hearing about their struggles of several years, wanting to learn from their experience. What was this experience? What did they learn themselves from this? What would they, with their past experience, advise the landless in other villages who might want to get organised? What was the relation of their present activities with the past ones? Or was it that they had nothing to teach me, with hardly a year's experience to talk about, doing little this and wanting to do little that, so that I should go away and maybe return after five years?

After a dead silence they opened up, one after another, getting stimulated as they narrated stories of their past struggles, their high and low points, and their ultimate frustration in cost–benefit terms. They had overspent their energy in pressure-group action before developing the necessary organisational and economic strength to confront their enemies and win more easily. This was the central lesson for new organisations: develop your own strength before confronting big enemies, and meanwhile accept some compromise or 'even some humiliation'. But, albeit at a high cost, their gain was also significant: they had established their status in the villages as an organised force; the elites had also been harassed and had suffered, and now treated them with much greater respect.

Would they not like to document their story, draw its lessons more systematically after thorough discussion in the base organisations, and disseminate them so that fellow landless in other villages would not need to start from zero and could benefit from their experience? Yes, they would, they had not thought about this before, and they could themselves also advance their own systematic collective knowledge to guide their subsequent action. How would they do it if they could not write? Why, they replied, this was the area of the late Ramesh Sheel, the country's most outstanding *kabial* (village poet–debater). They could document their story through *kabigans* (songs of such poets), dramas, etc.

Back in Dhaka I had the opportunity of interacting with a newly created drama society of students which was looking for ways of contributing to social change through a progressive theatre movement, and was planning to spend a few months every year in villages to collect current drama themes and involve villagers in playing them. We talked of the need for such a theatre movement to join hands with the rural poor's movement, to document and disseminate experiences of the rural poor's organised struggles for the benefit of rural poor elsewhere and of those who wish to contribute to their self-development. It is envisaged that collaboration between the two movements may start soon.

The gender question: separate or joint organisations?

There are many separate poor women's organisations under NGO programmes in the country, but I also noticed confusion among some male NGO workers as to the necessity for this. (There is debate even in trade-union and ILO quarters on this question.) I asked members of a poor women's organisation in a village whether they would like a merger with their menfolk's organisation. They replied that in a joint organisation many women members would not be able even to speak at meetings, for women are not supposed to speak in the presence of their *bhashurs* (elder brother of husband). The practical question in the cultural context of some societies is as simple as that.

Are the 'educated' more learned?

I was taken to an inauguration ceremony in a village of a programme of group-based bank credit for the rural landless, and was introduced to the gathering of landless as a 'very learned man'. What a fatal start to create (or strengthen) an inferiority complex among the people at the very beginning of their cooperation. As for the truth, I know that all my learning would be of no value if I were thrown in the village to make a living – I can neither cultivate nor build a hut with my own hands, and would have to learn from the rural poor how to do these and how to survive. I also know that the rural poor are developing from their organised struggles experience from which we all have to learn continuously if we wish to keep pace with life. Give them an inferiority complex and they will only wait for deliveries from outside, which will be the sole purpose of organising.

The need for a people's praxis
The above interactions pinpointed the great need for the people's own systematic review and evaluation of their ongoing experience – i.e. of a people's *praxis*, not merely people's action, to be evaluated and researched by others. The need for and the methods of helping this process are not well understood in all NGO quarters. While I was interacting in the field, Orlando Fals Borda, who was working for me in the ILO, completed editing his synthesis of experiences in participatory research in Colombia, Mexico and Nicaragua under a project in its PORP programme. This report, if soon published, will be timely for interested NGOs in Bangladesh.[2]

Reflections: NGO work organising the rural poor*

The Perspective
NGO work of organising the rural poor can have several different objectives. These will be discussed under four different headings.

Economic uplift
This means raising the incomes of the poor, giving them greater stability of income and some social security or insurance against unforeseen situations, old age, etc. If this is the only or the principal objective, an efficient 'external delivery system', coupled with an internal group savings scheme, is a good way of achieving it. External delivery can be in the form of credit, technology and expertise. The group savings scheme takes care of the social security objective.

But emphasis on the external delivery approach conflicts with the other objectives discussed below.

---

* This section was originally published also in *IFDA Dossier*, No. 50, November/December 1985, under the title 'NGO work of organising the rural poor: the perspective'.

Human development

Creativity is the distinctive human quality, and the human development objective aims to develop the creativity of the people. Creation is the product of thinking and action – i.e. of *participation*. This consists of investigation, reflection (analysis), decision-making and application of decision (action). Reflection upon action (review, evaluation) gives men and women the sense of creation and thus the sense of having developed as human beings.

Human development is a process of *self*-development – outsiders cannot develop the rural poor. Outsiders can have a role, however, in stimulating and assisting this development. This can be done by initiating and stimulating self-investigation and reflection by the rural poor; by stimulating them to take their own decisions and action, and to review and evaluate them themselves. The process may be assisted by external inputs (of ideas, points of views, materials) which the people can internalise or absorb in their self-development process without being overwhelmed by them.

Special questions of human development arise for poor *women*. They have a doubly subhuman status. To liberate their creativity (as also to liberate them from male domination and male oppression) they need to think and act independently of the menfolk to whom they are held to be subordinate. This requires separate base organisations of poor women which may collaborate with organisations of poor men at higher levels to promote common interests.

Achieving social and economic rights

This means elimination of economic and social oppression and injustices and achieving equity in the use of public resources. This implies the exercise of collective power of the poor, and often implies *struggle*.

Judicious struggle is conducted by assessing relative strengths, and by challenging oppressors/exploiters when sufficient strength is acquired to have a reasonable possibility of winning. The role of outsiders is not to make this assessment for the poor, but to make them aware that it is necessary, and to bring to them knowledge and considerations relevant in this assessment. Also to help develop a consciousness among the poor which sees short-run failures as a learning process upon which subsequent strategy is to be built. A struggle is never lost if constructive lessons are drawn from its failure – the process then moves forward even through a conscious decision for temporary retreat.

One role of outsiders in the context of this objective is to bring to the poor knowledge of what their rights are – by law, by national policy and by international agreements and conventions, etc.

The question of *right to public resources* is particularly important in relating this objective with the objective of economic uplift. An NGO which brings credit to the rural poor indefinitely, detracts from the need for more equitable use of the public credit system – it does not make sense that the poor's credit needs should be met by 'voluntary agencies' obtaining resources from special donors while the public credit system continues to serve the rich. (The same applies to other public resources.) An NGO may only bring credit to a group of the poor for a brief period, to demonstrate that the poor are creditworthy, and to develop among them confidence and the ability to handle outside credit. Simultaneously, the poor should be made aware of their right to receive credit from the banking system, and of how this system works. The NGO should aim to withdraw its credit operation for any single group early, leaving the group now to negotiate for credit from the banking system with their organised strength and management ability. In this negotiation also the NGO may assist, by helping develop contacts and by technical assistance, bearing in mind that this dependence may be terminated early.

The above three objectives become mutually complementary if they are pursued together. This implies care to pursue the economic uplift objective through primary reliance on the people's own resources and creativity, and channelling their organised effort towards obtaining their rightful share of normal public resources rather than relying indefinitely on special credit programmes for some 'privileged' target groups. This also implies care to avoid 'adventurist' approaches to struggle for economic and social rights rather than developing organisational and economic strength for taking on difficult social challenges. In all this, the emphasis must always be on stimulating people's reflection and analysis, assisted but not dominated by knowledge and considerations the external 'interveners' may have. In this way, people's consciousness will keep advancing.

Macro social transformation

Together, the above three objectives can be considered to be 'locally progressive' – i.e. progressive at the micro level. Their contribution to macro social transformation can be positive, if such micro work spreads on a broad enough scale, and has the requisite qualities as discussed below.

On a macro level, the chief obstacle to social development is control of social power by a non-productive class which is abusing and misusing domestic and external resources in alliance with certain external interests. Since the great bulk of the flow of external resources is controlled by external forces interested in dominating and exploiting the country rather than in its self-determination and development, a *self*-reliant development effort is an absolutely necessary element for the country to shape its own destiny and to stand up with pride. Self-reliance does not mean autarky, but it means that external resources are taken only when this does not imply any compromise with the right to self-determination. Needless to say, this is not in the interest of the non-productive class which is controlling social power today in alliance with domination-seeking foreign interests.

Self-reliance at the national level cannot be achieved without self-reliance at the grassroots level – in fact, at all levels. This by itself requires primary reliance on people's own effort and creativity rather than on external deliveries, because external deliveries imply dependence upon (and submission to) external forces. Limited amounts of external resources may be available from quarters who might not wish to control the country's destiny, but this will come nowhere near the amount of resources necessary to develop the country with a delivery-oriented strategy.

This applies to external credit as well as to other deliveries. The total supply of credit for uplift of the poor is, and will remain, limited. 'Soft' credit projects for the poor which provide ready credit indefinitely to a limited number of project groups take these people away from the hard struggle for economic uplift which the broad masses of the poor have to undergo. This would create 'privileged' groups among the poor and weaken their motivation to participate in the broader struggle for overall social and institutional change.

Social transformation requires transfer of social power from the present dominating non-producing class to the class of direct producers, and this transfer is a political process to be led only by a competent political organisation. However, successful social transformation, which includes social *reconstruction*, is much more than the mere act of formal transfer of political power: it requires a social psychology, culture and capability of self-reliant economic and social effort. If this is significantly lacking at the time of transfer of power, people will continue to wait upon deliveries from above, and the leadership will fail to lead social reconstruction without a massive inflow of external resources and eventual submission again to external interests.

A corollary of self-reliant grassroots (people's) effort is reliance on people's own *knowledge*. Examples of social change exist where transfer of macro power has been achieved in the name of direct producers, but new power has been appropriated by another class of non-producers – a class of professionals – who have possessed monopoly over development knowledge and expertise. Direct producers who have been mobilised for accomplishing a transfer of power have submitted to this class out of a sense of intellectual inferiority, not having developed the needed confidence in their own knowledge and abilities, and in their own ability to choose from among available outside knowledge and expertise, for their own development. The result becomes a return to the delivery mentality which must eventually bring back dependence on external resources, hence control. There is no self-reliant way of development without primary reliance on people's resources including their own knowledge, and professional knowledge has to play a complementary but not dominating role in such development.

Part of self-reliance consists of collective economic cooperation. By this means scarce resources, skills and talents are used to benefit not a few privileged individuals but all those who participate in such cooperation. Through this process resources thus get 'augmented'. Practice of collective economic cooperation and collective economic management develops skills and experience in such collective work which should be regarded as an important asset created in the 'womb of the old order', for self-reliant economic reconstruction of society.

With this perspective in view, work with the poor which seeks to develop their creativity primarily through their own collective effort, giving emphasis to both the people's self-reliant *thinking* and *action* through which collective action and consciousness both keep advancing, would be creating positive assets for the task of social transformation.

Some suggestions
For some NGOs at least, a greater clarity of objectives is necessary for a sharper direction of their work.

- The chosen objectives, and their rationale, should be discussed with the 'target groups'. They should be asked to reflect why development effort in the country has been a failure, notwithstanding so-called 'learned' men being in charge. They may not initially grasp all the issues, but a broad picture of the macro situation should be given to them – e.g. the man–land ratio and the land distribution situation; the national poverty picture; the extreme dependence of the country on foreign resources and yet the inability of such a heavy flow of external resources to develop the country; the 'basket-case' image of the country . . . there is a need to shock the people into a sense of self-esteem.

- The people should be asked to deliberate what they want to do in this overall context, and how the NGO can help them. They should be asked to formulate their own immediate objectives, and for collaboration with the NGO these should be consistent with the objectives formulated by the NGO.

- There should be educational sessions to make the target groups aware of their rights in law, government policy, international conventions, etc.

- From the very beginning an attitude of self-reliance must be stimulated in the people. They should ask questions such as 'What can we do ourselves to solve this problem?' 'Do we need the NGO worker to solve this problem?' 'If we absolutely need outside help for this now, how fast can we make ourselves independent in this respect, and what should we and the NGO do for this purpose?'

- The people should have the opportunity to discuss all such and other questions, and take action, in small groups. Only then can they participate and develop intellectually (necessary for human development). The idea of 'teams' or 'brigades' within the framework of larger organisations may be considered in this respect.

- The credit policy of the NGO should reward self-reliance, or a clear decision by the target group to move fast towards self-reliance. Priority in advancing credit should be given to groups who, among people of similar income situations, want less; to those who decide to plough back a higher percentage of profit into their group fund; to those initiating collective economic projects; to those engaged in production which may be combined with trade in self-produced goods rather than pure trade. This policy should be discussed with the people, and the rationale explained. As discussed, credit by an NGO to the poor should be seen as a temporary measure, to be replaced early by credit from the banking system and/or from group savings funds.

- The people must periodically evaluate their own experience and review their progress collectively, draw lessons from successes and failures, formulate a future course of action based on past experience, and formulate advice to the NGO staff as well as on how to achieve agreed objectives. They should be encouraged to document, store and disseminate their ongoing experience for progressive advancement of their collective knowledge based on their collective effort. They may be assisted by NGO staff, local educated youth, school teachers, etc., to document the results of their investigation and review ('participatory research') in simple language; they should also be encouraged to use their cultural traditions (e.g. kabigan, drama, ballads) to document and disseminate these, and to take their experiences themselves to other groups and villages.

- In areas where there is a past history of collective effort by the poor, this history should be collected (by the participatory process, in which the main researchers will be the people, assisted if necessary by others) and discussed, and lessons drawn from them as a guide to current effort. In new areas where work is to be initiated, this should be the very first task (except in cases where delving into the history of past struggle may create special difficulty for work to be initiated).

- Closely following the people's periodic review of their work, NGO workers will undertake their own periodic collective review, keeping clearly in view the chosen objectives of their work.

- It will be valuable to bring out a bulletin which will periodically print the people's as well as NGO workers' reviews of ongoing work. The bulletin should be oriented to print not just 'stories' but analytical reviews of ongoing work in the light of the objectives of such work, highlighting action and experiences most conducive to the promotion of these objectives, and to analysing failures in order to draw constructive lessons from them. Articles in the bulletin should be read and discussed in all base organisations.

• Needless to say, the NGO should work so as to make itself progressively redundant to any group or set of groups with which it has been working intensively.

Notes

1. A national organisation of rural landless was indeed created from out of organisations of the landless formed under the programme of another NGO (whose work was not visited in this trip). After creation of this organisation there was reportedly bitter struggle for its control between forces which wanted it immediately to take a radical political position and those which wanted it to function as a trade-union type organisation leaving its political articulation to evolve in due course through its own praxis. Eventually the organisation itself split, a section of its leadership being persuaded to rename the organisation with a more militant connotation to work in close alliance with left forces.

The autonomy of organisations of the landless to ally with political forces of their choice is not the point in question. But it appears that the formation of a national organisation of the landless was premature in terms of their self-development: the national organisation was created at the initiative of the NGO and not of the base organisations of the landless themselves from out of their own felt or self-reflected need. It became, therefore, highly susceptible to being hijacked by external forces: a clear lesson to other NGOs (and to the landless themselves) who are truly committed to self-development of the rural poor.

2. Subsequently published: Orlando Fals Borda, *Knowledge and People's Power, Lessons with Peasants in Nicaragua, Mexico and Colombia*, New Delhi: Indian Social Institute, 1985.

6. The theory and practice of participatory action research

*Consciousness of the oppressed**

- Do you know who Lakshmi is and who Swaraswati is?
  Adivasi: Yes.
- Who is Lakshmi?
  Adivasi: Rice; clothes; hut.
- And Swaraswati?
  Adivasi: Sawkar's knowledge.
- If you could have only one of them, what is your preference?
  Adivasi: Swaraswati.
- Why?
  Adivasi: If everyone has knowledge, then no one can cheat others. Then only can we have true equality.

Introduction

The tradition of intellectuals stimulating and assisting popular struggles is an age-old one. This tradition seems to have been gaining some momentum in recent times, and developing links not only within but also across national boundaries. Two major factors may be contributing to this: (a) convergence of national systems into elite domination over the masses, of both 'right' and

Paper prepared for presentation at the plenary session on 'Contradictions, conflicts and strategies of societal change', of the Tenth World Congress of Sociology held in Mexico in August 1982. The paper presents personal reflections of the author only, and in no way commits the ILO to them. The author will be grateful to receive feedback, particularly from participatory researchers and other grassroots activists.

The paper's opening passage is a dialogue with a tribal (*adivasi*) poor peasant in Junglepatti, Thana District, Maharastra, India. Lakshmi and Swaraswati are the Hindu goddesses of prosperity and knowledge respectively. A *sawkar* is the moneylending landlord/trader/rich farmer.

'left' varieties, which is generating its own counter-consciousness; and (b) increasing facilities for communication with the resulting counter-culture.

This counter-culture has taken a wide variety of characters, with some carrying a conscious research (knowledge-generation) interest. The latter variety has sometimes been referred to as 'action research', sometimes as 'participatory research'. The terminology has not yet converged.

Orlando Fals Borda chose the term 'participatory action research' – henceforth to be abbreviated to PAR – in inviting the present paper. I felt that this might be a useful term, making the point that we are talking about Action Research that is participatory, and participatory research that unites with action (for transforming reality).

It cannot be claimed that PAR has as yet a convergent theoretical position. But certain concerns are being increasingly shared in common, ideological positions are being taken (not necessarily in writing) that are broadly similar, and methodological similarities in action are being observed. From this, an ideological position may be inferred, and theoretical questions can be raised and discussed, all in a tentative way, as a contribution to the progressive articulation of the standpoint of PAR. This paper is a modest attempt in this direction.

There has been no attempt to do justice to the vast practice of PAR in this short paper, and I have a language barrier myself in undertaking such a job. In observing some highlights of this practice, I have confined myself to a few initiatives which are: (a) relatively recent, as these directly challenge us as contemporary intellectuals to respond; (b) relatively well documented; and (c) possessed of ideological concerns I have a good sense of, through a combination of reading and personal dialogue with the people involved in them.

These highlights from the practice of PAR are presented in the next section, 'The practice of PAR'. The third section discusses the emerging ideology of PAR and questions relating to its contribution to social transformation. The final section discusses PAR as a means of generating scientific knowledge for guidance in social practice.

The practice of PAR

[An account of Bhoomi Sena in the original version of this paper has been omitted in view of the presentation of this movement in Chapter 3 of this volume.]

The Change Agents Programme – Sri Lanka

The Change Agents Programme was initiated in 1978 as a pilot Action Research Project under the Ministry of Rural Development of the Sri

Lankan government (see Tilakaratna, 1982). It aimed at evolving a methodology for catalytic intervention in the rural sector, to stimulate self-reliant mobilisation of the rural poor to overcome their poverty through the generation of internal leaders (change agents) and participatory processes. Conceptual leadership in developing the methodology was provided by a Sri Lankan social scientist assisted by an Indian action researcher, both of whom had interacted intimately with the Bhoomi Sena movement in India.

A four-member team of development workers visited a village about thirty-five miles from Colombo, in which practically all the poor families were betel producers. The team established rapport with the villagers and settled down in the village, setting out to stimulate the poor betel producers to get together to investigate their socio-economic situation and discuss the causes of their poverty. A process of investigation and analysis by the people themselves followed, supplemented by research by the development workers. This revealed to the betel producers that the bulk of the surplus of their labour was being appropriated by the trading middlemen who carried their products to exporting organisations. Action followed, initiated by a group of producers in January 1979 who set up an informal Betel Producers' Association. After several attempts the Association succeeded in getting an export organisation to buy from them directly. The resulting benefit to the producers was considerable. Producers from a number of neighbouring villages started joining the Association, and its membership increased to over 200 by mid-1981 from 35 in March 1979. Resistance from private traders in collusion with other export organisations was faced and gradually overcome by various strategies and tactics.

As the Association grew in size, the issue of membership participation in its decision-making, *vis-à-vis* its office holders came to the fore. Eventually the Association split into five small organisations each undertaking its own marketing work and operating as an autonomous unit with active participation of its members. Together, they are developing into a force to reckon with in the area.

Similar methods of intervention in a village in the southern coastal belt of Sri Lanka resulted in a group of coir yarn producers getting together, first to build a small capital fund by saving in kind – i.e. by setting apart a few pieces of yarn as savings – out of each day's production. After building some savings the group sold the stock at a higher price to an outside trader bypassing the village trader, and used the proceeds to buy raw materials, also from a new source. Eventually, the group found direct market outlets for their product at a very favourable price in Colombo. Other small coir producers joined, and a collective marketing organisation was formed whose membership rose from 31 in March 1980 to 214 by December. By now, the process has spread into neighbouring villages, and similar marketing organisations have emerged in another six of them. The producers have evolved their own organisational forms – for example, in the first village the primary organisational unit is a small group of 15–20 families with ten such groups in all, linked together by a central committee consisting of representatives from each group. All members in each primary unit undertake the marketing and handling work on a rotating basis with no hierarchy of officials. All primary groups hold meetings every week, and the ten groups meet in a general session once a month.

The village organisations have federated into an inter-village organisation of coir producers to promote their common cause, through activities such as joint negotiation with export organisations, negotiation with the government for various facilities, and expansion of the movement into new villages.

Neither the betel producers' nor the coir producers' organisations are now dependent on the initial teams of development workers who stimulated their self-reliance. These development workers left the villages by June 1981 and have since been initiating similar processes in other areas, occasionally visiting the villages where they started their work.

As a whole, the Change Agents Programme is developing into a small-scale movement. It is now working also with other small rural producers such as tea and rubber smallholders, milk producers, rural artisans and fishermen. Besides the Ministry of Rural Development in the government, the programme is now being carried forward also by a newly formed NGO – the Participatory Institute for Development Alternatives (PIDA) – set up by a group of persons who were involved with the original pilot project. PIDA is being coordinated by a senior university professor after the untimely death of the programme's first intellectual leader.

Proshika, Bangladesh

Proshika was established in 1976 by a team of educated young activists, as a non-government development agency (see Hossain, 1981). The word 'Proshika' is an acronym signifying development education, training and action, three essential elements integral to Proshika's approach to rural development. It is funded by the CIDA (Canada) through CUSO. The primary aim of Proshika is to help the rural underprivileged achieve self-awareness, see their own problems and find their own ways of solving them. There are five main steps in Proshika's approach: (a) first, individuals and groups are identified from among the villagers who have expressed interest or shown initiative in sustained development activities; (b) these people are then invited to visit an existing Proshika 'development centre'; (c) Proshika then encourages them to receive training in leadership and organisational skills, with emphasis on analysis by the underprivileged themselves of the society, by drawing examples from their own life's situations; (d) after such initial training, Proshika encourages them to organise a group composed of members with homogeneous characteristics – e.g. landless or marginal farmers, fishermen, etc. A Proshika 'animator' works as a guide in the group formation process; (e) the group is urged from the outset to build a joint savings fund irrespective of what the initial contributions may be. It is asked also to meet regularly to discuss the problems of its members and to identify common action to solve them according to their own priorities. Emphasis is laid on the undertaking of cooperative income-generating projects; (f) after a group has identified a project, Proshika provides the specific skills training required by the group; (g) when the group is ready and able to take on an income-generating project with its own funds, Proshika makes available a small loan, if required, on a matching grant basis.

Proshika has established two regional centres and sixteen development centres in eight districts. Each of these centres offers training facilities to Proshika's field workers and members of Proshika groups, besides serving as places for review of experiences and exchanges between the trainers and group members. These development centres by now cover more than 4,000 Proshika groups of average size with 15–20 families in each group.

While emphasising group action for income generation, Proshika gives considerable importance to organisation building, group solidarity and collective action for realisation of the basic economic and social rights of the underprivileged. In different places several Proshika groups are meeting together to discuss acts of social injustice and oppression by the rural elites, and are taking coordinated action to resist them, often with significant success. In some places Proshika groups have federated into inter-group organisations. Through Proshika's intervention the underprivileged in the Proshika areas are emerging as a strong countervailing force at the local level.

Cross-fertilisation

The above are some of the more widely known attempts by educated activists to generate participatory grassroots processes for improvement of the economic and social status of the underprivileged in South Asia. But there are many more, and the number is growing (see Tandon, 1980). A process of cross-fertilisation between them is ongoing, both at the national and international levels. Workshops bringing together several NGOs/ voluntary groups engaged in such work is commonplace in India and Bangladesh. One NGO in India – the People's Institute for Development and Training (PIDT, New Delhi), itself engaged in PAR with the rural underprivileged in several parts of India – has initiated with the sponsorship of the ILO a process of 'People's Research on Forestry, Ecology and the Oppressed', in which ten forest-based poor people's movements (including Bhoomi Sena) in different parts of India are getting together over a series of grassroots workshops and are conducting joint fact-finding investigations with the assistance of sympathetic professionals who develop and articulate their joint position on the question of forestry management.

At an inter-country level, Proshika, PIDT and the Change Agents Programme have been interacting closely: the development workers in the Change Agents Programme visited the other two initiatives before starting their own work in Sri Lanka, and more recently these three have interacted systematically at the leadership level for cross-fertilisation in an ILO-sponsored exchange project. The latter also involved an initiative of the Rural Workers' Office of the Ministry of Labour in the government of the Philippines – Group Action Among Landless and Near-landless Workers in the Sugar Crop-dominated Regions – which was initially rather paternalistic in its approach oriented primarily towards the mobilisation of external resources to generate employment and incomes for the under-privileged; as a result of interaction with Proshika, PIDT and the Change Agents Programme, it is now working under the name of SARILAKAS (own strength), to stimulate grassroots self-reliance, seeking to generate processes of people's own deliberation and action according to their own priorities. A number of village-level rural workers' organisations have emerged as a result, with their self-deliberated efforts directed primarily at resisting injustice and exploitation by local and external vested interests. Needless to say, in the Philippines itself there are several other such initiatives.

Methodology
While such works, naturally, have many differences in their approaches, broad similarities can be observed in many of them. For those which are in close touch with one another, a methodological and, indeed, ideological convergence seems to be approaching. Methodologically, a converging trend in the following direction may be observed:

• Catalytic initiatives are taken by persons coming from the well-educated class (university graduates and above), independent of macro social organisations such as political parties, to promote self-mobilisation of the rural underprivileged for group or organised action to emerge from out of their own deliberations.

• The starting point in generating such grassroots processes is to encourage the underprivileged to get together to find out why they are poor and oppressed through social investigation and analysis of their own, thus promoting their critical awareness of their environment.

• The underprivileged are encouraged to discuss what they could do by uniting to overcome poverty and oppression. They are encouraged to form groups or organisations absolutely of their own, whose structure and functioning are to be decided by them, and through these to take economic and social action according to their self-deliberated priorities.

• Attempts are made to generate a self-reliance consciousness among the underprivileged, and an attitude of *assertion* of their knowledge, views and decisions *vis-à-vis* outsiders. Materially, external resources and expertise are not considered to be primary in solving their problems – these are offered only as supplements, when needed and available, for the mobilisation of the people's own resources and skills. In the use of external resources emphasis is placed on the further development of people's own resources and skills for them to achieve progressively greater self-reliance.

• The people are encouraged to meet periodically in 'camps' or 'people's workshops' to review their experiences, to undertake periodic fact-finding investigations on their environment, and to take decisions for subsequent action based on their own research thus conducted – seeking thereby to generate a process of *people's praxis*, i.e. a progressive action–reflection rhythm.

• The people, once they have developed experience in mobilising and in organised action, are encouraged to stimulate and assist other underprivileged people to start similar action, and to gradually form higher-level organisations by federating smaller ones, and to develop links with other organisations of this type.

• Dependence of the people on the initial catalysts is supposed to cease, through the generation and development of internal leadership, cadres and skills. This does not necessarily mean actual physical withdrawal of the catalysts from people's processes, but the people should within a reasonable time be able to carry on with their collective activities on their own, while a catalyst may continue his or her association with such processes and seek new roles in their progressive development.

• The initiators of such action have not only a practical but also a research interest, in generating and assisting such self-reliant people's processes. This includes a search for methodology of self-reliance-sensitive catalytic action, for a role for intellectuals in the development of people's praxis and 'people's power', and inquiry into the implication of such interaction for social transformation. This research, however, is subordinate to the people's collective interests as perceived by them, and to a commitment to protect information whose dissemination might be contrary to this interest.

The Freirian work

There are such activities in other parts of the world as well (Callaway, 1980; Mustafa, 1981) which can, however, be competently discussed only by colleagues more familiar with them. Mention may be made of the work of Paulo Freire, a legend in PAR, which has stimulated a worldwide movement in the pedagogy of literacy, besides influencing action research not directly focused on literacy as such. Indeed, most of the Asian initiatives referred to above have used the concept of 'conscientisation' in the same sense as Freire – i.e. stimulation of self-reflected critical awareness on the part of the oppressed people of their social reality and of their ability to transform it by their conscious action. The rejection of 'aid' and 'extension' as solutions to the problem of people's development ('liberation') which is implicit in the Asian initiatives has also found its sharpest expression in the Freirian work and thinking. However, the pedagogy of *literacy* as a method of conscientisation has not featured very much in the particular Asian cases observed; instead, the thrust has been the stimulation of *immediate social investigation and analysis by the oppressed people* – social research – collectively.

Work in Colombia

Among other PAR activities outside Asia, one of the most illuminating reviews has been done by Orlando Fals Borda of the work that he and his colleagues did with grassroots groups in Colombia (Fals Borda, 1979). A major focus of this work has been the legitimisation of popular knowledge and its development into 'scientific knowledge', with the aim of assisting in the development of a 'science of the proletariat' with which the masses could conduct their own struggle for social transformation. Orlando's self-critique of this work brings home the paramount care that is needed in the methodology of such effort. With his characteristic sensitivity and frankness, Orlando reports that the search for a way to achieve the intended objective has so far been inconclusive. While the intellectuals conducting this search were able to develop considerable rapport with the masses, the latter were not stimulated to take over the initiative in the intellectual inquiry. In the end,

> with characteristic impatience, it was the action researchers and their intellectual allies who were forced to define 'popular science' . . . and inject their own definition of it into the context of reality. . . . The result was a special application of the notion of insertion into the social process in order to 'place knowledge at the service of popular interests', but such knowledge did not derive from the objective conditions of the proletariat as would have been theoretically more correct. . . . As historical materialism was almost an exclusive heritage of action researchers and

committed intellectuals, they consequently had to diffuse it among the grassroots as an ideology. This led to the adoption as 'special mediating categories' of what, in a classic manner, are expounded upon as general Marxist postulates. In this manner, what was termed 'popular science' had to be an ideological replica of certain general theses of historical materialism as developed in other contexts and social formations. This is to say that the groups fell victim to the worst historical form of dogmatism, that of mimesis.

In the above, Orlando has touched the source of elite domination over the masses in many radical attempts at social transformation, and PAR continues in its search for ways of avoiding this tragic pitfall.

PAR and social transformation

The ideology

What with successes and failures, underlying all such work is the ideology that a self-conscious people, those who are currently poor and oppressed, will progressively transform their environment *by their own praxis*. In this process others may play a catalytic and supportive role, but will not dominate.

Many participatory action researchers claim to have been inspired by the ideals of historical materialism. Indeed, the notion of 'class struggle' as opposed to class harmony is implicit in PAR's approach which separates out the poor and oppressed for self-conscious mobilisation to assert themselves; the resulting actions of the oppressed are inevitably constituting class struggles of different forms, testifying to the inherent class consciousness of the oppressed.

Historical materialism, however, has passed through many hands, in theory as well as in its application, and there seems no longer to be any broad consensus as to its operational meaning. The recent growth of PAR as an activity independent from left political parties suggests that it is opposed at least to a certain interpretation of this ideology which views social transformation as primarily the task of a 'vanguard' party which will assume itself to have a consciousness that is 'advanced' relative to the consciousness of the oppressed masses, and who will mobilise the masses for social revolution and social reconstruction. One feels from interaction with PAR activists that, in fact, the growth of PAR owes itself to the *crisis of the left* as well as to the *crisis of the right*: application of the 'vanguard party' theory has produced structural change in a number of situations, but there is evidence that in several of them newer forms of domination over the masses have emerged, and to this the 'vanguards' have not shown much sensitivity.

People's liberation in many 'revolutionary' societies has as a result remained elusive. The ultimate caricature of the revolutionary ideal of liberation is visible today (January 1981) in Poland where a self-generated countervailing power of the working class *vis-à-vis* the vanguard is being militarily suppressed in the name of protecting 'socialism', apparently a strategy of development based on paternalistic deliveries to the people through expertise and with massive borrowed finance. Managed without involving the people, the strategy has failed even in its own terms and has led the country into economic and financial bankruptcy – a case of 'Bhoomi Sena', in its first phase, on a national scale.

Dual transformation

Historical experience of this nature calls for rethinking the meaning of 'liberation'. Liberation, surely, must be opposed to *all* forms of elite domination over the masses. The dominant view of social transformation has been preoccupied with the need for changing existing, oppressive structures of relations in *material* production. This is certainly a necessary task. But – and this is the distinctive viewpoint of PAR – domination of masses by elites is rooted not only in the polarisation of control over the means of material production but also over the means of *knowledge* production including, as in the former case, the social power to determine what is valid or useful knowledge. Irrespective of which of these two polarisations sets off a process of domination, it can be argued that one reinforces the other in augmenting and perpetuating this process. By now, in most polarised societies, the gap between those who have social power over the process of knowledge generation – an important form of 'capital' inasmuch as knowledge is a form of social power – and those who have not, have reached dimensions no less formidable than the gap in access to means of physical production. History shows that a convergence of the latter gap in no way ensures convergence of the former; on the contrary, existence of the latter has been seen to offset the advantages of revolutionary closures of the former and has set off processes of domination once again.

For improving the possibility of liberation, therefore, these two gaps should be attacked, wherever feasible, simultaneously. This is not accomplished by the masses merely being mobilised by a vanguard body with the latter's 'advanced' consciousness. People cannot be liberated by a consciousness and knowledge other than their own, and a strategy such as the above inevitably comprises seeds of new forms of domination. It is absolutely essential, therefore, that the people develop their own endogenous process of consciousness-raising and knowledge generation, and that this process acquires the social power to assert itself *vis-à-vis* all elite consciousness and knowledge. The theoretical basis for this assertion is discussed in the final section of this paper.

The change in the relations of knowledge that is being conceived goes beyond the concept of 'from the masses, to the masses' (Mao Tse-tung, 1968). The Chinese Revolution did seek to legitimise people's knowledge and thought, and asked elites to go to the masses and learn from them. But the task of systematising people's thought was given, it seems, to the elites (intellectuals) and not to the masses, with the presumption that the people are incapable of systematising their own thought – i.e. *building their own science*. In this view, revolutionary theory rests ultimately with the elites. Whether 'Mao Tse-tung thought' correctly reflected people's thought or not, the process of its systematisation was, apparently, external to the process of people's own collective reflection, and the knowledge that was built was in the end handed down to the people. The wisdom of all great religions can be traced to the wisdom of ordinary people revealed at some point or other in some or other context; but systematised religion descending from above and preached as a faith, rather than (scientifically) rationalised through processes of people's own (collective) self-reflection (see last section), is alienating rather than liberating. It can also be replaced by another religion if the faith does not work, or if the 'prophet' dies.

PAR and macro social structure

PAR is a search for ways of promoting the dual transformation process conceived above by generating and assisting processes of people's own praxis. It starts at the grass roots, as a micro level activity, and seeks to stimulate and assist grassroots processes to develop into a wider movement. How far this can go from any given situation cannot be usefully speculated in the abstract – PAR, and the development of people's praxis which it seeks to promote, are creative acts that must move with skill and tact in order to create and expand space for its own continued growth. In this sense there is no theory of how PAR may, if at all, bring about macro structural change by itself, or through the processes that it generates. In fact, the notion of praxis is opposed to such theorising which asks and presumes to answer questions on the course of progressive creative encounters between social forces.

In places where sustained PAR is proving possible, there is evidence of the generation of social transformation processes at the local level, in terms of both of the two relations mentioned above. This shows that objective conditions are favourable for the development of such processes in these places, at least up to a point. For the Asian experiences in particular, it appears that a sporting chance exists for the oppressed to be able to unite and for their collective power to wrest significant gains from their immediate exploiters at least.

Specific explanation for the existence of such space in any given country should be derived from the specific socio-political context, and this will not be attempted in this short paper. Broadly speaking, one would surmise that the strength of the link between the status quo of macro power and the local elites will be a factor in explaining this phenomenon. The stronger this link is, the likelier it is for macro forces to come to the protection of local vested interests in the event of any threat to the latter from organised action by the oppressed, thereby making it difficult for local action by itself to achieve much. On the face of it, this link is a question of the dynamics of political alliance between national and local elites, a relation that by itself may vary both over time and space, permitting independent grassroots mobilisation, more at certain times and in certain areas than at other times and in other areas. There may be some relation in a more basic sense between the economic worth of local elites and the national elites, by way of the dependence of the privileges of the latter on the appropriation of economic surplus by the former at the local level.

For Bhoomi Sena, the above conjecture is corroborated by a participatory study (de Silva *et al.*, 1979) of the movement which observes that the moneylending *sawkars* are an unproductive class which has been contributing little to developing the productive forces of Junglepatti in order to be able to make any significant surplus available for use at 'higher' levels. Indeed, one of the reasons Bhoomi Sena has come as far as it has may be ascribed to the contradiction between the feudal moneylending class against whom the tribals' struggle is chiefly aimed, and the emerging class of capitalist farmers in the area, with power at the state level no longer committed to bail out the former parasitic class. In Sri Lanka, attempts (now being withdrawn) to create a welfare state rather than develop the productive forces resulted in the creation of a generally soft society where the 'traditional' sector was subsidised with resources raised through taxation of the 'modern' sector supplemented by foreign aid (Haque *et al.*, 1977). And in Bangladesh the rulers in recent times have given the impression of being quite content with the image of an 'international basket case', with success of government policy often equated with the amount of foreign aid it is able to obtain, domestic resource mobilisation remaining at an acutely low level (Alamgir). In such situations, the economic worth of local-level elites to the national elites is low and in places negative, so that popular movements confronting the former alone may not be viewed by the latter as an immediate threat to its material interests. Within limits, the national elites may actually be induced to patronise such movements as examples of democratic tolerance and concern for the wellbeing and rights of the poor, a gesture that may be stimulated also by the support to such movements of foreign donor agencies, for obvious reasons. It is, however, also not improbable that sections within the national elites may cherish some nationalist sentiments, and may be attracted by initiatives seeking an alternative development strategy with greater national self-reliance, and the support of such quarters may actually have played a role in the development of grassroots people's processes in the Asian region.

Notwithstanding objective conditions such as the above favouring the growth of PAR in some countries, there may be limits to its growth in any one country, placed ultimately by the macro structure of the society which progressive development of grassroots processes and their interlinking may eventually confront. In other societies with different objective conditions very little activity of this nature may be possible at all. When such a limit is reached, it would be necessary to seek to change the macro structure by appropriate means in order to enable the further development of people's praxis. Unless people's self-conscious mobilisation itself has developed already to the point of being able to take on this task, PAR has the responsibility to ally with other progressive social forces for confronting the macro structure at appropriate times.

PAR in the 'womb of the old order'

It is important, however, to note that the development of genuine people's praxis after macro structural change is likely to be limited by the kind of social processes that have preceded it. The classic work of Bettelheim (1976) on the Soviet Revolution reveals, sector by sector, the almost total unpreparedness of the Soviet working class to self-manage the task of post-revolutionary reconstruction, so that 'experts' were able to take over and consolidate their power, and eventually establish a dictatorship over the people. All revolutions witness this struggle for power, after the old order is overthrown, between forces committed to the release of people's initiatives and those seeking to dominate the people in new ways. It may be suggested that a crucial factor by which this struggle may be won or lost is the *relations of knowledge* – more specifically whether the people can assert their right to apply their own knowledge in reconstructing society, and their autonomy in the choice of outside knowledge, rather than submitting to external expertise in a state of helplessness.

The earlier people's praxis starts, the greater should be the consciousness and confidence of the people at any stage to resist an invasion of expertise. Accordingly, the liberational potential of the destruction of an old order should be greater the more advanced is people's praxis at the time of this act of the revolution. It is therefore never too early to start PAR, if space for this exists or can be created. Under such conditions, *vanguard praxis* cannot be viewed as a substitute for people's praxis, if liberation indeed is the objective. The growth of PAR, and for that matter popular movements, in several countries in recent times demonstrates that people's praxis is possible, right now. This is a challenge to all 'vanguards' to clarify their commitment. The possibility exists, unfortunately, that the further development of PAR, which even reactionary social structures may permit, may be pre-empted by the action of other macro social forces committed to some kind of structural change but indifferent to the development of self-assertive people's initiatives.

Notwithstanding many obstacles that are being and will be encountered, there is some assurance that the ongoing PAR in different countries may not be in vain. There is evidence already of the impact of Freirian work on revolutionary thinking, and if it has not by itself yet made a 'revolution' in any single country, revolutionary leaderships after coming into power are seeking to adapt the Freirian method in educational programmes for reconstructing society (e.g. in Cuba, Nicaragua, Guinea-Bissau). Thus even micro level experiments within restricted space can develop liberation-promoting knowledge and methods that may find macro level application after space for this has been created by revolutionary action. The same may be said of the micro level initiatives that are ongoing in Asia: any national leadership in such countries which may search for ways of social reconstruction that may not end up with an inglorious and often hopeless strategy of delivery of development from above and outside will do well to consider the methodology of generating such self-reliant people's processes as some of these initiatives are developing.

PAR's own tension

> At times this congress sounds like an intellectuals' meeting. If they want to hold a congress then let the intellectuals hold one without us.
>
> Jan Jedrezejewski, a worker from Gdansk, in Solidarity's Congress on 29th September 1981 (*The Financial Times*, 30 September 1981).

But PAR itself needs to be modest about its own role. It should be admitted that it constitutes a rather unusual interaction between two social classes: in terms of material production intellectuals are primarily a consumer class, *vis-à-vis* the class of direct producers, and in terms of knowledge production it is, traditionally, the opposite. It is significant to observe that PAR postulates eliminating the second class distinction but not the first, in so far as intellectuals are not supposed to engage in manual labour (Fals Borda, 1981). Thus PAR postulates perpetuation of one of the 'great contradictions' in society. This must imply deep tensions in terms of the distribution of material privileges and social power from which PAR cannot be claimed to be immune.

PAR, after all, is threatening to become a respectable intellectual movement, and participatory researchers are gaining in social status, within and across national frontiers. PAR is getting institutionalised, and this will corrupt some in this movement at the same time as promoting its growth.

Finally, PAR constitutes praxis of the participatory researcher as well as that of the people, and the two processes are different, rooted in the respective traditions and accumulated wisdoms of the two parties in this interaction. The consequent pairs of knowledge-building and self-transformative processes may not always be in harmony, aggravating the tension that is inherent in this interaction.

As one participatory action researcher – a 'community facilitator' in the SARILAKAS project in the Philippines – told me recently 'In this work you have to constantly fight your enemies, and the greatest enemy is yourself.'

PAR as research

Because PAR is viewed as a kind of research as well, a discussion of this aspect of the activity is in order.

As Paul Oquist (1977) has observed, the epistemological premises of 'action research' conform to those of pragmatism and dialectical materialism as schools of scientific research. These schools hold that science should be purposive, aimed at the modification of reality, and should unite with such efforts. This also means that research should be value (ideology) directed, a standpoint that is explicit in the research of these two schools. The specific ideology of PAR that is elaborated in this paper separates it from pragmatism which keeps the choice of ideology as an open question; the ideology of PAR may be considered, if one wishes, to be one of the several interpretations of dialectical (historical) materialism, but this is an immaterial question of labelling.

Value bias

The epistemological standpoint of PAR opposes that of other schools such as empiricism, logical positivism and structuralism, which reject (social) value bias in what is considered to be 'scientific' research, and from the same principle adopt the detached observational method of social inquiry. It may be argued, however, that no research in the final analysis can be value-free, although some specific inquiries may not be consciously so.

In the first place, although research may be considered by some schools to be valid for its own sake irrespective of its social use, the 'social value-added' by research – i.e. the social effects of the application of the knowledge produced by those who are in a position to apply it – is an observable fact which cannot be dismissed. Given the structure of society, the products of specific research activities will be used more by some social classes than by others, naturally to the greater intended benefit of the former. It is in general possible by relatively elementary social analysis (which even the 'illiterate' oppressed poor are capable of) to know which social class will be in a position to use a particular knowledge in efforts to promote its own interests. In this sense all research whose results may be applied in practice, have class bias, and this ideological responsibility of research cannot be avoided.

In the second place, there can be value bias, more subtle to observe, implicit in the choice of the logical system of analysis in social research. Consider, for example, the system of formal logic *vis-à-vis* dialectical logic. Formal logic postulates that something that is observed to be *a* cannot be not-*a* at the same time, thereby ruling out the possibility of a change from *a* to not-*a* in certain ways which are considered to be possible by dialectical logic. Policy conclusions from research on the same phenomenon by the two logical systems may therefore differ, with possible ideological implications that may be important. Thus, for example, if the poor are observed to be incapable of carrying out social analysis, formal logic would tend to conclude that they should therefore *receive* education to do so; but dialectical logic, postulating that the observed incapability unites with its opposite into which it may transform itself in response to appropriate stimulation, might suggest a different kind of pedagogy (the kind discussed in the section 'The practice of PAR') to provide this stimulation – an act of *liberating the thought process* – to the people rather than for outsiders to *educate* the poor. The profound ideological difference between the two conclusions should be obvious.

In the third place, ideological bias is direct in the detached observational method of social research which implies a 'subject–object' relationship between the researcher and the researched (the people) in contrast to the 'subject–subject' relationship of participatory action research. Research on the oppressed people by external researchers with a subject–object relationship assumes and asserts the myth of incapability of the people to participate in the research as equals. This humiliates the people, and alienates them from their own power of generating knowledge relevant for transforming their environment by their own initiative. This makes them wait upon elite researchers to come and find the facts about them, to write about them and make policy recommendations for outsiders to solve their problems. This helps perpetuation of domination of the people for which, as we have observed, not only their economic dependence, but also their intellectual dependence on privileged elites, are responsible. In this way this research methodology has contributed to inaction of the people and has invited action by others, and has had therefore profound action as well as ideological consequences. Needless to say, 'radical' research by the *nonparticipatory method*, including 'vanguard praxis' that has not involved the people, also has its responsibility in this matter.

Finally, the methodological premise that knowledge must be produced by detached observation has also contributed to the creation and perpetuation of a 'class' of intellectuals (experts, technocrats) distinct from the masses of direct producers, constituting a separation of mental from manual labour, a class which has been seen to be politically active in controlling or influencing social power to promote their own privileges in both pre- and post-'revolutionary' situations. In this sense non-involvement is a myth – the social researcher is involved consciously or unconsciously in his/her own bid for social power, and the observational method of research serves as an instrument to promote this interest.

Objectivity

One may also question a claim to 'objectivity' in research if this were to mean being free from *subjective bias*. The methodological biases discussed above are subjective biases. Such bias is inherent also in conceptualising and categorising most human phenomena, and full communicability of such concepts and categories requires a sharing of sensuous (subjective) perceptions – i.e. communication at a subjective level in addition to formal definitions if these are so defined.

There is, however, another sense in which research may be defined as objective (or, for that matter, 'scientific'), i.e. in the sense of the methodology and product having passed a process of *social* verification. This produces social knowledge which is distinct from knowledge that is purely individual, i.e. subjective. Objectivity in this sense requires transition from the individual to a collective. This in turn requires that:

(a) a collective is defined;
(b) codes of communication (language) exist or are developed within the collective; and
(c) agreement be reached within the collective as to valid methods of investigation, reasoning and refutation of observations and arguments.

Research in all well-established schools has a verification system of the above nature, explicitly or implicitly, and is objective, if verified within its own paradigm. In the more advanced schools the method of verification has by now become more or less standardised, and verification is often possible by mechanical application of certain rules or arguments so that interpersonal communication may not be necessary for establishing its objectivity. It is important to recognise, however, that objectivity in this sense is *relative*, internal to the collective concerned (e.g. a research profession). For those not belonging to this collective, either because of a lack of communicability or because they do not accept its premises or rules, this knowledge either has no meaning or is not acceptable. There is in this sense no universality in any 'science' in so far as the entire human race does not constitute a collective for the purpose of scientific knowledge generation. If the Chinese have not followed the verification system of some Western schools in developing their knowledge, this does not make acupuncture, for example, a piece of 'unscientific' knowledge in the endogenous development of the Chinese medical science.

PAR, an emerging school of research also generates objective (scientific) knowledge in the above sense. Moser (undated, 1981) has discussed the verification process in people's collectives. It is in general the dialogical process of collective reflection, when people 'withdraw' from action for review and decision-making in their action–reflection rhythm (Fals Borda, 1981). It is argumentative, and dependent on consensus rather than on pre-established rules to be applied mechanically. This does not make this process any less objective (scientific) than other types of research, as long as the necessary criteria for objectivity are satisfied. The people are entitled to see their 'ghosts', as professional researchers see theirs (Cain, 1977) and regard them as part of their objective reality, a scientific truth for them in their endogenous knowledge-building process, as long as their existence can be *collectively* verified, tentatively at a point of time, open to subsequent refutation.

An immediate objective of PAR is to return to the people the legitimacy of the knowledge they are capable of producing, through their own collectives and the verification systems *they may decide to establish themselves*, as fully scientific, and their right to use this knowledge – not excluding any other knowledge but not dictated by them – as a guide in their own action. The reappropriation of this right by the people and its assertion is considered by PAR to be fundamental in the promotion of its ideology of dual social transformation, for the elimination of a major source of dependence that is standing in the way of people's liberation in both pre- and post-'revolutionary' societies.

Two research streams

PAR also involves a knowledge-generation process for the participatory researchers, a scientific process in its own right. However, participatory researchers being in general intellectuals coming from a tradition very different from the underprivileged masses with whom they work, communication between the two may not be good enough for the two research processes to converge into a single stream of knowledge-building. PAR therefore may involve two different knowledge-generation streams, and this has implications for social relations between the people and participatory researchers to which reference has been made in the previous section.

Summary

By Participatory Action Research (PAR) we mean action research that is participatory, and participatory research that unites with action.

Short glimpses are given of PAR with the Bhoomi Sena movement in India, the Change Agents Programme in Sri Lanka and the work of Proshika in Bangladesh. Cross-fertilisation between such activities within and across national boundaries is mentioned. A converging trend in the methodology of such work is observed, in the direction of catalytic work of educated activists to generate and promote self-organisation development of the rural poor and processes of their own praxis, which becomes progressively independent of outside assistance.

Mention is made of the Freirian work whose concept of conscientisation is reflected in the Asian initiatives, which have, however, used literacy as a method of conscientisation to a lesser extent but have stimulated immediate social investigation and analysis by the oppressed people. Finally, the work in Colombia is cited, which sought to generate an endogenous 'science of the proletariat' but ended up with the reformulation by radical intellectuals of revolutionary dogmas developed in other contexts.

The ideological trend in PAR is elaborated, as is the view that a self-conscious people will transform their environment *by their own praxis*, as opposed to social revolution attempted by a 'vanguard party' with 'advanced' consciousness primarily through vanguard praxis; the latter may produce structural change but has the seeds of newer forms of domination. It is suggested that *liberation* opposes domination of all forms, and requires the dual transformation of relations of production in both physical goods and *knowledge*, to be attempted simultaneously. PAR is a search for ways of promoting this.

PAR, it is observed, starts as a micro level activity and confronts vested interests at the local level. Its growth may be facilitated by a weak link between national elites and local elites, probably depending in part upon the economic worth of the latter in preserving the former's privileges. Eventually macro constraints have to be encountered, to be overcome by macro action. The dialectical relation between PAR and macro structural change is discussed, observing in particular the role of PAR before structural change in advancing the possibility of liberational activity after such change.

It is noted that PAR has its own tensions, arising out of the differences in the two traditions involved in this interaction – the intellectual and the popular. It constitutes praxis of both the parties, and the two may not necessarily converge.

As a method of research, PAR and people's praxis are frankly social value-biased. It is argued that the ideological burden of the mainstream of research is also heavy: the application of all research is class-biased and the bias may be anticipated, so that responsibility for this cannot be avoided; and the methodology of all social inquiry has ideological implications which are discussed. This, it is observed, nevertheless permits research to be 'objective', in the sense of passing through a process of *social verification*. PAR, and people's praxis, are in this sense a valid, objective research method. An immediate objective of PAR is to return to the people as part of the dual transformation process the scientific legitimacy of the knowledge they are capable of producing by creating their own system of social verification.

References

Alamgir, Mohiuddin *Economy of Bangladesh: Which Way Are We Moving?*
Bettelheim, Charles (1976) *Class Struggles in the USSR First Period: 1917–1923*, Monthly Review Press.
Cain, Bonnie J. (1977) *Participatory Research: Research With Historic Consciousness*, Participatory Research Working Paper No. 3, International Council for Adult Education, Toronto, April 1977.
Callaway, Helen (ed.) (1980) *Participation in Research, Case Studies of Participatory Research in Adult Education*, Netherlands Centre for Research and Development in Adult Education.
de Silva, G. V. S. *et al.* (1979) 'Bhoomi Sena: a struggle for people's power', *Development Dialogue*, No. 2.
Fals Borda, Orlando (1979) 'Investigating reality in order to transform it: the Colombian experience', *Dialectical Anthropology*.
Fals Borda, Orlando (1981) 'The challenge of action research', in Rahman (1981).
The Financial Times, London, 30 September 1981.
Haque, Wahidul, *et al.* (1977) 'Towards a theory of rural development', *Development Dialogue*, No. 2.
Hossain, Mosharraf (1981) *Conscientising Rural Disadvantaged Peasants in Bangladesh: Intervention Through Group Action – A Case Study of Proshika*, study done for ESCAP.
Mao Tse-tung (1968) 'Several questions on the method of direction', *Selected Works*, Vol. III, Peking.
Moser, Heinz *Action Research as a New Research Paradigm in the Social Sciences* (mimeograph).
Moser, Heinz (1981) *Participatory Action Research – the aspect of research*, Paper presented at the International Seminar on Participatory Research and Training in Local Level Development, Lepolampi, Finland, September 1981.
Mustafa, Kemal (1981) *Participatory Research Amongst Pastoralist Peasants in Tanzania: The Experience of the Jipemoyo Project in Bagamoyo District*, Report prepared for the ILO, Geneva, May 1981.
Oquist, Paul (1977) *The Epistemology of Action Research*, ISA Symposium on Action Research and Scientific Analysis, Cartagena, April 1977.
Rahman, Md. Anisur (1981) *Some Dimensions of People's Participation in the Bhoomi Sena Movement* (in English and Spanish), Participation Occasional Paper, Geneva: UNRISD. (Chapter 3 of this book.)

Tandon, Rajesh (1980) *Participatory Research in Asia*, New Delhi: Centre for Continuing Education.

Tilakaratna, S. (1982) *Grass Roots Self Reliance in Two Rural Locations in Sri Lanka: Organisations of Betel and Coir Yarn Producers*, WEP Working Paper, Geneva: ILO.

7. Further news from 'nowhere'

During October–November 1985 I had the opportunity to visit the work of a non-governmental organisation (NGO) in Bangladesh which is engaged in organising work with the poorest classes in many parts of the country. I travelled with varying sets of the NGO's staff, to visit samples of their work in a number of *upazillas* (sub-districts), interacting as a rule with unstructured sessions and meetings of the base groups of the poor, representatives of such groups from different places who assembled together to meet us or among themselves, and sessions of field workers of the NGO, and I also sat through two training courses for group representatives, one (for women) at a primary level and the other more advanced.

My field notes are presented in the following pages, followed by some reflections. The various upazillas are numbered in the chronological order in which they were visited.

Field notes

Upazilla 1

Organisational work in this upazilla started in 1982. There are twenty groups now – nine women's and eleven men's. There are on average about twenty members in each. They have federated into a central organisation with a central committee of eleven – three women and eight men elected once a year.

Members of the groups have a variety of different occupations – e.g. agricultural worker, livestock grower, rice mill worker, domestic attendant, cook in officers' houses, vendor. Members started with a subscription of one taka each per month; now raised to 10 taka in most organisations. Some put aside one fistful of rice a day, and later sell this saving to pay the subscription.

The base groups meet once a fortnight. Men's and women's groups of the same village hold a joint meeting once a month. Members of all groups meet periodically – two to three times a year – in meetings convened by the central committee.

Group activities are mostly economic, e.g. fish farming, cottage industries. One women's group I visited is engaged in group cane work. Individuals get paid according to labour, earning from 90 to 120 taka a month. This earning they generally keep in the bank as individual savings. The profit goes to the group fund, with which they plan to buy a sewing machine for which they have taken training.

Not much pressure-group activity reported in this area. Such mobilisation said to be difficult due to prevalence of kinship ties between elites and the poor which blurs the class consciousness of the poor.

Encouraging awareness reported of the oppression of women – both among male and female members. Members of men's groups do not take dowry on marriage. Divorce cases involving members are settled by the groups themselves, through negotiation and moral persuasion.

Upazilla 2
103 groups, being facilitated by two male workers of the NGO.

Visited a women's group of about thirty-one members, which was about one year old. About twenty are regular members. They meet twice a month, and have made a saving of 2,000 taka. They have purchased a sewing machine and are planning to start sewing work.

Question: What benefits have they got from the organisation so far?
Answer: We are less shy now to talk in public; our husbands do not beat us
    any more; polygamy has stopped; so has marriage dowry. On marriage
    we make it a condition that the husband cannot leave the wife, and will
    not have a second wife.

Visited a 'colony' of thirty-two refugee families who had migrated from India nineteen years back. Working male members are mostly rickshaw pullers and mechanics. They have one men's organisation of twenty members, and one women's of twenty-eight members.

In a joint meeting we had with them both male and female members talked. The women's group is about one year old, and so far is mainly collecting subscriptions, which started with one taka per month and is now five taka. Male members have started taking loans from their own group fund. They have also taken some land on lease. Half of this land is used for individual cultivation; on the other half, low land, the group is doing collective fish farming.

Meetings of the two groups are held jointly, with a male chairman.

Discussion with the leader of one male organisation in the area who runs a homoeopathic store and was eager that we visit it. He is emphasising saving in his group, and the subscription is now 10 taka each per month. He thinks the members have become landless as they had not saved. There was no sense of exploitation as a cause of impoverishment. His group meets once a month rather than twice as the other groups do, because *he* is unable to make time to give to the group meeting more than once a month. The idea that the group could and should meet more often, even in his absence, had not occurred to him. An altogether discouraging model of a leader.

Met also the leader of a female group in his store who had come there on her way to attend a three-day training programme for group representatives in the divisional centre of the NGO. Her group started with a saving of 5 taka each per month, which has now been raised to 10 taka. They plan to buy a sewing machine when they have enough. They are aware and active in safeguarding women's rights. When asked to give an example, she reported that a man had sent his wife away to her parents' home, whereupon all the women of the group went to the husband and his father and persuaded them to take the woman back.

'Basic' training

Three-day training programme in the divisional centre of the NGO. Twenty-five women representatives attended from five upazillas.

Two of the trainees who came from the same village were very young – studying in classes V and VI. Their potential to absorb the training was questioned, and initially the training authorities asked them to go back. But in the end they were asked to sit through the training to avoid the embarrassment they might face if they returned without attending it. It was evident later that they were playing leading roles in their group notwithstanding their age, in view of their literacy and in particular their ability to handle the accounting of the group's fund, a group whose principal activity so far was to build a fund.

The training course consisted of:

(a) presentation of life's struggles of the participants;
(b) identification of and discussion on 'basic needs' (food, shelter, clothing, medical care and education);
(c) social analysis of the causes of poverty and its relation with the distribution of power;
(d) special problems of women and the need for women's organisations;
(e) organisational questions.

Almost all the participants were extremely poor, and their stories of life's struggles were deeply touching. Extreme poverty mixed with extreme insecurity, oppression by elites and often by their own menfolk; sexual harassment; some struggling alone with small children without male relatives in hostile environments; some putting up heroic battles, working long hours as domestic servants in others' houses, somehow to manage to send a son to school, and struggling to keep themselves 'chaste', exhibiting some of the finest human values of dignity, hard work, rejection of charity. Here in this group they were at least able to talk freely and release themselves and they wanted to keep on talking – this was, even if momentarily, a 'liberation'.

They had to be almost forced to stop and enter into an analysis of the causes of their plight. Initially, some fatalist ideas were aired, leading to a discussion as to whether their condition was a divine design or man-made. The consciousness of human responsibility for poverty was there in every one, but it needed encouragement to come out – the courage to think that it was legitimate to talk in these terms. Once it came out, it was easy to see the need for the poor to unite, to resist exploitation and oppression, and to make collective efforts to improve their status. This included consciousness of men oppressing women and the need for women to organise.

In the analytical discussion, however, only a handful of women dominated, and this was not surprising. For many, this was the first time ever, and they leaned too much on the trainers (the director of training, a male, and a female co-trainer) to answer the questions. There were repeated attempts to make the trainees recapitulate what they had discussed and concluded previously: few could respond with any clarity and articulation.

Personal discussion with a senior staff member revealed some deep tensions of NGO workers in this kind of work. The work is sensitive, challenging the traditional power and privileges of vested interests, who often are ruthless and would try even to physically liquidate 'disturbing elements'. The field worker walks through the village late at night in fear of assault. His work has no job security (this NGO's funds come from foreign donors) or any insurance to protect his family in the event of something untoward happening. It is a very deep and restless commitment which is keeping him in this work – a deeply religious young man who cannot tolerate any injustice and spends sleepless nights over it, and draws support from the Koran in his fight against social polarisation. As he read out to the trainees at the concluding session of the training course: 'Wealth should not be distributed in a way that it keeps rotating in the hands of one small class.' 'When people are in want, no Muslim has the right to keep more than the minimum he needs.'

Upazilla 3

Work of the NGO in this coastal area is linked with a foreign-funded land reclamation project which is building an embankment against salt water. Government policy grants reclaimed land to the landless, but *jotdars* (rich farmers/landlords) are illegally occupying much land here. The NGO is doing organisational work among the landless and assisting them in their struggle for land against the jotdars. About 200 groups have been formed, membership varying from 20 to 30. The groups have federated into a central association, with an elderly chairman who has a trade union background from his early life as a coalmine worker in Calcutta.

Some 686 acres of land reclaimed in the project have been officially granted to the landless groups. Of these, some 354 acres are under the occupation of the groups; the remaining 332 acres are still being occupied by the jotdars who are resisting their transfer to the landless.

The groups are doing collective farming on the land in their possession (they are not landless anymore!): 40 acres, 60 acres, of this order, allotted to the individual groups. Bank loans have been obtained to purchase ploughs, draught animals. Borrowing in groups' names, guaranteed by the project. Group funds are also being used as working capital.

Organisational mobilisation, coupled perhaps with the status of the foreign-funded project (and presence of foreign consultants in the project), has made government functionaries (e.g. police, upazilla administrator) gradually side with the groups in public. The President of the country once visited the area, and in a public meeting attended by thousands declared that reclaimed land in this area belonged to the government who had granted it to the landless, not to the jotdars. The jotdars nevertheless are finding ways to resist the actual occupation by the landless of much of the land.

A discussion with the chairman of the federation:

Question: How easy was it to persuade the members into collective farming? How is the output being distributed?

Answer: Some persuasion had been necessary initially. It had to be argued that brothers should work together and help each other. In times of sudden need one would not have to go to the jotdar but could be helped from the fund created out of the profits of collective farming.

Participation in collective production had strengthened the bond and sense of family among the members – they are now united to protect the honour of their womenfolk, coming to support each other against thieves and dacoits; the jotdars are unable to harm them any more. 'For the last three years they have been unable to molest our women.'

The groups are keeping regular accounts of individual contributions – plough, draught animal, fertiliser, medicine, labour. A supervisor records these contributions every day, and presents the whole record to weekly meetings. Surplus paddy is presented as 'cash' of the group. When the price rises, the group decides in a meeting to sell it, keeping a portion as seed. The money is used again in production. Some is distributed *equally* among the members for family consumption.

Question: Does this create a problem of equity?

Answer: No, we have resolved this by taking as a rule only one member from each family in the group who gives the same amount of labour as others in the field; only if a family is very large do we take more than one member from it.

The chairman had a word of criticism for the NGO which is helping them. After the flood this year the NGO brought relief materials and these were distributed by the NGO workers rather than by the groups. As a result many undeserving families got help while more deserving families were left out. This generated a lot of adverse comments.

In a session with the NGO workers working in different unions of the upazilla, more insights into the oppressive situation in the area and the dynamics of the people's struggles were revealed:

Union 1

Organisational work for one and a half years. Low land often submerged under water. Habitation since 1974. Absentee jotdars occupy most of the land, using some of the landless themselves as their *lathials* (club men) to whom they give half to one acre of land. The other landless work as sharecroppers from whom half or more of the output is taken by the jotdar.

The jotdars used also to take money from the landless on the pretext of arranging for land registration in their names, which was never done. The landless had to sell their assets (e.g. cow and household goods) to raise this money, and the jotdars, from time to time, only told them that progress was being made in the matter of registration. But nothing ever happened.

With the development of organisation and awareness, such extortion of money is now stopping. Being new settlers, the people do not have kinship ties with the jotdars (or among themselves), so that the sense of enmity is sharp. The jotdars are afraid of the NGO because of its status and connections (e.g. link with the foreign-funded official reclamation project). A test of strength is coming when in the next harvest time the people will claim their rightful share more militantly.

On the women's front little progress has been made. They are oppressed severely by their own menfolk – beating, polygamy, 'wife-shedding' are common; in the absence of kinship ties the rape rate is high. The women are kept firmly under purdah so that the NGO's male workers cannot reach them. It has not yet been possible to engage a female worker in this area.

Union 2

Twenty-seven groups; two women's. No land, no homestead. Many live in or around the moneylender's house, and the moneylenders use them any way they like. Some live on WAPDA (Water and Power Development

Authority) land, and are periodically driven off by WAPDA officers.

After getting organised some groups launched a collective struggle to raise their wages. Some succeeded in raising the wage from 6 to 10 taka for a day's work, both for women and men (men get in addition one meal and $\frac{1}{2}$ seer of rice). The jotdars had tried to bring labour from outside, but the groups were able to persuade outside labour not to cooperate. While the jotdars were forced to raise wages, they also retaliated and created conditions in which nine families had to leave whatever they had as 'homes'.

Another small gain: the jotdars used to engage the landless without payment as night watchmen against robbers. The groups discussed this, and collective negotiation with the jotdars has resulted in agreement to pay 5 taka and a meal to each night watchman per night.

Oppression of women by their own menfolk is severe, but some progress has begun for those who are now organised. Awareness has increased among the women, they mobilise themselves to negotiate with oppressive husbands. Purdah has reduced a little for these women.

In a meeting with representatives of four organisations more accounts of struggles and work and achievements were given.

A jotdar beat a member of a group. The group went on strike; rickshaw wallahs also would not carry the jotdar anywhere. Thus ostracised, the jotdar wanted a settlement, but the people wanted him to appear before a people's court in front of the group's office, nowhere else. Finally, the jotdar's father, a person of high standing, came to the group and apologised on behalf of his son. The people accepted this.

Seeing this victory, others also approached them for help in organising.

People's courts settle internal disputes now. Often elites, who used to settle such disputes previously, are invited to sit as observers. If a group is unable to settle a dispute, the case is taken to the area federation rather than to the elites.

The group leaders talked proudly of their gains from organising:

> When some 'poor brother' is now taken into police custody, we can bring him out. Now we do not have to bribe the police, and we have access to the magistrate.
> But we cannot do without the NGO. We cannot go far out to other places, we do not have the time. We cannot present our cases well in offices and courts because we are not literate.

Question: What is your thinking about becoming literate?
Answer: We do not have enough money for that.

Cyclonic weather. Many houses had been submerged in the last few days, and last night 50–60 women took shelter with their children in the office of the NGO.

Casual talks with stray visitors to the office. The groups had put up their own candidate in the 1983 election for the Union Council chairman. He lost by 400 votes. (The women did not vote because it is a highly conservative place and they had not yet been organised.) In another union two group members were elected as members of the union council, but they are not able to do very much.

Organising women has been a difficult and slow process in this highly conservative area. A woman worker of the NGO recruited from within the area reported that she has to wear a *burqah* herself while moving in public, and has had to face a lot of character assassination campaigns.

Upazilla 4

Twenty-three groups – sixteen men's and seven women's. Work started in 1982.

Here the NGO has male workers only. It has been difficult to get female workers because of transportation difficulties; during the monsoon it is difficult even to walk in the villages. Yet women's groups have been formed.

Initially men's groups were conscientised about the need for women's organisations, which were then initiated by the men's groups. Leaders of women's groups, once formed, later initiated the formation of other women's groups. The purdah culture is still prevalent, so that the male workers of the NGO have to sit at a distance to talk to some women's groups.

It has been difficult to generate much social awareness among the women members – they expect some material gain from the organisation, and some leave when social analysis is initiated. Those who have gone to the basic training course did gain some social awareness, but have not been able to spread this among fellow members. The groups are concentrating on building their savings fund, from which they help weak members of their own and other groups in times of acute distress, marriage, etc.

The NGO's field workers are mostly recruited locally from among the rural educated youth. They live in their own houses. It is difficult to imagine workers from outside coming and living in such areas to work among the poorest under difficult living conditions.

A men's organisation we talked to had started first as a village-wide organisation open to all. This did not last, as the well-to-do tried to use the organisation's funds to promote their interests only. That organisation broke up, and now it is an organisation of the landless only. The members are socially aware, see and discuss the various ways they are being exploited: resources come to the Union Council in the name of the poor but they do not get anything; they are made to work for the Food for Works Programme but are not paid fully; the elites come at the time of election and make big promises, and after winning the election cheat them. While aware, they do not yet see how they can resist such exploitation. They need union-wide organisation, but do not see how this can be developed. They need, they said, the workers of the NGO to confront big enemies (e.g. the chairman of the Union Council) – they do not have the courage to confront them by themselves.

Upazilla 5

The groups in this upazilla did not show any social awareness. They talked only of savings.

One group, one year old, has saved about 2,500 taka. They are engaged in moneylending, at 10 per cent interest for members, and 20 per cent for non-members. Are they not exploiting non-members? 'Yes, but otherwise our fund cannot grow fast'!

One women's group of twenty members has saved about 1,500 taka. A member stops paying after she has contributed 50 taka. The fund is conceived to grow thereafter through moneylending. Money is being lent at 50 per cent interest for a period of eight months. Group discussions focus mainly on how the fund can be increased. Awareness even about women's rights is low. There has been a case of oral divorce of one of the members; the group has discussed this, but does not know what can be done about it – they are not even aware of the recent laws about divorce, according to which oral divorce has no standing.

It had not yet been possible to recruit a female worker in this area.

Upazilla 6

Visited a women's group with sixteen members. Very, very poor. Six are beggars, particularly in slack employment seasons when they find no work; nor do their husbands, who drive them away, being unable to feed them. They are unable to come to the group meetings when they are on begging errands but try to save whatever they can (some 2, some 5 taka, a month) to keep in the group fund in the hope that they may get some help from the group on occasions like daughters' marriage, etc.

The group was started by a male member of the village who had taken the basic training course. He keeps the accounts for the group. Two of the group members have some literacy and have recently started looking after the accounts, taking help from the above person when needed.

A meeting of representatives of six men's groups (about forty present). The men's groups had mobilised to confront the Union Council chairman about distribution of World Food Programme wheat for distressed women which the women were not getting. They succeeded in getting some wheat for the women.

Awareness among the men about oppression of women is increasing. Men's organisations themselves initiated the formation of three women's organisations. Men's awareness about marriage dowry was evident in the meeting. They said that they are against exploitation, and dowry is exploitation. Members of the groups were reported to be marrying without dowry.

Asked to report worthwhile specific activities that they are doing, these responses followed.

One group of fifty-three members, ten months old, has savings of about 4,000 taka. With part of this they have leased a plot of land which has been given to a poor member of the group on a sharecropping basis – this helps the member as well as increasing the group's fund.

Another group, twenty-three members, also ten months old, has savings of about 1,500 taka. With this they give loans, to members at 10 per cent interest, to outsiders at 15 per cent unless the borrower is very poor, when the interest rate is reduced. Not everyone is repaying properly.

A third group of fourteen members is having problems with its cashier who is trying to usurp the group's fund (about 1,800 taka) by denying that he has it. He is not poor – he is the brother of a Union Council member. This group does not have all landless members – the group had been formed before the NGO came here, and joined the NGO's network after it came. Pressure is being put on the cashier for recovery of the fund.

A fourth group of sixteen members has savings of about 1,500 taka. With 1,000 taka they have purchased a saw for wood-cutting and are renting it to members.

Question: For what purpose do the groups need the NGO workers most?
Answer: To negotiate with government functionaries at the *thana* and
  higher levels.

Upazilla 7

Tribal people in hilly area near the northern border. Once living with and upon forests, have now lost control over forests to the government, and reduced to wood-cutting (illegally by bribing the forest guard), and farm work for non-tribal landowners. Very poor. (Yet these tribals are giving priority to literacy for their children.)

The non-tribal population settled below the hills are mostly (80 per cent) refugees from India who came after 1947. The NGO recruited a worker from one such family for work in this area. Transportation into and within the area are very poor; no electricity. These, and ethnic specificity (language of the tribals is also different and not all can speak Bengali), would have made it difficult for an outsider to come and do organisational work in this area.

On the way to a general meeting we visited the house of the leader of women's organisations in the area, popularly known as 'Mashi' ('Auntie'), an energetic tribal woman. Mashi was previously with another NGO which started work in this area in 1974. But the field worker of that NGO did not give a satisfactory account of the money the women had deposited with him. So she and many other women left that NGO, and joined this one in 1982. They now have sixteen women's groups, membership varying from fifteen to twenty-five or so.

Meeting on top of a hill in a tribal village, in front of a church and primary school. Not many had been able to come because of other work: twelve tribals were present.

One men's group had been formed in 1982, before this NGO came. It later joined this NGO. It has some 1,700 taka and 26 maunds of paddy as savings. Cash loans are given to members at 10 per cent interest; paddy loans against 50 per cent in paddy. Previously, the village moneylender used to charge 2 maunds of paddy as interest against a loan of 1 maund and would appropriate land if one could not repay. This is the principal reason why they formed their organisation.

Forest guards have taken away the land they used to cultivate (paddy, potato, egg plant, turmeric), from which they had a decent living. Now they are reduced to dire poverty.

A youth group (nine boys and nine girls) is engaged in just building their fund. They contribute 2 taka each per week, have purchased 500 maunds of paddy with their fund, and lend paddy out at 100 per cent interest in paddy.

An evening session with field workers of the NGO working in different upazillas in the district who had come to meet us.

Upazilla 8

Work is among rickshaw workers, small store-keepers, fishermen. Fifty-one groups formed – twenty-nine men's, twenty-two women's, in twenty-five out of eighty-seven villages in the upazilla. Two NGO workers, one male and one female, working here. Twenty-two male and twenty-seven female group members have taken the basic training course.

Many of the groups were preoccupied with building their fund rather than with social rights. Four groups had broken up after mismanagement of funds.

Those who take the basic training course themselves develop in social awareness, but are unable to explain these matters to others – they cannot remember everything or articulate well, and then become frustrated and give up trying. Those who are literate do better, but some of them become arrogant with their knowledge and behave badly with others.

Asked to give examples of social struggles if any:

1. A woman was beaten by a Union Council member. All members of the women's group came and *gheraoed* (encircled) him; other officials of the Union Council came and made him apologise.
2. Another struggle failed. A *khas* [derelict pond] was promised to a group

for fish cultivation. After they dug it and brought it back to life they were not allowed to use it without registration, and registration required a heavy bribe. They have not been able to do anything about it.

Upazilla 9
There are 182 groups – 48 women's and 134 men's.

In 1984 one tribal woman (whose parents are members of a group) had been raped by a police officer, and then the people had gheraoed the thana office. Men's and women's organisations and also the unorganised poor had all joined in. DC (District Commissioner) and SP (Superintendent of Police) came. The people demanded the police officer be handcuffed; SP carried him away in his jeep at which the people threw bricks. Case was filed against the police officer. This is still pending, while the offender is sending messages of apology. He is now under suspension.

Another successful struggle in a flood-savaged area: people demanded the building of embankments from the UNO (Upazilla Administrative Officer) to protect their houses, but the UNO did not respond. Then people gheraoed the UNO with 300 signatures demanding embankments. They got them.

The groups have linked up at the union level in a committee of twenty-nine meets once a month, exchanges reports from different groups, and discusses common issues and strategy for joint struggle.

Upazilla 10
Twenty-two groups – nineteen women's and three men's, in twelve villages in four unions. Work started in 1983.

The focus initially was too much on saving and growth of the fund through moneylending. In some groups members took back their own contributions and kept the profits in the fund after they became sizeable. Seeing this excessive saving orientation, the NGO workers intervened for some groups to reduce their saving and to initiate discussion on social rights as an objective of organising.

Awareness of women's rights is emerging slowly – in two marriage cases dowry has been stopped; laws about divorce are now known to the women.

Upazilla 11
Fifteen women's and seven men's organisations in three unions where work started in 1982 under two female workers and one male worker. Basic training has been taken by twenty-six women and twenty-seven men. Advanced training taken by six from each sex. Four people's theatres have been produced.

Progress in organisational development was initially slow because of the presence of another NGO and the Grameen Bank in the area. These agencies give financial resources to the groups they create, whereas this

NGO does not. Organisational development under this NGO picked up after potential leaders were identified and sent to take the basic training. Activities so far have been confined to saving and social discussion in weekly meetings. Small-scale social action on such issues as divorce, marriage dowry, have been staged by women's groups. But no major social action yet. Discussions are initiated on exploitation, mollahism, oppression of women, and this is slowly developing the awareness that the organisation has more fundamental objectives than saving alone. But the confidence to launch a major social struggle has not yet come.

The people's theatres depict processes of exploitation, by the moneylender, doctor, members and chairman of the Union Council. The people want to see more, and then they are asked to organise. Three groups have been formed through such stimulation.

Attended a meeting of representatives from groups of Upazilla 8 (the location of the above discussions). This was the first meeting of representatives in this area. It had not been possible to give timely intimation to all groups, so the attendance was thin (about twenty).

Initially the discussion was dominated by Mashi. She had a lot of complaints. She (a natural leader) has to give a lot of time to guidance of a number of women's groups, supervising their accounts, etc. Almost each group had a 'trained' member by now (taken the basic training), but they are unable to give much time to work for the group. A lot of harassment has to be handled by Mashi alone in social struggles, and she is unable to give so much time. She herself suffered in one struggle for land when her son and another relative were falsely implicated in a murder case and were taken into custody, and she had to raise 10,000 taka of her own by borrowing and selling assets for their release. The groups later offered to raise the money to pay her, but she declined this offer. Her own house has also been set on fire.

I asked Mashi whether before paying the bribe she had sought the support of the groups who might have mobilised themselves to resist the police harassment and help get her son and relative released. She replied she had become panicky upon knowing about her son's arrest, ran to the police station, and agreed to whatever they demanded for his release. A very human response, but perhaps an opportunity missed to test the collective strength of the people?

There was nothing exciting reported by representatives from the other groups. After the meeting it was resolved that such meetings of representatives should be held once every month, with adequate prior notice.

Advanced training

Four-day advanced training for group leaders. It was planned that twenty-five would be trained, from among groups in two divisions. The team from one division never arrived, due, as was learnt later, to non-delivery of mail. So only twelve received training, nine males and three females.

The training was conducted by a male director and a female co-trainer. Each day was divided into two sessions chaired by one from among the trainees. The training themes included:

(a) review of basic training;
(b) advanced social analysis dealing with processes of exploitation and underdevelopment;
(c) history of peasant struggles in Bangladesh and its independence struggle;
(d) history of popular struggles in other countries;
(e) roles of heroic women in popular struggles;
(f) advanced organisational questions (leadership, structure, tactics, planning, need for national-level organisation of workers).

Although the course was intended to have maximum participation from the trainees, some of the subjects were rather complex or heavy, and the trainees had no previous preparation or systematic thinking on them. The first two days were reduced virtually to one-way lectures by the trainers, except for an unprepared talk upon request by me on the underdevelopment of Bangladesh. Some of the trainees appeared to think that I was supposed to have answers to all questions and pressed me at times to give them. I declined stubbornly. The dependence on the trainers continued throughout the first two days.

Participation of the trainees improved in the last two days when, after we had a discussion about their poor participation, the trainees were formed into two groups and were left to themselves for a period to discuss each major question and report back to the full class. It was only when they were thus 'liberated' from the presence of 'overwhelming' teachers that they revealed their ability to think, deliberate and draw conclusions, at least as groups.

Individually, some were clearly more articulate than others, and three who were literate (and thus *could take notes*) had a distinct edge over the others in recapitulation of discussions of previous sessions. The three female trainees were particularly weak and did not appear to have absorbed any substance from the training. When asked to recapitulate at the beginning of different sessions, they could hardly say much beyond 'We are poor, our needs are rice and clothing; what else can we say? *You* know best how our lot can be improved.'

I was told that this was one of the weakest groups of trainees – normally their participation in the discussions is of a much higher quality, sometimes involving considerable excitement and heat. But this group, on the whole, certainly, showed disturbing lack of self-confidence and wanted to be told rather than to participate in the deliberations.

Among stories of social struggle that were recounted in the discussion was the interesting one of confronting corruption in a hospital. There is medicine for free injections, but the doctor would not give it. A women's group mobilised about 100 women to go to the hospital to protest, complained to the chairman of the Union Council, and forcefully got the medicines out. The doctor had to apologise in public. 'Why is the hospital there – only for the rich?'

Another male group leader had challenged local touts who had been appropriating relief wheat meant for distressed mothers. The touts misrepresented to the Union Council chairman that he (group leader) was trying to snatch away wheat meant for the distressed mothers! The group leader faced this with courage, mobilised support from among the poor to seize the wheat and measure the stock in public, made a list of the distressed and gave a petition to the chairman stating that they would go on resisting if the distribution was not fair. 'I have gone to jail nineteen times previously for protesting against injustices, and shall go on protesting.'

The NGO's cultural wing put on a programme in the evening of songs on organisation and struggles, and a puppet theatre depicting a moneylender's exploitation tactics. A very effective awareness raiser.

Upazilla 12

Organisational development in this area is 7–8 years old. It started under local initiative of the educated youth, and spread to many villages. Later the groups joined this NGO and a leading youth activist who had been guiding them became an officer of the NGO. After a few years' association with the NGO local youth, activists working with the groups initiated a resolution that they did not need the NGO any more. The NGO withdrew from this area, the first instance of complete withdrawal according to the principle of self-reliance organisation development.

Our visit, however, revealed a discouraging situation. In an ad hoc evening, gathering in one village, it was reported that 7–8 years' of struggle for the five 'basic needs' had yielded nothing and there was a great sense of frustration. Large mass mobilisations had been organised, thousands had marched to the city to gherao the DC's office and present their demands. The DC had promised that the demands would be met, but nothing happened. They do not know what more they can do to improve their lot. They are also unhappy that the NGO workers do not come any more.

Others said that there still have been gains, and those who deny this are agents of the enemy. Now if one poor brother is in difficulty, others come to help him. No disputes in the village can be settled without involving the groups. The UNO and the DC come and meet them, seek their opinions. This had never happened before.

A meeting of representatives of different organisations in the area had been arranged on the occasion of our visit. This was rather too formal. The chairman of the meeting – an unemployed youth activist – requested the help of the ILO in getting trade union rights for the rural workers. (I explained to them that while I would pass on this request to the ILO, I was not visiting them as an ILO representative.)

Representatives of organisations of different villages were invited to make statements. Eleven representatives spoke, reporting briefly on the various mass demonstrations that had been launched to demand the 'basic needs', in some places to get khas land which got them involved in court cases and other social struggles. All these brought them a lot of harassment, but their fate had not changed. They are frustrated, they do not know what to do, and request 'workers at the top' to tell them which way they should go. All the eleven speakers, men and women leaders of the village organisations, virtually repeated the same statement, in such unison that it appeared they had rehearsed this together!

Upazilla 13

Struggle for khas *beel* (marshy) land had started in 1978, before the NGO had come to the area. The jotdars were using the land when 50–60 landless decided to assert their right to khas land and launched a crop seizure action. They got involved in court cases, and made temporary peace by paying some money. But the struggle for land continued, and they got organised under the NGO's guidance. More land seizures; court cases; raising funds to fight the court cases and make mass representations to the court; houses of landless set on fire; mass gherao of Martial Law office with no effect. Meanwhile they have sizeable land under their control which they are cultivating, and some land they have seized but are unable to cultivate because of a court injunction.

They have put the land under collective cultivation, allotting land to hamlet-based groups – a large number of groups with membership ranging from six to sixty. They have a central committee at the union level. Local school teachers are now with them, helping them in dealing with the court, etc. They feel strengthened when the worker of the NGO is with them, but even without him they think they can continue in their struggle and are not going to give up.

They took us around to see the land they are cultivating, and the land under injunction. Relaxed militancy, enjoying the taste of collective power and collective work even if they are being harassed and have not seen the end of their struggle.

Collective funds? They have none. They had started something, but could not manage it well and stopped it. They do not save from the project of collective farming either. When they need money for their struggle they raise it on an ad hoc basis, raise thousands of Taka, if necessary by selling livestock and other household goods, or by borrowing. At times of personal distress they borrow from the moneylender: 'even this is better than borrowing from a group fund and defaulting, and risk impairing relations with our organisation as the organisation will press for repayment'!

While the self-assured militancy and collective production endeavour were impressive, the attitude to the question of collective funds was rather unconstructive.

There were no women's groups in this area, and a female worker of the NGO who accompanied us there took the militant men up on this: 'Can you go to the district headquarters if your bullock cart has only one wheel?' 'No, we cannot.' 'Then where is the other wheel?' The men promised that they would make the other wheel – the women's organisation – and asked the female worker to return after a few months to see it.

The pedagogy of 'conscientising the men' was most interesting.

Upazilla 14

Visited one upazilla in the Delta area, where organisational work of the NGO is linked with a foreign-funded project for construction of polders and irrigation to bring very fertile land under cultivation. Organisational work started in 1981. Land being brought under cultivation in the project is auctioned for lease every year, and organisations of the landless have been able to get some of these initially with their collective funds, and subsequently with the profit from collective production on these lands.

The organisations are also involved in struggle with contractors for a fair wage for the earth work in which the landless are engaged. Last year the contractors brought labourers from other areas to replace them when they demanded better wages. They were able to explain to these outside labourers why they should not play into the hands of the contractor in this way, but the outsiders still could not stop work because the shrewd contractor had already paid them advance wages. They are hoping that next year such advances will be refused and they will win.

A high rate, 25 per cent, of the profit from collective production (paddy and fish) is retained in the group funds. This is used to lease new land, to provide working capital, and also in a literacy project for children: they have constructed a primary school with their own labour and resources, and are paying two teachers from their collective funds (several base groups have combined to implement this project). The men's groups here have a distinctly constructive orientation.

There are five women's groups in the area with 130 members. Meeting with one of them was distressing, to hear of their stark poverty and how they are being discriminated against. The flood had struck some families hard, but the chairman of the Union Council would give relief wheat only to those who were not organised, as a punishment for organising. Yet organisational awareness is high. Do they still prefer to stay in the organisation? 'Yes, for what is the value of two days' relief wheat? If instead we can build some fund of our own it may give us some lasting benefit.'

The group is registered with BRDP (Bangladesh Rural Development Programme) which in principle entitles it to loans from a government bank. It has to keep its savings with the BRDP, and its representative has to report to the BRDP office once a week to deposit the weekly saving. For this she is entitled to 16 taka for transportation and food. But she does not get this allowance – it is usurped by the officers.

The Union Council chairman also discriminates against them in recruiting women for earth work, because they are organised. That they still want to stay organised reflects a deep class awareness among these women and a sense of dignity which refuses to submit to injustice.

Engaged in profitable production, the men's organisations are the more animated. But the limits of their consciousness were revealed in two sessions with representatives of a number of men's organisations.

One was convened to discuss some grievance the organisations had against the NGO. The NGO workers invited them to spell out their grievances frankly, and judge if they had done any wrong. The main grievance appeared to be that while a previous field worker of the NGO used to keep much closer contact with them, he had been replaced by another who gave them less time. They look upon the NGO workers as 'masters' of whom they are 'disciples', and expect close presence of the 'masters'. A disturbing lack of self-confidence, although they are doing good work.

I felt that, in part, the tendency of the base groups to cling onto the NGO workers is derived from the general sense of helplessness they feel in a deeply oppressive environment: in the NGO they have, at last, found a *friend*. However, the awareness had not dawned on them that it is in their own interest to want to release the NGO workers early (and, therefore, to prepare themselves for this) for organisational work in other places, so that their collective struggle can expand over a wider area and be effective in representing their interests at higher levels of social decision-making and power.

The other session was a general one, to discuss what the groups were doing. They were presenting the five 'basic needs' as their principal demands 'because we are human beings'. I challenged:

'What is human in these? These are needs of animals as well. How do you prove that you are truly human?'
'We do not understand your questions.'

'All right, imagine that a man is drowning. There are two alternative ways of saving him. One is to lift him with two hands and put him on the shore. He will possibly thank you for saving his life, but deep inside him will he also feel a little humiliated?'

'Not a little, but deeply,' said a senior leader of the people sitting in a corner in the front row.

'The other alternative is to ask him to hold you by one hand while you swim, and ask him also to swim with his other hand. Then once on the shore, he will thank you for saving his life, but he will also thank you for something else . . . for saving his dignity, for giving him a role in the process. Because man does not want to have others do things for him. Because man is a *creator*. Isn't the greatest quality of labour that he/she creates, and not merely consumes (the "basic needs")? Isn't this the difference between a human being and an animal?'

There was a man, somewhat eccentric, who had been standing on the side all the time while we had all been sitting, and had been making assertive but apparently irrelevant interventions from time to time. This time he showed his genius and shouted out to the others: 'I say, don't listen to him – he is talking in *High Bengali*!' Obviously, his equilibrium had been disturbed.

The response of the senior leader sitting in the corner was more direct: 'We have never heard anything like this before. Can I request you to say some more like this?'

We saw that it is possible to touch the creative chord which exists deep inside every person, often forgotten and rusting.

Reflections

Positive elements

Albeit based on observations of an impressionistic nature, the organising work reported above has a number of positive elements. Some of these are:

- The base groups are becoming aware that their plight is caused by social exploitation rather than by 'destiny'.

- Awareness is developing that social exploitation and oppression should be resisted by organised action. Whether over a given period of time such struggle is being successful or not, in all places that I visited the members of the base organisations have in general shown strong commitment to staying organised. This illustrates that organisational motivation of the oppressed classes can be sustained without any financial inputs from the outside, by competent work towards the promotion of awareness, stimulating collective action for achieving the economic and social rights of the oppressed, and efforts towards economic betterment primarily through the mobilisation of the internal resources of the poverty groups. The evidence suggests that class organisations of the oppressed are a higher social formation by themselves in their struggle for a better life.

• Different types of local-level exploitation and oppression are being resisted, in many cases successfully; rights are being achieved, and injustices are being dealt with in 'people's courts'. The record is not uniform in these matters in all places, but over the canvas as a whole the achievement seems to be positive.

• There has been visible improvement in the social status of the poverty groups after they become organised. Local elites, staff of government agencies, etc. treat them with greater respect than they customarily treat the poor, and the self-esteem of the poverty groups also seems to have increased.

• In many cases broader linkages between different base organisations have been established for issue-based struggles.

• Separate organisations of rural poor women are promoting women's specific rights and resisting such exploitation and oppression over women, and progress in this respect in many cases is encouraging. It is particularly noteworthy that this is being achieved without creating a confrontational situation between men and women among the poverty groups. The strategy has been to motivate and 'conscientise' the men of the poverty ranks in respecting the rights of the women rather than to provoke confrontations between the two groups, in order that their common struggle against poverty and class oppression is not weakened. In this strategy visible success has been achieved.

The perspective of social change
One is, however, stimulated by the above experience to reflect on the relevance of such effort in grassroots organising for fundamental social change.

As one understands Marxist theory, radical social change occurs when the most creative class in the society considers the existing production relations as an obstacle to the fulfilment of its creative urges and acts to destroy this obstacle. Social change does not occur because of exploitation only; if the exploiting class engages the resources appropriated by exploitation in rapidly developing the productive forces, it thereby releases a dynamism in the society which absorbs other contradictions. The possibility of radical social change in such a case arises only when this class becomes incapable of further developing the productive forces so that the above dynamism fades out, and a new creative class appears on the scene capable of taking the productive forces further forward under a radically different system of production relations.

Has the time for radical social change come in the country? If so, then which is that new creative class which will have the principal role in constructing the new social order? Some progressive quarters characterise the present social phase in the country as a phase of 'undeveloped capitalism'. There has been a lot to debate on this proposition in the country in recent times. However, if this characterisation were correct, then the first important question which arises is whether this 'undeveloped' capitalism is showing such dynamism as to promise a vigorous growth of the productive forces within a capitalist framework. The answer is perhaps still in the negative. Then the second question arises, i.e. is any other social class visible which possesses the requisite creative qualities, through whom, therefore, a radical development of the productive forces under some other framework of production relations may be possible? The poorest labouring class in the society whose organised struggles we have reported upon above – is this the 'revolutionary' class in this sense?

This question concerns the *creative* capability, mentality and preparedness of a class, not its *destructive* capability. Through mass mobilisation of an oppressed labouring class it may be possible to destroy an old social order; this does not necessarily mean that this class has the capability to build, and failing this control over the new society will inevitably slip from its hands to the hands of some other class. The history of social revolutions has many experiences of this nature. It is particularly noteworthy that the Soviet Revolution did not transfer social power to the class of direct producers. In particular, the 'proletariat', whose 'dictatorship' the new social order was supposed to be, was not prepared to lead constructive initiatives, and power was progressively transferred to a class of technocracy (Bettelheim, 1976), and in this sense a 'counter-revolution' was eventually victorious.

In a given country with an oppressive social structure, organised struggle by the oppressed classes may bring down the prevailing social order. But unless the masses can take a leading role in rebuilding the society they will be liable to become subordinate again to some other social class or classes and lose the power to *participate* in the process of social reconstruction and development as full subjects. To be able to take such a role, the masses must have a creative mentality, a self-confidence not merely in emotional militancy but in their ability to construct, and an urge to acquire the needed knowledge and skills to stay at the frontier of developmental creativity to plan, implement and manage economic and social programmes. Revolutionary social change liberates creative forces whose fulfilment has been blocked by the prevailing relations of production. But *in order to be liberated, a force must be already active* – in fact, it is not a *force* unless it is active. A sleeping 'force' cannot be liberated by opening the door: this will only invite some other active force to take over control.

Among the base organisations which were visited, some have taken spontaneous constructive initiatives, and this is a matter of hope. Some have failed to manage a simple collective fund, and instead of constructively reviewing their failure and creatively devising ways to prevent such mismanagement in the future, have agreed to the closing down of the fund, and thereby the vital process of internal resource mobilisation.

Organising work of this nature needs to make more conscious effort to rouse the creative urge among the base groups. Indeed, the basic demand of the oppressed should be that they must be given the opportunity not just to participate in the consumerist benefits of development – satisfaction of the five 'basic needs' to start with – but to take development initiatives of their own. Their basic struggle should be not against the exploiters of their surplus labour as such but against the obstacles to the fulfilment of their creative potentials. There is not much point in demanding the five 'basic needs' from a (ruling) class which is unproductive itself and, therefore, cannot deliver these to the people. The people's demand should instead be: 'We can produce all these things that we need; give us this power and opportunity.' At the same time, effort should be oriented to raise their capability to deliver these to themselves.

'Training'
What should be the elements of a 'training' programme for base groups' leaders and members, oriented to promoting a creative role of the exploited and oppressed classes, i.e. to promoting their participation as true subjects in the economic and social development process? I suggest the following:

• Establishment of the creative identity of human beings.

• Analysis of the reason why productive forces in the society are not developing, e.g. the country could be self-sufficient in food production; governments have made five-year plans, two-year plans, etc. to make it so – why has this not happened? What is standing in the way of the needed production of the other 'basic needs' goods and services?

• If control over resources by a certain class has failed to develop the productive forces, which class could give a constructive leadership in this respect? Is it 'us' (the oppressed working class)? Some searching self-analysis on this question.

• If indeed 'we' want to make a bid for this leadership, or even to participate as equals in the leadership, how must 'we' prepare ourselves, by way of attitudes, acquiring the needed knowledge and skills, managerial experience and ability, etc.?

- Analysis of social change in other countries from the point of view of what classes in fact come into power in the new social order. How much creative initiative were the toiling masses able to take in reconstructing society? What are the lessons of history in this respect? What precautions and preparations must be taken in conducting struggles for social change with such lessons of history?

With the above perspective, field animation work to stimulate purposeful initiatives and struggles of oppressed classes, aiming at promoting the participation of these classes as builders of a new society, should focus not on promoting mass demands for delivery of 'basic needs' by others, but on what the masses can do themselves in meeting these needs. Deliberations by the base groups should be stimulated to inquire: (a) what in the local context are the potentials for developing the productive forces concretely, to increase radically the production of the essential needs of the society; (b) to what extent official plans and programmes for a specific area are designed to realise these potentials; and (c) what alternative programmes could do better in this regard. In the country itself there are examples of local-level mass initiatives or participatory programmes for raising food production, providing basic health care and literacy, etc., which have done much better than conventional progammes in meeting these needs; these should be discussed to draw inspiration and ideas.

Stimulated in this way, the base organisations would in some places be able to take initiatives to produce for themselves and for their communities some of the essential goods and services, where necessary with the cooperation and help of people-oriented professionals with whom contact may be established. Success in this regard will increase self-confidence as well as positive experience and skills. In other places there would be obstacles coming from the prevailing structure, bureaucratic regulations, lack of access to resources, etc., in the way of realisation of such constructive plans of the masses. Mass struggles and demonstrations could then be addressed to the removal of such barriers to the people's ability to take constructive initiatives. In this way, mass struggles would become creativity-oriented rather than consumption and external delivery-oriented, and would develop greater potential for the masses to participate in and contribute to a constructive effort for social change. Such struggles would also, one suggests, draw greater respect and support from the wider society as well.

Reference

Bettelheim, Charles (1976) *Class Struggles in the USSR, First Period: 1917–1923*, Monthly Review Press.

8. Glimpses of the 'Other Africa'

Introduction

Africa was staggered by the recent drought. But even before and without the drought, development in Africa did not show much dynamism. This was possibly one reason why the drought became such a killer: neither material not institutional reserves were there to absorb such a shock.

The international development assistance system is eager to assist African development so that a calamity of the nature of the last crisis does not recur. There are few examples, however, where massive international assistance has generated a development dynamism in a country where the society has not mobilised itself. There are many examples, on the contrary, of such assistance distorting the very orientation of a society's development thinking and effort. The distortion is towards spending energy more on waiting for and upon outside resources rather than on mobilising domestic resources, waiting for the foreign consultant to show his or her wisdom rather than taking initiatives based on indigenous knowledge and skills, and towards misusing outside resources much of whose accountability is tied to formal spending rather than with creating worthwhile material and human assets.

The only hope of generating a development dynamism in Africa is through stimulating domestic mobilisation of social energy and resources. These may be supplemented by outside resources sensitively, so as not to destroy or disorient domestic initiative but to provide complementary skills and release critical bottlenecks.

How does such mobilisation take place? It does not take place if the state assumes the primary responsibility for initiating and implementing

The author is grateful to Philippe Egger, who is working closely, for the ILO's PORP programme, with the movements in Senegal, Burkina Faso and Rwanda reported in this paper, for checking the summary descriptions of these movements. Peter Peek and Adrina Van-Ommering made some useful suggestions towards a revision of an earlier draft.

development, for then two negative things happen. One, the people wait for the state agencies to 'deliver' development; like the state waiting upon international assistance, the people then waste resources, time and energy in lobbying and waiting for such deliveries instead of mobilising their own resources and taking initiatives of their own. Two, the state itself fails to deliver. This is because, first, it never can have the resources to deliver, on a national scale, because its resources are comprised only of (a) what it can get from the people, a politically dismal prospect if the people expect the state to give them more than they can pay for; and (b) international capital flows which are never a full substitute for domestic resources. Second, state bureaucracies are typically unable to display the dynamism, innovativeness and flexibility in their functioning, needed to become the 'leading sector' in development.

Domestic mobilisation can only take place (in non-regimented societies) through *people's self-mobilisation*. This means the people, in convenient units of similarly situated persons/families living together as a community, getting together, reflecting upon their problems, forming some kind of a collective structure if this does not already exist, and taking initiatives as a group by pooling their brains, muscles and other resources together to achieve some jointly conceived objectives, and to keep on doing so, and thus *developing authentically* (discussed more fully in the concluding section). Such structures may link at higher levels for coordinating, planning and implementing action on a wider scale. The pace of such development may come faster if some complementary outside resources, by way of brains, skills and physical resources, become available. But a forward-moving development process need not be contingent on the availability of outside assistance if a community would resolve to pool whatever they have, first to accomplish something that it can accomplish with these; this then becomes a psychological, proficiencial and material basis for the next step forward.

The poverty and underdevelopment of Africa is well and widely known. Not so are some of the outstanding and inspiring initiatives of people's self-mobilisation for development in Africa and, hence, the potential of the African people. In this paper information collected by the ILO's Programme on Participatory Organisations of the Rural Poor (PORP) on such initiatives in West Africa, in Rwanda and in Zimbabwe with which PORP is collaborating, and the experience of an ongoing project in Tanzania, are presented briefly, to give some glimpses of this 'Other Africa'. The author reflects upon these experiences in the concluding section.

The Committee for Development Action in the Villages of the Zone of Bamba-Thialene, Senegal

The zone of Bamba-Thialene in the eastern part of Senegal was struck by successive years of drought starting in the early 1970s. The villagers in this traditionally agricultural and pastoral area grew worried as their livestock was decimated, agricultural productivity diminished drastically, the forests were threatened with extinction, and productive work was drastically reduced. Many travelled, and those who went to the north brought back chilling stories of the fate of the villagers there who had been hit even harder by the drought.

The fear of suffering the same fate generated the awareness that collective action to fight the situation was needed. This resulted in a movement for collective self-development in sixteen villages in the zone, which is today spreading to other areas of the country.

The process started in 1975 with a nucleus of persons who had returned to the region from a trip to the north. They initiated discussions in the rooms of some friends as they dared not at first pose the questions in public in a society traditionally governed by the village elders. They guided the people to pose questions such as:

Where would they get the products which they could not get in sufficient quantity from the forest, e.g. game-bird, millet, cassava, wood etc.?

Why was the bush not sufficient for grazing the animals?

What would happen if they had the kind of difficulties that the north had?

Why did the zone lack collective infrastructure?

Why did they not have productive work all the twelve months?

The team thereafter designed a delegation to different parts of the zone for conducting a census of the population, livestock, supply of seeds and other agricultural inputs from the government store, and of all the collective needs of the population. The census was done in sixteen villages which were served by the government store. The people continued to reflect on the situation and on the problems revealed by the census.

By a happy coincidence, early in 1976 the nucleus team met an educated professional who had rich ideas and experience on people's self-development, and who had resigned from his salaried job in search of more fulfilling work. This 'animator' started visiting the group and listening to the people discussing their problems, and eventually integrated with them to guide their struggle. Towards the end of that year the first 'sub-committee' was formed in Bamba village.

The word spread to other villages where people also got interested in deepening the survey and the ongoing analysis. Many inter-village reflection sessions were held, and sub-committees started being formed in these other villages. After the setting up of fifteen sub-committees, the Committee for

Development Action in the Villages of the Zone of Bamba-Thialene (henceforth the Committee) was formed in 1977 as an apex body of these sub-committees.

There was an initial period of difficulty consolidating the organisation as collective reflection was not converging to a direction for action. The people were getting frustrated, and most sub-committees remained non-functional or disbanded. The spirit was gradually revived as the first sub-committee of Bamba village started collective poultry farming in 1978 with the subscriptions of its members. Other sub-committees started getting busy, and initiated similar self-help projects in agriculture or animal husbandry. In agriculture, the traditional use of horses for ploughing was found inefficient and was replaced first by oxen and then by cows. This increased the return from the members' investment many times over as the cows provided offspring, milk and hides. Loans were provided to members in the form of cattle, with repayments in the form of calves, thus building a revolving fund to support newer activities. In poultry, sheep and cattle, fattening programmes were introduced, combined with marketing programmes.

After an initial period of fully self-financed activities, external financial help started coming, and the activities expanded. Training programmes in management and accounting, adult education, reforestation for environmental protection and community health programmes were added. The Committee, however, is wary of becoming too dependent on outside funding, and gives great importance to the financial contribution made to the running costs of the various programmes out of collective projects such as communal fields.

In all this development, collective reflection has remained a most important methodological element. A lot of collective discussion precedes the launching of any project. In these reflections, special attention is given to the cultural implications of a project, to ensure that it would not introduce a cultural shock but would be in tune with local traditional and religious values. Development is not conceived as simply material change but is seen as an evolution of the totality of the people's life.

With assistance from the ILO's PORP programme, the Committee in 1987 initiated a people's self-review of their ongoing experiences.

This was the first systematic self-review undertaken in the Committee's work, and consisted of six phases as follows:

First phase: meeting of the Central Committee to discuss the objectives of the self-review and to design its methodology, and to draw up a questionnaire.
Second phase: discussion of the questionnaire by the sixteen sub-committees and in general assembly meetings, and filling in the questionnaires with the

animators and with the active participation of the people.

Third phase: discussion of specific activities of the sub-committees with members of specialised commissions.

Fourth phase: processing and analysing the filled-in questionnaires, interpretation of the results, and preparing their presentation in appropriate pedagogic forms with the participation of the animators.

Fifth phase: presentation of the results to the general assembly for discussion, modification and validation.

Sixth phase: a synthesis at the level of the Central Committee for preparation of the final report.

The following are some of the lessons highlighted in the review:

• One should not await state action. The financial means of the state are limited in relation to the needs of the different zones. It is, therefore, necessary that each group reflect on ways to take charge themselves to improve the conditions of their life, search for solutions and get organised.

• The people have to organise themselves. The organisation cannot be imposed from outside, with rigid rules. It is easy for a leader to organise the people, but then such organisation risks being dominated by the more able. It is better to let the people seek out the path themselves slowly so as to reduce this risk, taking into account their traditional modes, and develop a natural process of discussion and review. The process is more important than the result for obtaining and sustaining the solidarity of the group.

• Effective participation of the members is essential. This needs time and space for discussion and for amendment of modes of thinking. This requires that the people confront and collectively analyse the problems, and deepen the understanding that each has of them.

• One should first of all count on one's own forces. The experiment of self-development should necessarily start with the mobilisation of internal resources of the group including: their capacity to reflect; their subscriptions and savings; their latent capacity to work.

• The process of self-development has different phases which are a slow evolution at the rhythm of the life of the people concerned, accompanied by the acquisition and accumulation of knowledge and other resources with a view to achieving liberation from all forms of dependence. This process gives to all the right to decision-making, and enables the taking of action immediately without waiting for outside help.

- It is vitally necessary at the very beginning to avoid looking for aid, which kills local initiatives and puts the people in a complacent mood. Aid is necessary, but it should not inhibit the evolution of the group.

- Information and training should form the basis of the activities conducted by the groups. Training will respond to the preoccupations of the people. It will not reject traditional knowledge, but will seek to strike a balance between what is positive in traditional knowledge and modern knowledge. In this process new privileges should not be created in the form of repository of knowledge.

- As for information, this completes the training, and starts with the base – from the base towards the top and vice versa. This should facilitate the taking of decisions. Then the groups should spread the information to other groups in the country and beyond, for exchanging and comparing the experiences.

- The base groups should be made responsible for their activities, by starting with appropriate training and laying the permanent structure of participation in decision-making. The nearer decision-making is to the base, the more involved are the people at the base, and the more responsible, therefore, they become.

- After some experience of a few years, there would be reasons for satisfaction, but also for disappointment. For the members of the group, what is essential is to have tried something together, and encountered the obstacles, which should, far from dividing them, strengthen their confidence and solidarity. The actions undertaken would permit the launching of others, initially unbelievable or doubted, the people not believing that they were truly the agents of their own development, that it was possible to count upon themselves and to accomplish tasks which benefit all.

The Six-S movement in West Africa

In Burkina Faso there has been a tradition of mutual cooperation and community work in what are known as 'Naam' groups, which are in particular youth groups among the Mossi people. In 1976 a group of Naam leaders and some of their European friends formed the Six-S Association[1] to address the following question: how can one take as much advantage as possible of the time available during the dry season? The dry season in the Sahel region is long – October to May – when the rate of unemployment of the labour force is high, explaining much of the poverty of the peasantry and migration of their youth to the urban areas.

While addressing this basic economic question, Six-S held the view that 'all action should start from what the peasants are, what they know, what they can do, where they live, and what they want.'

With motivational work and external resource assistance, Six-S has today developed into the largest people's self-development movement in Africa. Its headquarters are in Burkina Faso where the movement started and where it has (as of March 1987) more than 2,000 groups with an average of about 50 members in 33 zones, of which about 800 are women's groups. Each Six-S zone is under the direction of one official coming from the ranks of the peasantry, who is paid by Six-S for the eight dry months of each year. The official is given one or more training courses in animation and technical skills, and is assisted by a management committee elected by the Naam groups in the zone. The apex body of Six-S, a council of administration, is composed of seven founder members and the zone officials.

Basically, Six-S is promoting the development of the traditional Naam groups into development-oriented organisations, stimulating them to maximise the mobilisation of their internal resources and supplying technical, material and financial assistance to release critical bottlenecks. The local groups themselves define their programmes of activities, which are concentrated in the dry, hitherto slack season. These include: (a) group *income-generating activities* such as vegetable gardening, stock farming, handicrafts, millet mills, grain banks, production and sale of horse carts, fencing, etc.; (b) activities of *communal benefit* such as constructing water dams and dykes, anti-erosion works, wells, afforestation, most of which contribute significantly to raising the production of cereals in the rainy season also; (c) *social activities*: rural pharmacies, primary health care, schools, theatre, etc.

Six-S provides credit to partially support a large number of such activities. Activities of communal benefit are subsidised, through limited cash remuneration and food for work, and free supply of the needed equipment. In turn, Six-S gets funds from member groups' contributions and external donors. All Six-S groups have a savings fund built with member subscriptions and receipts from income-generating activities. Six-S's financial assistance to any group decreases over time as a matter of policy with the growth of the groups' collective fund and assets.

A particularly innovative dimension of Six-S's work is in the area of skills promotion. When some members of Six-S's groups master a certain technique or technology, they form a mobile 'labour-yard' school to teach the skill to other groups. Such mobile schools exist in each of the thirty-three zones of Six-S, and every group in a zone can request the schools to come and train them. Through this process new skills are spreading fast among Six-S groups in all kinds of fields, e.g. agriculture, handicrafts, health care, well construction and maintenance, etc.

In addition, farmer–technicians are employed by Six-S during the slack season to advise the groups and assist their activities. The groups can also propose to have one or more of their members trained in a certain field, and Six-S arranges the desired training with some other group under apprenticeship, or at some specialised institution. At a general level, Six-S strongly encourages and facilitates the interaction between its groups for exchange of experience and knowledge and is also organising exchanges between countries. Self-evaluation of their experiences by the Six-S groups is being promoted with assistance from PORP, ILO, as a key educational and human developmental method.

The visible improvement in employment, income and socio-economic security in the villages covered by Six-S (accompanied by a drastic reduction of youth migration from these villages), and the demonstration of such fulfilling self-mobilisation by the people, are contributing to a fast growth of Six-S groups. The movement has spread into Senegal, Mali and Mauritania as well, and is also linking with other self-development-oriented peasant organisations in these countries. Today, an initiative has also been taken to introduce the Six-S regional movement into Niger and Chad.

From Twese Hamwe to ADRI, Rwanda

In 1979 an agronomist (hereafter the 'promoter') initiated 'animation' work with the people of Murambi in the Giciye commune of Kabaya district in Rwanda. His aim was to generate awareness among the people about their potential and to stimulate action towards their self-development.

There had already been informal groups, and a tradition of mutual cooperation, in the area. The promoter's work soon stimulated twenty-five peasant women, who had been informally organised since 1976, to constitute a cooperative called Twese Hamwe with some forty members.

Twese Hamwe first initiated collective activities in the agricultural field – collective production of vegetables, maize, etc. – on land lent by the commune or rented. Gradually, other activities were launched: marketing, milling, a rural pharmacy, artisanal production of baked bricks, a grocery store, grain storage, poultry, etc.

Seeing these initiatives, two other women's groups pooled their savings, and with the help of the promoter managed to get some external credit from an agency, to set up another grinding mill which they managed themselves.

Other groups in Giciye and another commune, Gaseke, had also become interested in initiating such activities, and had been approaching the promoter for help. The promoter convened a general meeting of all groups in the two communes, seventeen in all, who sought his help. A second meeting was held after a few weeks, and an inter-group organisation,

'Impuzamiryango Tuzamuke Twese (ITT), was formed with two representatives from each group making up its council. The task of ITT, defined as a peasant organisation for assisting its members, was conceived as being: (a) to study action proposals of the member groups; (b) to grant credits to the groups for launching their projects; (c) to offer various other related services.

Twelve groups joined the ITT. The total membership of all the groups taken together was close to 300, the membership of individual groups ranging from six to seventy. This included three exclusive women's groups, totalling among themselves 159 members.

Numerous people's collective initiatives have sprung up in the two communes since then. Initial actions were in general taken in agriculture, comprising collective production of cash crops to gain cash. Tree cultivation (cypress, eucalyptus, apple, tea) was very popular and nearly every group engaged in one or more community afforestation projects. Some other activities gradually initiated were grain storage, a consumer store, livestock marketing, furniture making, brick making for sale, one more mill set up jointly by four groups and the manufacture and sale of beer. The mill was a particularly great relief to the women as a facility for mill-grinding had not previously been available within about 20 km and the women had to spend considerable time and energy in manual grinding. Another relief was the opening of a rural pharmacy by several groups together, to meet a need for which the people had hitherto walked long distances to the urban centres.

A new innovation was to develop the people's own savings and credit system. All groups have had a savings programme. Their savings were initially deposited in the Banque Populaire which had been opened in Kabaya in 1978. But due to lack of legal status the groups had no access to the bank's credit facilities to finance their projects, and due to the bureaucratic high-handedness of the bank officials they had difficulty even in withdrawing their own deposits. The groups, therefore, were provoked to search for an alternative solution to this problem. After analysing the problem, they decided to have their own autonomous system of saving and credit called Caisse de Solidarité (Solidarity Bank). This bank takes deposits from the members, and advances credit to the groups. The deposits get 3 per cent interest per annum, and credit is given at 10 per cent.

The Solidarity Bank plays a particularly important role in the management of external funds for group projects. External funds to support income-earning activities for the groups are now channelled through this bank, which is considered to be the collective liability of all the groups and not only of the group using the funds. This serves the dual purpose of providing a credible guarantee to the donor against default, and wider collective interest that the activity of every group financed by external credit is managed properly so as to generate the income to enable repayment.

Credit from the Solidarity Bank has so far been given for the purchase of mills, to set up a revolving fund for one group and another, for a pharmaceutical store, for the purchase of livestock for family breeding and improvement of housing.

On the basis of the experience in Kabaya district, the promoter and other colleagues and members of ITT established contact with other groups of the rural poor in the country interested in learning and adopting the approach followed. This led to the formation of an agency called Action pour le Développement Rural Intégré (ADRI). The task of this development NGO is conceived as stimulating and assisting self-development efforts of the rural population. Four directions of work have been identified, namely to assist animation work in the formation of associations of the rural poor, to consolidate such associations through advice, training and exchange visits, to facilitate the emergence of a federation of associations, and finally to provide direct support to base groups on funding and implementing collective projects of a social or economic nature.

The actions of ADRI have contributed significantly to the promotion of organisation development of the poor peasantry and collective initiatives by them in several areas, and to the development of linkages among them. Assisted by ADRI, representatives of ITT visited peasant groups in other regions and explained to them their method of organisation and collective action. This stimulated the formation of inter-group associations in two other areas – several groups of potato growers in Kanama formed an inter-group association called Impuzabahinzi, and groups of sugar-cane growers in the Nyabarongo valley formed an inter-group association called Abihuje. Abihuje subsequently called upon ADRI to assist them in community animation work and in training and research on the processing and marketing of sugar cane.

ADRI also contributed to the creation in 1983 of an inter-group fund called the Fondation Abbé Gervais Rutunganga (FAGR), covering groups of peasantry in Karago and Giciye totalling more than 2,300 in number. The fund is built by donations from the peasants particularly at harvest time, in cash or kind, and is used to serve as distress insurance to the members of FAGR against such events as death, fire, natural disasters, accident and sickness, and inability to finance children's secondary education.

ADRI, officially registered in 1985, is now actively working in several other areas (Gafunzo, Muyira, Satinskyi-Nyakabanda, Lake Muhazi, Mboge and others), assisting in the consolidation of local associations and providing animation work to develop awareness among the peasantry of their self-development potentials.

The Organisation of Rural Associations for Progress, Zimbabwe

Matabeleland is one of the most depressed areas in Zimbabwe with acute poverty and the highest rate of illiteracy in the country. In 1980 a group of concerned persons in Matabeleland got together to initiate a new development strategy in the area. The philosophy was that the rural people were to be encouraged to question and understand their total situation – poverty, underdevelopment, dependence – become aware of their potential and regain their sense of dignity, and to take collective initiatives for their self-development. The Organisation of Rural Associations for Progress (ORAP) was registered in 1981.

PAR and animation work by the initiators of ORAP invoked the traditional culture of *amalima*, which means the people getting together to work and help themselves; and also *ilima*, the traditional concept of rural mutual help groups. This resulted in the formation of people's groups in the villages, some growing out of the village committees formed during the liberation struggle, and some out of the women's clubs which already existed. These groups spent a lot of time discussing their situations, problems, needs and what they wanted to do. Gradually they initiated developmental action in different fields, mobilising their labour and skills, with material and financial assistance from external donors through ORAP. Village groups federated into 'umbrellas'; umbrellas federated into 'associations'. Elected representatives from the associations and, if an association has not yet been formed, umbrellas, become members of the Advisory Board of ORAP, the apex body, whose elected chairman comes from the rank of the ordinary villagers. A set of professionals and semi-professionals work as the staff of ORAP.

Today ORAP is one of the most inspiring examples of people's self-mobilisation for their own development in East Africa. As of June 1987 it had about 500 village groups, with membership of a group varying from about 50 to 100; 30–40 umbrellas, and 10 associations.

A wide variety of group projects have been launched, e.g. carpentry, netwire making, sewing, building, basketry, wood carving, livestock grazing, school uniform making, vegetable gardening, poultry-keeping, sisal and cement sheet making, knitting, mat making, ox-yoke making, baking, grinding mills, food storage, water and sanitation, etc. Most of these projects have been initiated at the group level, with some at the inter-group level.

An imaginative development is taking place at the association level – the creation of 'development centres'. A development centre is a centre where ORAP communities come together to deliberate, plan and consolidate their development efforts. A development centre is located in physical space where the people construct an assembly hall for mass deliberations; a market-place to sell their products, also serving as a place for interaction, exchange and discussion among the people on their ongoing developmental experience; a community kitchen to serve participants in mass meetings and rallies; and 'workshops' in various technical areas, e.g. bakery, building, blacksmithing, tinsmithing, mother and child care, etc. The development centre is designed by the member umbrellas: the people make their own drawings to construct traditional-type buildings with their oval shape and thatched roofs; the kitchens are designed by the women to serve 300 people or more.

The workshops are an innovative idea in themselves: the association identifies people from among the community with some technical skill and social leadership quality to be the 'promoters'. ORAP organises a training programme to give them some modern knowledge in their respective fields. The promoters then return to the development centre of their association and construct a physical structure to locate the workshop in the field concerned. The communities spontaneously participate in its construction, by giving free labour, the service of donkey carts to carry materials, contributing tools, etc. for running the workshop, with ORAP providing the bulk of the material and financial inputs. The promoters then start the workshop to experiment with 'appropriate technology' in the field concerned, combining people's indigenous skills with the modern knowledge which they have acquired to meet the community's real needs, and in the process upgrading people's indigenous skills. The promoters are paid by the communities, to ensure that they really serve the communities.

ORAP itself ran a drought-relief programme during the drought of 1985–6, transporting grains from surplus to deficit areas, buying from the former and selling at cost price to the latter.

With the experience of the drought, ORAP's Advisory Board gives high priority to developing a comprehensive food and water programme, with a four-point strategy: recourse to traditional seeds and fertilisers which have a lower risk factor than the modern ones; emphasis on quantity and variety of foods produced; improved food storage and food banks in the villages; improved water storage and local irrigation schemes. By June 1987 three associations had already begun the process of integrated food production.

A part of ORAP's vibrancy consists of a systematic critical review by the people, at different levels of the ORAP structure, of their experiences. Sensing some frustrations at the lower levels, two review workshops were organised by ORAP with the association leaders and ORAP staff, following a series of the people's own collective inquiries at the grassroots levels. The first one addressed the question of factors which frustrate their development, and the second looked into the structures which facilitate or hinder people's participation. The first workshop identified too much dependence on outside donors, which orients the accountability of leaders towards the donors rather than to the people, thereby tending to create bad leadership, as a major factor in hindering the process of people's development. ORAP is assisted by many (non-government) donors, and it is now embarking on a campaign to raise funds locally through such activities as music concerts, village markets, local private contributions, etc. to minimise this dependence on outside aid.

The second workshop identified the 'project approach' which had so far been adopted in many groups as well as at higher levels, as one that creates hierarchical control of communal activity, strengthening leaders, 'project managers' and 'committees' at the expense of the general membership who are often bypassed in thinking through issues, planning and implementation. The size of many groups was also considered too big for effective participation by the member families in their deliberations. It was accordingly decided to create a smaller primary unit called the 'family unit', meaning a collective of a smaller number of families (men, women and children all together), five to ten or so. The creation of family units since late 1986 has added another dimension to ORAP's work, with the family units first taking up collective activities from which the benefits to the member families are direct and immediate: members of a family unit are mobilising their labour to construct for each member household some of the basic amenities they need, e.g. a well for drinking water, a sanitary latrine and improved bath, an improved kitchen, etc., as well as to help each other in tasks such as clearing land, ploughing, cultivation, harvesting and threshing corn. In the family units participation by the member families in both deliberation and collective action is direct. This also is raising, specifically, the level of participation of the women members of the families.

Animators at work in Tanzania

In 1984, a government project was launched in Tanzania to 'identify the planning and implementation needs of Tanzanian villages with a view of enabling them to initiate a self-sustaining development based on the villagers' own resources and ultimately fulfilling the objective of self-reliance'. The methodology that was conceived was for a multidisciplinary team of researchers to work closely in dialogue with the villagers in thirty pilot villages in three districts. The project, however, degenerated into an academic research exercise, with social researchers paying occasional visits to villages treating the villagers as objects of inquiry and presenting papers in seminars and meetings for academic discussions without any clear purpose.

After drifting aimlessly for more than two years, the project asked the ILO for assistance in the form of methodological guidance to stimulate self-reliant people's action. The ILO responded by sending an expert (Mr Tilakaratna) from the Participatory Institute for Development Alternatives (PIDA) in Sri Lanka, with which the ILO has been working closely to develop its conception and methodology for promoting participatory rural development. This gave the Tanzanian project a radically new turn.

Fourteen 'animators' were recruited in April 1986 from among the field staff of a number of ministries, having demonstrated the following qualities: a sense of commitment and a willingness to live and work in the villages; innovativeness in work and willingness to experiment with new approaches; communication skills, in particular an ability to dialogue, discuss and listen to the people; flexibility and readiness to learn from one's own and others' experiences; and intellectual ability and emotional maturity. These animators were given a six-day 'training' in a workshop in animation work to stimulate people's self-reliant collective action. The training consisted of no lectures but exercises in collective reflection and analysis. In particular, this interaction worked out and analysed the implications of two models (methods of action) of field work, one an anti-participatory model with paternalistic development workers, and another on a participatory model with animators trying to promote people's self-deliberation and initiatives and learning from them. The trainees thereafter drew up a programme of action to immerse themselves in specific village situations, to understand these situations thoroughly, identify basic issues of concern to the people's livelihood, and analyse them *with the people* to explore possibilities of collective action. They then moved into fourteen different villages in the three districts to implement this work programme.

The difference between the 'culture' of these animators and that of government and political functionaries who used to visit them before was immediately apparent to the villagers who started responding positively by actively participating in the social inquiry and started forming groups and taking collective economic action without any financial input from the project. The story of what the Tanzanian peasantry can do when appropriately 'animated' is revealing and is best told in the following extracts from a report by Tilakaratna:

The overall performance of the Planning Rural Development at the Village Level project in its first year has proved to be very satisfactory in comparison with the experiences of similar projects that I am familiar with in Asia. In most project villages the animation process has taken off and the methodology has been well accepted by the people. . . . The overall picture may be summarised as follows:

1. There are 63 active grass-roots groups in the 14 villages which are in varying stages of evolution. Some have initiated the first set of self-reliant

activities using their own resources and distributed the benefits while channelling a part for accumulation, others have built up group funds and are beginning to embark on development actions, and still others have planned concrete actions and are collecting funds to initiate them.

2. The size of these groups vary from three to 30 members with a concentration in the range of six to 15. About 30 per cent of the membership of these groups is women.

3. The primary focus of group actions currently is improvement of production and incomes. Most groups have obtained land from the village governments to start group farms in extents varying from one acre to more than 30 acres. In the 1986–87 season, these groups cultivated more than 300 acres as group farms and in the 1987–88 season, the total extent of group farms is estimated to rise over 500 acres. Apart from agriculture, group activities cover a range of industrial and service activities such as brick making, timber and carpentry, blacksmithy, pottery, basket/mat weaving, grain milling, tailoring, consumer shops and kiosks.

4. All group activity is self-financed. Currently there is no dependence on outside finances except in the case of two groups which have obtained bank credit. Practically all groups have built up group funds through individual contributions (in cash or kind) and by channelling a portion of the income from group activity. The total capital accumulated by these groups as at the end of June 1987 can be roughly estimated at about 1.3 million shillings (that is an average of about 2,000 shillings (US$30) per member) and the planned accumulation of these groups amounts to nearly 3 million shillings (about 4,000 shillings (US$60) per member). These amounts include the group funds and the purchases of capital equipment for the use of the groups.

Some examples of group activity and capital accumulation are given below:

A 24-member group in *Ukwamani* village built up a group fund by contributing one head of cattle by each member (cattle are a symbol of wealth and social status and are not used in cultivation). The proceeds from the sale of cattle financed half the cost of a tractor; the balance half was financed by a loan obtained from a bank on a guarantee provided by the village government. This group cultivated a collective farm of 69 acres using the tractor and assisted another group of 15 members to cultivate a 41-acre group farm. This second group is now planning to buy a tractor using the same strategy adopted by the first group. The activities of these two groups has created a demonstration effect leading to the emergence of several new groups in the village.

A 13-member group in *Mhenda* village cultivated a group farm with rice. Out of the total harvest of 104 bags, 39 bags were put in a group fund, the sale proceeds of which the group intends to use for the hiring of a tractor and purchase of agro-inputs to improve cultivation in the next season. The pioneering effort of this group led to the emergence of three other groups which will initiate group farms in the next cultivation season.

A 14-member group of women in *Kimamba* (a sisal plantation area) who had hitherto engaged in casual labour negotiated with the local authorities and obtained swampy land for rice cultivation. All cultivation work was done manually. Of the total harvest of 84 bags of rice, 14 bags were kept as a group fund and the balance was distributed among the members (average of five bags per member) which is adequate to provide food security for thee households until the next harvest. This was the first time that these households were able to obtain access to such a stock of food. The sale proceeds from the group fund will be used by this group to hire a tractor in the next cultivation season to expand the group cultivation and to reduce the workload of the (women) group members. The demonstration effect created by this group activity led to the emergence of two other groups (casual workers) who will also initiate group farms in the next season.

In *Kipenzelo* village, 12 organised groups cultivated group farms totalling some 78 acres in the 1986–87 season. These groups faced similar problems such as obtaining fertiliser in time for the cultivation. In a joint effort to solve their problems, these groups formed a committee (called the Village Implementation Committee) consisting of a representative from each of the groups with an elected chairman. This committee negotiated with the village co-operative to obtain fertiliser on a loan for repayment after the harvest and sorted out other common problems faced by the groups. It also identified the lack of a consumer shop in the village as a common problem and it was decided that each member-group will contribute three bags of maize to provide the initial capital to start a consumer shop. In addition, each group will have its own group fund to purchase farm inputs and to plough the group farms by using oxen in the next season. The demonstration effect created has led to the emergence of 11 new groups.

A 22-member group in *Mwanawota* village are collecting maize from the members to build up a group fund of 110,000 shillings to provide a down payment for the purchase of a grain-milling machine – the group hopes to raise the balance money from a bank for which it is negotiating with the village government to provide a guarantee.

The context in which the above group initiatives are taking place has to be noted. In most villages, communal farms and village projects initiated by village governments have not been successful and in general villagers have lost confidence in total village activity. In some villages coercive methods are being used (e.g. fines) to obtain labour for village farms. At the other extreme, the peasant cultivating an individual plot of land has continued to be of low productivity and cannot rise above bare subsistence. On the other hand, small groups which are voluntary and relatively homogeneous in character have proven viable in raising productivity as well as in accumulation. In general, the productivity in the group farms has been higher than that in private plots as well as village communal farms. (Tilakaratna, 1987)

To 'guide' the above process Tilakaratna, after 'training' the animators in April 1986, visited the project only once more, for two weeks in September 1986. This suggests the basic power of the conception and methodology of 'training' of the animators which was applied in this project. (See Postscript below.)

Reflections: What is 'development'?

People's collective self-development initiatives of the nature of the above cases not only point to a way out of the African development impasse, they also suggest the need for reflection on the very notion of 'development'. For a long time, and even today, development has been identified in many influential quarters with the mechanistic notion of the development of physical assets and increasing the flow of economic and social goods and services. Much of the activities of the people's groups in the cases reported above are indeed also addressed to such 'development'. But there is a fundamental philosophical question – and the choice of the meaning of development is a philosophical choice, a value judgement – as to whether the fact of the people mobilising themselves, inquiring, deciding and taking initiatives of their own to meet their 'felt needs', is to be regarded only as a matter of the means of 'development' and not as an *end* in itself.

A value judgement concerning society derives its validity from significant social consensus. Certain professional classes and other elite quarters may have consensus among themselves around the above mechanistic view of development and also around the view that this is what the people – the 'poor' – need and want most. The people, however, have seldom been asked to contribute to a social articulation of the meaning of development.

A study of ORAP by a team of four professionals presents the following revealing observation:

Significantly, the translation of the concept of development into Sindebele [local language of Matabeleland] is 'taking control over what you need to work with'. The names of most of the ORAP groups also reflect these concerns. A few chosen at random are: Siwasivuka (We fall and stand up), Siyaphambili (We go forward), Dingimpilo (Search for life), Sivamerzela (We're doing it ourselves), Vusanani (Support each other to get up). (Chavunduka *et al.*, 1985)

In apparently simple-minded words these popular articulations of people's collective self-identity reflect deep conceptualisations of popular aspirations and, hence, what must be viewed as authentic development. The people want to *stand up*, *take control* over what they need to work with, *to do things themselves* in their own *search for life*, to *move forward, supporting each other*. The different articulations link with each other as if parts of the same whole. The present author with all his sophisticated training could not give a better articulation of the whole which is thereby expressed. One can perhaps only try to elaborate (in the author's hopelessly elitist language): authentic development is an organic process of self-propelled forward evolution. Some dimensions of this evolution may be suggested as the development of a collective *structure*, to serve as an instrument of reflection and action; development of *skills and faculties*; a progressively widening range of *creative application* of skills and faculties in accomplishing self-defined tasks; and development of an *understanding* of this process of evolution in the context of its surrounding reality, thus developing as a human *personality*. A community/society which would be moving in this way, defining its tasks in favourable and unfavourable weather, becoming engaged in doing them, and reviewing their experiences to promote their self-knowledge and asserting that this is what they want to do – who would say that they should be 'developing' differently?

In such an evolution the concept of 'basic needs' (food, clothing, shelter, medical care and education), with which much of so-called 'development' thinking and planning are engaged today, gets absorbed as a question of what the people would want to create, by taking charge of their own lives. These 'basic needs' are not to be delivered to them, but to be created by them (directly, or through production and exchange). But the basic *human need*, one may suggest, is not any of these: it is 'to do things ourselves', i.e. to create, for being human is being creative, and this is what distinguishes the human from the animal in oneself. The animal, indeed, needs to be fed and clothed and sheltered and medically cared for and taught how to find all these; but the human needs to be fulfilled by creative acts.

The tragedy of underdevelopment is not that the ordinary people have remained poor and are becoming poor, but that they have been inhibited from authentic development as humans. In many countries elites in the first instance have appropriated the people's resources, and then have taken over the right to 'develop' society. In others, indigenous resources may be at the command of the people, but the 'development expertise' is assumed to rest with official bureaucracies and the technocracy. This has distorted the natural and profound popular notion of (authentic) development. For no one can develop others; one can only stretch or diminish others by trying to 'develop' them. True to this maxim, the elites who are in charge of social direction have only 'developed' themselves at the cost of society. This has been a brilliant performance: the evolution of elite capabilities, including the capability and accomplishment of mass impoverishment and under-development the world over through domination, exploitation and environmental destruction.

One might even say that the very notion of 'poverty', conventionally conceived in *consumeristic* terms, distracts from the human need to be fulfilled by creative acts. The first man, or woman, or the first human community, was not 'poor' for not having any clothes to put on or shelter to house the body: it was the beginning of life, to move forward from there, by creating and constructing with one's own priorities, i.e. with self-determination. People become poor when their resources are appropriated by others, thereby denying them not only the basic material means of survival but more fundamentally, through dependence on others for survival, *their self-determination*. The communities whose efforts at authentic development are reported in this chapter may be 'poor' by the material standards of the so-called 'rich', but are immensely rich themselves in the culture and values they are showing in the way they are moving forward as part of a self-determined collective endeavour.

Some further observations
Philosophy apart, the initiatives reported in this paper are a few examples in Africa of attempts to reverse the process of underdevelopment. They are rich in lessons. One is that where some traditional culture and form of mutual cooperation still exist, the process of authentic development can start from there, giving those cultures a sense of aspiration, possibilities and assertion. Once this sense is enthused, people's imaginativeness reveals that means of action exist to promote the satisfaction of the 'basic needs', very few of which are conceived in conventional, externally designed and controlled projects: the collective fund as an instrument of banking and social insurance; the people's own bank; collective marketing and storage; pooling human energy and talents (collective fund of human resources) otherwise available for individual pursuits only, in mutual cooperation and joint action to promote everyone's needs satisfaction; skill spreading from people to people; and so on.

An important message lies in most such initiatives being non-governmental projects. The essence of this message is also confirmed in the Tanzanian case where the initiative came in a government project, and the contradiction which emerged between the conception of the project and forces against it. It took more than two years of aimless drifting to realise that a drastic orientation was needed. Mention may be made here of the experience in both Sri Lanka and the Philippines where such field animation methodology was initially tried in government projects with equally inspiring results but also where the field animators saw the limits of working in the framework of government bureaucracy and formed non-government agencies (PIDA in Sri Lanka and PROCESS in the Philippines) to carry the work further forward. The limits in the Tanzanian project may also soon be reached, and the question of further forward movement of the initiative rests upon the possibility of forming a non-government agency with greater flexibility of operation to take over the task of animating and facilitating people's self-reliant action.

Leaving aside the Tanzanian project which is but a small and relatively recent experiment in grassroots animation work, whose institutional unfolding is yet to mature, a noteworthy feature of the other cases of people's self-development initiatives is indeed the extent of people's self-direction and control of their collective activities. The Six-S originated out of the vision of the people's own leaders in dialogue with some outside friends, and is a people's organisation with a few of these friends in the Council of Administration as 'organic intellectuals'. The Committee for Development Action in Senegal is a people's organisation. ORAP originated out of the conception of a few middle-class activists who, however, allowed people's structures to develop assertively and eventually absorb the activists as 'organic intellectuals' working for ORAP, the apex body, the majority of whom are people's representatives. The fact of such structurally organic relations between these two trends – middle-class activists and people's leaders – stands in sharp contrast to the relations observed in most South and South-East Asian cases of such activism known to the author, where middle-class activists serve under a separate structure of their own, commonly known as NGOs (non-governmental organisations). This dichotomy between people's structures and structures of middle-class activists who work to promote people's structures carries with it its own questions of balance of power in the overall movement, of relative privilege, structural dependence of one upon another, etc. It is noteworthy that in the Rwandan case also there was no formal structure of middle-class activists for a considerable period initially, and work was concentrated on promoting people's structures and linking them with one another. While ADRI has been formed more recently as a separate middle-class structure to service the people's movement, it seems to have been born out of a felt need of an evolving and vibrant grassroots movement for some special services rather than, as in many other cases, as a structure existing prior to the grassroots movement. This should, at least, give the grassroots movement a lead in the dialectics between the two trends.

The question of the relation between the two trends in initiatives to promote people's authentic development assisted significantly by middle-class activists is important because the middle class in general can at best commit only one part of their being to the cause of the people; the other part remains committed to a lot of 'middle-class culture and aspirations'. In this sense one is at most *both* a *friend* and an *enemy* of the people. The best possibility of keeping the negative trends in check lies in the control of an aware and vigilant people over everybody's actions. It is curious that in some of the pioneering African cases of initiating people's self-development the 'balance of power' seems to be more on the side of the people than in the average of such cases. One would like to understand the social, historical and cultural factors that bring about such development, a subject perhaps for a socio-anthropological inquiry – an agenda for the ongoing PAR.

Africa can indeed show cases of vibrant and assertive people's self-development efforts in rural areas which are at the frontier of all such efforts anywhere and from which much inspiration can be taken and a lot can be learnt, and African activists assisting such efforts are showing an inspiring culture of working with the people to promote such authentic development. The task is perhaps made easier in communities where rural class polarisation is not acute, and land as such is not a constraint, as is the case in all the examples presented in this paper. With sharp rural class polarisation, as is the case in most South/South-East Asian and Latin American countries, initiatives towards collective self-development of the ordinary rural people are handicapped by generally stiff, often violent resistance from elites (feudal, semi-feudal or capitalist) whose privileged lives thrive on class exploitation of the underprivileged; as well as by the ordinary people's lack of access to some basic means of production to survive independently. In such situations collective initiatives by the people are often directed of necessity to militant action to assert human rights and gain access to some basic economic resources (Rahman, 1986, 1987). In the African scenario of the above type, the main source of resistance to such initiatives would perhaps be the state and professional bureaucracy whose privileged status depends in part on the power they have either to deliver or to sermonise on how to deliver 'development'.

Postscript

I visited the Tanzania project with Tilakaratna in July 1989 to participate in a review of its progress and deliberations on its future, with the animators, the government and UNICEF which was supporting the project. By then the number of groups in the 14 villages was about 125 (with a number of separate women's groups), and groups within the same village had started federating. Revolving funds had been created with government and

UNICEF contributions to advance loans to the groups for group projects beyond the means of their own funds, but against a matching 50 per cent contribution from their savings funds. In a gathering in one village which I attended, the chairman of the village government had the following to say: 'My task as the village government chairman was to mobilise the villagers, but I could not do it; now I do not have to do it – the villagers are mobilising themselves. I request the government and the party not to take this project away.'

Following the review, the government undertook a plan to extend the project to other villages in the three districts, sending the initial animators to other villages, with 'internal animators' from within the existing groups taking over the task of animation in the pilot villages, and by training new animators.

[*This postscript giving more recent information on the Tanzania project is not part of the original paper published by the ILO.*]

Note

1. Six-S stands for the more elaborate French name 'Se servir de la saison sèche en Savane et au Sahel' (Making good use of the dry season in the Savanna and the Sahel).

References

Committee for Development Action, Senegal
Dia, Marius (1987) 'L'expérience en matière d'auto-développement du Comité d'action pour le développement des Villages de la Zone Bamba-Thialene', Report on people's self-review, in Egger (1988).
Sharing Experiences in Development, Report of a Workshop for Development Leaders, Silveira House and Innovations et Réseaux pour le Développement, Harare, 18–23 June 1984, pp. 28–35.

Six-S
Egger, Philippe (1987) *L'Association Six 'S' – Se servir de la saison sèche en Savane et au Sahel – et les groupements Naam, note sur quelques observations*, mimeograph, Geneva: ILO, February 1987.
Sawadogo, A. R. and Ouedraogo, B. L. (1988) 'Auto-évaluation de Six-S groupements Naam dans la province du Yatenga', in Egger (1988).
Teuben, H. *et al.* (1983) *Rapport final sur les résultats de l'auto-évaluation assistée des unions des groupements des zones 6S au Sénégal*, mimeograph.

ADRI
Egger, Philippe (1987) *La leçon de Jomba, trois tableaux pour une conclusion sur l'emploi rural au Rwanda*, mimeograph, Geneva: ILO, March 1987.

Musengimana, Siméon (1988) 'La dynamique des organisations paysannes au Rwanda: le cas de l'intergroupement Tuzamuke de Kabaya', in Egger (1988).

ORAP
Chavunduka, D. M. *et al.* (1985) *Khuluma Usenza, the Story of ORAP in Zimbabwe's Rural Development: An Interpretative Study*, Bulawayo: ORAP, July 1985.
Khabo, J. H. *Fieldwork Report, 1986–87*, mimeograph, ORAP, April 1987.
Nyoni, Sithembiso *ORAP since 'Khuluma Usenza': A Review and Self-Assessment*, mimeograph, Bulawayo: ORAP, October 1986.

Tanzania
Project documents in ILO files.
Tilakaratna, S. (1987) *The Animator in Participatory Rural Development (Concept and Practice)*, Chapter 4, Annex: Animator training (first phase) in Tanzania, Geneva: ILO.
Egger, Philippe (1988) *Des initiatives paysannes de développement en Afrique: une auto-évaluation de trois expériences au Sénégal, au Burkina Faso et au Rwanda*, World Employment Programme Research Working Paper, WEP 10/WEP.47, Geneva: ILO.
Rahman, M. A. (1983) *SARILAKAS, a Pilot Project for Stimulating Grass-roots Participation in the Philippines, Technical Co-operation Evaluation Report*, Geneva: ILO.
Rahman, M. A. (1986) *Organising the Unorganised Rural Poor (Bangladesh Field Notes, October–November 1985)*, mimeograph, Geneva: ILO.
Rahman, M. A. (1987) *Further Interaction with Grass-roots Organising Work*, mimeograph, Geneva: ILO, December 1987.
Tilakaratna, S. (1985) *The Animator in Participatory Rural Development: Some Experiences from Sri Lanka*, World Employment Programme Research Working Paper WEP 10/WP 37, Geneva: ILO, December 1985.

# 9.	The praxis of PORP: a programme in participatory rural development

Introduction

This paper reviews the experience and understanding of the subject of people's participation in rural development, gained in the sub-programme on 'Participatory Organisations of the Rural Poor' (PORP) of the ILO's World Employment Programme from its work since the beginning of this sub-programme in 1977 until mid-1989. This experience and understanding have been developed in part through formal research which has been supported mostly by the Swedish Agency for Research and Economic Cooperation (SAREC). As a part of this very understanding, PORP's 'research' has united with action, and many insights have been obtained from collaboration with grassroots work in several countries in experimenting with methodological approaches to promote popular participation and in systematically reviewing the results thereof. Another instrument of research has been collective reflections among and with grassroots practitioners which have promoted collective syntheses of grassroots experiences and advanced the collective articulation of the underlying visions and viewpoints.

In this paper, the term 'people' has been used in the sense of the bulk of the rural population in most so-called 'developing' countries who have subordinate status in the society, due to economic and social deprivation *vis-à-vis* privileged 'elites' who control disproportionate shares of material resources and thereby control the dominant economic, social and political structures of society.

Research on people's participation has been considered to require unconventional modes of inquiry which seek research partnership with the people, and the evolution of experience and thinking in this regard is

This chapter was originally published as a paper by the ILO and presented in the ILO's Workshop on the Inter-relationship between Macro-Economic Policies and Rural Development, Geneva, 11–13 December 1989.

reviewed in the next section, 'In search of a research paradigm'. The concept of participation followed in PORP's work is discussed in the section 'The concept of participation'. The problematic of external intervention to promote people's participation, and the principles and art of what has come to be termed as 'animation-facilitation' work by external interveners, are reviewed in the section 'Promoting participation'. The characteristic expressions of people's initiatives when they are self-mobilised for collective action and which reveal their material as well as more holistic human urges, are reviewed in the section 'Expressions of people's initiatives'. The final section discusses the significance of grassroots initiatives for overall social change.

In search of a research paradigm

In the beginning, research on participation aimed to seek illumination, on the basis of concrete experiences, on some of the basic issues in this subject (see Rahman, 1978, for a conception of PORP's initial research programme). The field was considered to be multidisciplinary. Scattered literature on the subject existed, but this did not constitute a coherent base from which further research could take off. The subject being intimately human, conventional research methodology which seeks to collect data through detached observations and questioning was considered inappropriate to understand it. In particular, the perceptions and understanding of the people whose participation is in question were considered to be crucially important in understanding the problematic of participation. These perceptions and understanding were not considered to be static but subject to dynamic processes of people's reflection. Considering all these, the *dialogical* method of inquiry, in which the people would be drawn into critical reflection in group as well as individual-to-individual interaction, was considered to be the most appropriate method of research, without precluding, however, the role of more conventional research methodology to collect other kinds of data.

A search for people who could undertake such research was initially not very successful. Conventional social researchers were not as a rule oriented to dialogical research which required a different human relations approach to the inquiry. Some offered to try, but in the end fell back upon more conventional methods of inquiry, collecting quantitative and human perceptional data more by methods of surveys, questionnaires and interviews than by in-depth dialogues with the people. On the other hand activist-researchers existed who had the competence and skill to undertake dialogical research, but would not see the value of undertaking such research on participation for an external agency whose benefit to the people concerned was not immediately apparent. In the end, with the bureaucratic imperatives of a research programme which had to be 'delivered' within a pre-determined time, a set of case studies was collected most of which followed conventional research methods (Bhaduri and Rahman 1982), with the exception of one study, that of the 'Bhoomi Sena' ('Land Army') movement of tribals in Maharastra, India, in which the coordinator of PORP participated.

Participatory research
The Bhoomi Sena study (de Silva *et al.*, 1979) was more than dialogical research. It constituted a research partnership with the leaders of the movement, and thus constituted an approach to participatory research which was in the meanwhile being propagated and articulated by the Toronto-based International Council for Adult Education (ICAE) and its global network (Hall *et al.*, 1981). This research process evolved as follows:

1. A Bombay-based Indian activist-researcher who was in close contact with the Bhoomi Sena movement initiated a four-day workshop for an external research team and the leaders and some cadres of Bhoomi Sena to discuss the movement. This workshop (de Silva *et al.*, 1979: Chapter 5) generated mutual interest in forming a research partnership to study, analyse and document the Bhoomi Sena movement.
2. A series of visits were undertaken by members of the external research team, individually and in groups, to the Bhoomi Sena area for dialogical investigation on various aspects of the movement, including participant observation of village-level poor peasants' assemblies and inter-village 'conscientisation' camps.
3. Members of the Bhoomi Sena leadership themselves collected information on the movement for the study and prepared background papers in the Marathi language as inputs into the study.
4. Workshops were held for the external research team and the Bhoomi Sena leadership to discuss and analyse together different aspects of the movement.
5. The external research team collected and processed information for the movement available in official documents and in the published literature.
6. Responsibility was divided between the external research team and a senior activist in the movement for drafting chapters for the final study.
7. The draft study was presented to the full body of the Bhoomi Sena leadership for comments and for clearance, and information and discussion considered by the leadership to be of a sensitive nature were edited out.
8. Bhoomi Sena got parts of the study translated into the Marathi language for use as an awareness-raising measure within the movement.

This study demonstrated a research which was of value both to the external social researchers and to their constituencies, and to the grassroots movement itself which was studied. With this inspiration, PORP abandoned the idea of researching on participation through professional social researchers who are not involved with popular initiatives and movements and can, therefore, only do research *upon* the people, and sought to initiate more research of a participatory character through activist-researchers already working *with* the people.

'Participatory research' (PR), naturally, could not be designed in advance. Its methodology emerges spontaneously, from out of the joint imaginativeness of the activist-researchers and the people or their leaders with whom the research partnership is forged. An illustrative sample of the variety of methodologies which emerged from subsequent research is given below.

A PR study of a grassroots initiative in Sri Lanka was coordinated by a social scientist who was himself assisting this initiative (Tilakaratna, 1984). In this, the basic village investigations were carried out by two teams of village cadres in the initiative. These teams collected socio-economic data on the village households through discussions with the villagers and direct observations rather than through formal questioning. A number of collective discussion sessions with the villagers participating in the initiative were thereafter held, in which the findings of the household survey conducted by the cadre team were placed before the villagers for collective verification, and for analysis together with the cadres and a number of other outside researchers. Issues were generated in these collective reflection sessions based on the findings of the household surveys, upon which the villagers had not reflected before. This raised the level of their collective awareness and analytical understanding of these issues, over which they continued to reflect together after the research terminated, and this influenced their subsequent collective decisions and action.

A different kind of model was developed by activists involved with a tribal peasant movement in Maharastra, India. Here, the research theme was conceived as the tensions and contradictions in self-reliant development of the movement, and the aim of the research was not only to promote the people's understanding of these tensions but also, in the very process of understanding, to promote their resolution. The core of the research methodology consisted of organising a series of grassroots workshops for which the participants were first asked to develop polar, alternative positions on a set of major issues in the question of self-reliance, e.g. individual vs. collective self-reliance, participation in the wider labour movement in issue-based joint fronts vs. a more permanent affiliation to a larger federation. These polar positions were presented in the workshops and debated by the people. This made the people aware of the contradictions and alternatives in their struggle, and also of the need for concrete choices among alternative positions. On some of the issues thus debated, concrete choices were made in the process of the PR exercise itself; and a heightened level of awareness gained in this exercise contributed to reaching a conscious or unconscious synthesis of other contradictions subsequently. The research report (Paranjape *et al.*, 1984) was translated into the local language for use by the movement.

In another PR study of a poor women settlers' movement in Luzon province in the Philippines, an activists' organisation which had been associated with the movement initiated the formation of a research coordination team (all women) with two members taken from the leadership of a fourteen-member 'vanguard group' of the women settlers and two from the activists' organisation. Members of the vanguard group provided inputs into the research using reports and minutes of weekly meetings of the women settlers, initiating group discussions with the women on different aspects of their life and struggle, and preparing papers on the profile of the community, the history of the women's organisations and the activities of the vanguard group. These inputs were woven into two dramas which were staged by the women settlers, and all women participants in the movement were invited to witness these dramas which validated the data collected and synthesised their experiences. The final study incorporated the feedback which was received from the audience and discussed the benefits from the research:

> To the vanguard group, participation in this study provided an opportunity for a first comprehensive review of their first two years of organising effort, from which the strengths and weaknesses of their effort could be identified. The process of research enabled the residents, particularly the vanguard group, to develop their capacity to understand immediate micro issues in relation to broader macro issues. Furthermore, cognisant of similar efforts and movements in other communities, the women appreciated that their experiences would be lessons for other groups as well. (Women's Research Committee *et al.*, 1984)

PR was taken to another dimension in a research project in India in which a number of forest-based poor people's movements and organisations got together, for joint inquiry and articulation on the subject of 'forest, ecology and the oppressed'. Coordinated by a 'voluntary agency', representatives of these organisations first met in a ten-day workshop, to formulate issues for investigation and to design ways of recording people's perceptions. They then returned to their respective areas for detailed investigations. While doing this they were also visited by members from two of the participating organisations from other areas. The data thus collected were passed on to a smaller research team composed of social activists in contact with these movements, who analysed the data and interviewed those who had visited the various movements. On the basis of these, the above research team developed a set of case studies on the experiences of life and struggle of the people involved, problemwise analysis, and an analytical statement on the basis of all these. These were presented in a second workshop attended by all groups who had participated in the first. The final report was prepared by the research team incorporating the deliberations of this workshop (Dasgupta, 1986).

In a different socio-political setting in Nicaragua, a PR project was undertaken in El Regadío with a peasant community which had become organised and had been trying to play its own role in the wider society's effort at social reconstruction. A research team was formed, composed and coordinated by an educationist, and some coordinators of the Programme of Adult Education and representatives of mass organisations and cooperatives, to undertake the initial task of investigation. The team drafted the design of an inquiry into the history of the community, and a survey on the current socio-economic characteristics of El Regadío – demographic, educational, migratory, those relating to production, access to land, etc., as well as those concerning the levels of organisation and ideological transformation of the community. The draft design was presented to a larger coordination committee constituted for the research which discussed and modified it. Members of the larger committee were given training in survey work in a number of workshops. They made a map of the community and marked the houses, to survey them over approximately a period of one week. They explained the participatory character of the whole exercise to the members of the households with the promise to return the information obtained to each house for their reflection and analysis.

After the survey the results were tabulated in workshops where other members of the community also participated. The value of the information, the need to organise it, and the importance of theoretical analysis and reflection, were explained to them. After some tabulation was done, the whole community was invited to an assembly where the information obtained was presented on boards for the people, who participated intensely in discussing the data that were thus presented. Finally, delegates of the state institutions and mass organisations at the municipality level were invited to a meeting with the community to coordinate their programmes in the light of the findings of the survey, and to jointly seek solutions to problems. The coordination committee also planned methods for disseminating the information and knowledge obtained through the survey, and the idea of the whole project. It was decided to bring out a pamphlet and audio-visual documentation. For the purpose of producing the pamphlet, members of the committee learnt to use wooden mimeographing as explained in an adult education magazine, and also learnt diagrammatic techniques and other methods for presenting data, and improved their writing ability (de Montis, 1987).

Synthesising the experiences of such participatory research in three Latin American countries, Orlando Fals Borda (1985) presented possibly the first comprehensive methodological guidance in such work. The key elements of this are as follows.

Data gathering and validation
Socio-economic data are collected by the poor community through team visits to households, and in group or community events such as meetings, assemblies, committees, etc. through collective interchange and discussion. In this collective and dialogical manner data are obtained which may be immediately corrected or verified in the same process as their collection, or validated in community gatherings convened for the purpose.

Critical recovery of history
The community inquires about its past history in the context of the broad history of the country, and seeks to selectively discover those elements and social forces of the past which were useful for defending the interests of the underprivileged and exploited classes, elements which could be recovered in order to feed present-day efforts to improve their conditions. Techniques found useful for this purpose are: oral tradition and story-telling; elders' testimonies; family-trunk archives and depositories; ideological projection, imputation and other expressions of collective memory. In this way popular heroes of past days are recovered, data and facts are presented which may correct, supplement and clarify official or academic accounts written with other interests in mind; and completely new information is obtained for regional or national history, for the purpose of upholding the interest of the underprivileged.

Valuing and using popular culture
The essential or core values of the ordinary people are recognised, to enhance popular self-mobilisation. This technique incorporates important cultural elements often forgotten or discarded in elite social and political practices, such as music, sport, beliefs, myths, folk tales and other expressions related to popular sentiment, imagination and similar tendencies.

Production and diffusion of new knowledge
This technique is not seen as distinct from the research procedure as such because it is an integral part of the feedback and validation procedures of participatory research. It recognises an intellectual division of labour

between and within base groups. Four broad levels of communication are identified: (a) when the information and systematised knowledge is addressed to 'pre-literate' peoples. The means of communication in this case are predominantly audio-visual, e.g. 'talking maps', 'social trees', etc.; (b) when the material is addressed to semi-literate peoples, who may be reached by such means as illustrated booklets; (c) for middle-range leaders and cadres, through more elaborate treatises; (d) for advanced cadres and intellectuals, through essays, conceptual and theoretical writings.

Other forms of communication are based on holistic or intentional language such as image, sound, painting, mimesis, body gestures, photographs, etc. Also, there are material forms for returning systematic knowledge developed by or with the people to the people, such as in the organisation of cooperatives, shops, training centres, action teams, etc. considered as applied results of research.

Participatory research does not reject a flexible use of other practices for information gathering from the sociological or anthropological tradition such as open interview, survey, systematic observation, field diary, data files, cartography, primary and secondary source materials. Skilled participatory researchers would not only know how to handle these conventional techniques but also be able to popularise them in simple, direct ways at as many of the above levels as possible.

Finally, participatory research considers it to be a right of the communities by and from which information is gathered that the systematised knowledge developed be returned to them, to be used by them in their collective endeavour for their self-development. In publishing the results of such research for a wider public it is important to consider that no information is published if this might prejudice the interests of the communities concerned, with whom, at least, the question should be cleared.

Epistemological premises
Parallel with such experimentation and articulation at the pratical level, theoretical examination of the epistemological premises of participatory research was also undertaken (Chapter 6 of this book; Rahman, 1982). The epistemological standpoint of PR has been opposed to that of other schools such as empiricism, logical positivism and structuralism, which reject (social) value bias in what is considered to be 'scientific' research, and from the same principle adopt the detached observational method of social inquiry. It has been argued, in fact by many scholars (Shadish and Reichardt, 1987: Part V), that no research is or can be value-free. The claim to 'objectivity' in research is also untenable if this were to mean being free from *subjective bias*. Such bias is inherent in conceptualising and categorising most human phenomena, and full communicability of such

concepts and categories requires a sharing of sensuous (subjective) perceptions, i.e. communication at a subjective level in addition to formal categorisations and definitions. There is, however, another sense in which research may be defined as objective (and 'scientific'), i.e. in the sense of the methodology and product having passed a process of *social* (collective) verification. This produces social knowledge which is distinct from knowledge that is purely individual, i.e. 'subjective'. Objectivity in this sense requires transition from the individual to a collective. This in turn requires that: (a) a collective is defined; (b) codes of communication (language) exist or are developed within the collective; and (c) agreement is reached within the collective as to valid methods of investigation, reasoning and refutation of observations and arguments.

Research in well-established schools has a verification system of the above nature, explicitly or implicitly, the needed collective being constituted by the 'school'. Such research thus is objective, if verified within its own paradigm. In the more advanced schools the method of verification has by now become more or less standardised, and verification is often possible by mechanical application of certain rules or arguments so that interpersonal communication may not be necessary afresh every time for establishing its objectivity. It is important to recognise, however, that objectivity in this sense is *relative*, internal to the collective (paradigm) concerned. For those not belonging to this collective, either because of a lack of communicability or because they do not accept its premises or rules, this knowledge either has no meaning or is not acceptable. There is in this sense no universality of any 'science', i.e. there is no absolute truth.

With the above premises, participatory research generates objective (scientific) knowledge in the same sense that more conventional researches do. The verification process in PR is in general the dialogical process of collective reflection, when people 'withdraw' from action for social inquiry and review. It is argumentative, and dependent on current consensus rather than on pre-established rules (derived from past consensus) to be applied mechanically. While being objective in this sense, participatory research produces social knowledge as an organic element of the very movement of life, i.e. 'organic knowledge', and hence of immediate and direct service to life, unlike knowledge produced by 'observing' life from a discreet distance, which may not necessarily serve life.

Participatory research is a widely followed approach to social research today, but the 'participatory' character of participatory research also varies widely. In principle, the task is to establish a subject–subject relation between the external researcher/activist and the people for undertaking a joint inquiry. In practice, it is not always easy to establish a truly subject–subject relation with people who are traditionally victims of dominating structures: the inertia of traditional attitudes and images of self and of others may keep the people implicitly subordinate in a research (as well as decision-making) process in which formidable outside researcher/activists are present. And for outside professionals also it is not easy to avoid often being carried away by their own self-images and imposing their own ideas on the people consciously or unconsciously. Participatory research comes closest to its ideal if the people concerned have already been 'animated', in the sense to be explained, so as to have developed a sense of self-reliance and assertion. This animation work, discussed in the section 'Promoting participation', has been identified in PORP's research and action research as the key conceptual and methodological element in efforts to promote people's authentic participation in the forward movement of their lives.

The concept of participation

The notion of participation varies widely, and the spread of views has been studied (Oakley and Marsden, 1984: Chapter 2). In its inquiries, PORP has followed its own notion of participation, developed in the course of collaboration with certain trends in the grassroots movement. An initial articulation of this view made jointly with a number of other agencies was as follows:

> what gives real meaning to popular participation is the collective effort by the people concerned in an organised framework to pool their efforts and whatever other resources they decide to pool together, to attain objectives they set for themselves. In this regard participation is viewed as an active process in which the participants take initiatives and take action that is stimulated by their own thinking and deliberation and over which they can exert effective control. (ACC Task Force, 1978)

The key concepts in this view are: (a) participation as an organised activity of the people concerned: the primary unit of participation is thus conceived to be a collective of persons; (b) the taking of initiatives by the collective; (c) people's own thinking and deliberations direct their collective activities; (d) the people control the process of action thus initiated.

Together, these concepts belong to the view of participation as the exercise of *people's power* in thinking and acting, and controlling their action in a collective framework.

Implicit in this concept of participation is the concept of *self-reliance*. This does not mean autarky, but possession of a sufficient combination of mental and material resources to be able to resist the dictates of others on one's own course of action.

Subsequent research revealed that the above conception has its own internal tension, with respect particularly to the relation between organisation and spontaneity. While participation is viewed as an organised activity, in a basic sense the concept of participation is also 'opposed' to organisation, not in the sense of negating, but in the sense of a dialectical duality of opposites in which one requires the other for one's own identity and development at the same time that one may constrain the other's freedom and development. Organisations create *formal power* which is conceptually distinct from the power of those whose organisation it is. While 'people's power' needs organisation for purposeful action, the concept of people's power transcends that of people's organisations which vest power in offices which can be abused, and create rules of operation which may inhibit initiative and may also become outmoded over time. There may be circumstances when a rigid adherence to organisational discipline becomes necessary and is perceived by the people to be so for the attainment of specific objectives set by the people. Organisation or formal power then becomes the instrument through which people's power is exercised in order to achieve the objective in question. But there is a danger of distortion if there is a continued domination of organisation over people, as this is liable to create vested interest in the organisation *as such*, and to consolidate the power and privileges of such interests. When an organisation thus ceases to serve the basic interest of releasing people's *initiatives*, people's power needs to be reasserted as a 'countervailing power' *vis-à-vis* its own organisation (Rahman, 1981).

A basic requirement of such countervailing power is a consciousness of and vigilance against the possibility of internal authoritarianism. This may be sufficient if formal power is responsive to spontaneous expressions of the people's concern over the misuse of authority or of their desire to seek newer institutional forms to articulate their initiatives. But if such responsiveness and flexibility are lacking, then the people – i.e. the rank and file membership – need to confront their own formal power. In some cases this may be done successfully by spontaneous mobilisation: this has happened, e.g. in grassroots initiatives in Sri Lanka (Tilakaratna, 1984) and Zimbabwe (Chapter 8 of this book; Rahman, 1989a), where the people, after deliberations about their organisations' tendency to become hierarchical and non-participatory, have split them into smaller primary units or instituted a system of rotating leadership. But it is not always possible to reconstitute formal power in this way, and the need then arises for the people to create alternative institutions to confront their existing formal power or to break away from it. This is the more difficult task for keeping participation alive when distortions set in, and there is as yet no adequate practical or theoretical guidance on this question.

Promoting participation

People's participation has often been generated 'spontaneously'. This does not mean that it has not been led or guided by leaders or initiators. Spontaneity in this context means a process that emerges from out of the organic impulses of communities as distinct from a process that emerges as a result of a discreet act of *intervention* by some external force with the conscious objective of promoting participation. Participation has also been generated by such conscious intervention, and in recent times such intervention has increased as a response, in part at least, of concerned quarters to the perceived failure of conventional approaches to development. PORP's research has been focused particularly on participation thus generated by external intervention, and indeed on the problematic of promoting participation by such intervention.

Creating new forms of dependence

For the people, the image of 'friendly' external interveners is usually that of those who bring material resources, 'wisdom' and the status for improving the conditions of people's lives. Even those who do not bring material resources but are able to show the people a way to move forward by participating, i.e. by getting organised and taking collective initiatives, obviously possess something which the people do not have (or did not recognise that they had), that is some combination of special wisdom, knowledge, skills, as well as some status and contacts which help nurse the people's participatory efforts through various kinds of resistances that such initiatives often face. This puts the external intervener in a position of importance and tends to create a relation of *dependence* of the people on him/her in the collective activities that are initiated. Such dependence is inherently a force against the release of people's own initiatives, and also against the development of the people's own collective capabilities – a force, that is, against participation itself. Any external intervener who comes to promote participation also brings this anti-participation force with him/her. There is, thus, a question of the methodology and style of work of such external intervention aimed at promoting people's participation and avoiding creating new forms of dependence which might inhibit people's initiatives.

Numerous instances have been observed of the power of this force for creating new forms of dependence and eventual degeneration of relations between the people and the external intervener into anti-participatory, hierarchical modes. In several countries there are voluntary agencies working with the rural poor with impressive results in many ways, and some of them are explicitly committed to promoting people's participation and self-reliance. But there are relatively few examples of the resulting people's processes demonstrating, either in spirit or in substance, a sense of self-reliance and independence *vis-à-vis* the intervening agencies even after years of collective activity. In some, financial and material deliveries and technical assistance have become the dominant service of the external agency, and the people concerned are clinging to such agencies for continuous material improvement of their lives in a new patron–client relationship. In such a relation even the institutional forms of 'participation' – e.g. the class composition of the base groups (whether the landless can form groups of their own or should form groups jointly with the small farmers), the size of membership of the primary units, etc. – are determined by the external agency (Chapter 5 of this book; Rahman, 1987a; PORP, 1988). Some agencies impose collective forms of productive activity (collective farming), which by itself is not necessarily participatory unless this is the result of a voluntary decision of the participants themselves. Many intervening agencies impose or steer people's collective action towards an exclusively economistic orientation, whereas the people often have other coexisting priorities (e.g. questions of equitable access to economic assets, and social and human rights). Similarly, some intervening agencies decide that women and men will belong to the same base organisations, instead of leaving the question of women's participation, as regards gender-mixed or gender-specific organisation, to the women concerned. There are instances also of intervening agencies taking policy decisions at critical moments on behalf of the base groups, e.g. deciding to discontinue the savings fund of a group which mismanages such a fund, rather than leaving the group itself to review its experience in this regard and decide for itself whether it wants to stop the fund or try to improve its management.

Such impositions by intervening agencies are often prompted by their concern for showing 'success' in their work. They also imply, in many cases, a presumption of *superior wisdom* on the part of the intervening agency *vis-à-vis* the people whose participation they seek to promote, justifying, therefore, an encroachment on the autonomy of the base groups even in matters which are of direct concern to these groups. For their own part, the base groups also often submit to this implied superiority of educated, more well-to-do friends who come to help them, and the relations between the two parties then tend to become vertical (one deciding for the other and the latter looking up to the former for advice and guidance) rather than horizontal (a relation of equality with two-way dialogue and exchange).

The presumption of superior wisdom of middle-class educated activists working with the people is often explicit. Often it is inherent, arising from the ego of the educated; often it is observed to be a result of the 'vanguardist' notion of the left-wing intelligentsia inspired by the Leninist theory of revolution (see section 'Significance for social change'). Specific points of superiority are sometimes explicitly claimed, e.g. a claim was made in a study for PORP by animators in a Philippines programme that the people need educated intelligentsia permanently to conceptualise their problems, to understand the macro questions and to understand the link between their immediate, micro problems and the macro reality (Gregorio, 1985). With such a sense of superiority, many so-called 'conscientisation' programmes which are initiated by intervening agencies supposedly to promote *self-reflected* awareness of the people as the term was conceived by Paulo Freire (Freire, 1972) are observed to be attempts to transfer social knowledge (indoctrination) to the people in a vertical educational relationship.

Self-reliance-promoting intervention

On the other hand, there are cases where external intervention to promote people's participation has resulted in the development of people's organisations and processes with a high degree of autonomy exercised by the base groups. Bhoomi Sena submitted initially to external paternalism from a group of social workers who brought massive bank finance and modern technology. After the project collapsed due to management by these social workers, an external educationist with a few associates introduced a methodology for raising people's self-reflected social awareness. This resulted in a highly self-aware and assertive independent movement of the tribals which acknowledges help from outsiders in promoting their skill in social analysis but jealously asserts its autonomy in decision-making in all spheres (de Silva *et al.*, 1979). In Sri Lanka, the Participatory Institute for Development Alternatives (PIDA), with which PORP has been collaborating closely, has been highly successful in promoting people's participatory self-development processes in a number of village clusters, with external 'animation' work in each location for an initial period of about two years on average, thereafter the people's organisations moving on independently with collective economic and social action without further formal presence of the PIDA workers (Tilakaratna, 1985). In the work of PROCESS (Participatory Research for Organisation, Community Education and Self-reliance), a rural development agency in the Philippines which grew out of a pilot PORP project (SARILAKAS) in four villages and which is now working in more than 300 villages and towns in different parts of the country, external animators cover increasingly large areas promoting and assisting people's organisations which handle more and more tasks by themselves; the external animators then work more with newer base groups, and base organisations form their own federations to handle higher-level operations themselves (PORP, 1988). In Thailand, external interventions in NET (Toward Self-reliance in Northeast Thailand) and GRID (Grassroots Integrated Development Project) projects in villages in Surin province and north-east Thailand respectively which have been studied by PORP have resulted in the formation and development of people's organisations whose progress towards self-reliance is monitored closely. Eighty per cent of the village organisations in the NET project are continuing collective activities of their own after initial periods of NET presence, and GRID workers do not stay in the project villages after an initial period (PORP, 1988; Tilakaratna, 1989).

A different pattern of relations between external interveners and the people is observed in some African grassroots mobilisations with which PORP is collaborating, e.g. the Organisation of Rural Associations for Progress (ORAP), Zimbabwe, and the Six-S movement in Burkina Faso and other Francophone African countries. In these, external activists, sometimes in association with the people's own leaders, initiate the formation of people's organisations which are often transformations of traditional communal formations of some kind or other. The base organisations federate into higher-level bodies, and the apex bodies of such mobilisations include people's representatives as well as external activists, the latter as staff or advisers as an organic element of these structures. The dichotomy between a structure of external interveners and structures of people's institutions as observed generally in cases of grassroots interventions do not exist in these cases, with the external activists bound by the constitutional rules and procedures of the apex people's bodies. In a sense, the external activists thus become a part of the strata of 'organic intellectuals' (Gramsci, 1971) of the people's movements, so that the question of relations between the people and these activists becomes an internal question for these movements.

In terms of actual decision-making, there are examples, both in cases of dichotomous relations between external activists and people's organisations as in the Asian examples mentioned above and in the cases of organic relations between the two as in the African cases referred to, not only of base groups and higher-level people's bodies taking critical decisions and initiatives independently of the external interveners, but also of the people reviewing the nature and extent of participation in their organisations, modifying institutional forms to promote greater participation (e.g. splitting bigger groups into smaller ones), and devising imaginative checks on the abuse of authority by their own leaders such as the quick rotation of leadership or ad hoc appointment of functionaries for specific tasks only, rather than creating standing offices.

Animation and facilitation

Observations of and reflections on such cases, by means of participatory research as well as action research (practical field experimentation and review thereof), of negative as well as positive experiences in external efforts to promote people's initiatives and self-reliance, have over the years converged into a particular conception of 'animation' and 'facilitation' work in the minds of external interveners promoting participatory people's development, and of the methodology of training external animators for such a task.

The term 'animation', with its specific connotation in some recent grassroots work, means, in the very literal spirit of the word, *animating* the underprivileged people to regard themselves as the principal actors in their lives and not as subordinates to other social classes, to stand up with self-esteem, to develop a critical understanding of the conditions of their lives and to express and assert themselves through collective action to meet life's challenges. The central spirit behind this concept of animation in grassroots work is the view of men and women as *creative beings* and a desire to see the creative possibilities of the underprivileged people released – people who are often locked in states of mental dependence and/or apathy and do not exercise their creative potential as much as they could in a given social situation. The scope of creative action to solve problems and to face difficult situations is considerably greater for the poor and underprivileged through collective rather than through individual (family) action, so that animation is particularly addressed to generating a spirit of solidarity and collective action among these people.

This notion of animation, which has been elaborated in a synthesis of PORP's philosophy and experiences (Tilakaratna, 1987), defines some of the basic parameters in the style of work of an external animator and, in particular, in his/her relations with the people. Obviously, an external animator coming with the image of a charitable friend offering resources as well as 'wisdom' and advice, revealing, or with the presumption that, he/she has the means or the wisdom to solve the people's problems, cannot animate the people into self-esteem and creative self-action. The animator must, therefore, dispel in the very beginning any sense of expectation among the people that he or she has brought or has access to resources or expertise which will improve the people's condition. This is not to deny any knowledge or resources, including status and contacts, that the animator may have which may be handy in helping to advance people's initiatives at some stage ('facilitation' work as discussed below); but the basic relations between the animator and the people will not be built upon such resources of the animator, but on the premise that it is for the people to solve their own problems through collective endeavours in which the animator, when he/she is there, can only be a friend, and that the most important resource to help the people move forward is their own collective strength, thinking and capabilities.

Thus charged to stimulate a sense of self-esteem among the people, and of reliance on their own abilities, and to stimulate them to get collectively engaged in seeking and administering creative solutions to their problems, one of the first tasks of the animator is to stimulate in the people a sense of confidence in the knowledge that they already possess. It is important to assert that popular knowledge, developed through generations of life's experience and struggle, is inferior to no other knowledge. This is not to say that one stream of knowledge has nothing to learn from another; but this applies both ways, and professional knowledge has as much to take from popular knowledge and wisdom as the other way round. This desirable mutual enrichment is possible only in a relation of equality between the two knowledge streams and not in a presupposition of superiority of one over the other.

At the same time, the animator's task is to stimulate the people in systematically advancing their knowledge further. Thus the animator seeks to stimulate the people to undertake a *collective inquiry* of their own into the circumstances of their lives – their poverty, the socio-economic processes that are generating and reproducing this condition – and an intellectual search for possibilities of improving their situation by collective action. As Tilakaratna has observed,

> People operate as animated subjects when they are able to investigate, critically reflect on and analyse the social reality on their own, perceive self-possibilities for change, take initiatives and engage in critical review of their ongoing actions as a regular practice. The role of animation is therefore to assist the people to build up the above capacities, and a knowledge base to think and act creatively to transform their realities. (Tilakaratna, 1987: 23)

Animation work is combined with what has come to be known as 'facilitation'. As Tilakaratna has explained,

> While animation by breaking mental barriers begins to show possibilities for change, facilitation is a task of assisting the poor to break the practical barriers to action. External intervenors with their formal education, wider knowledge of social contexts, social contacts and status derived from affiliation to a formal organisation such as a 'development agency', are able to act as resource persons to people's groups to help overcome some of their practical problems.

This includes, according to specific contexts,

> Facilitation in the acquisition of basic skills, in particular literacy, management skills (such as accounts keeping, auditing, record keeping, correspondence . . . and related matters needed for effective operation of organisations and collective undertakings) and technical skills (in fields such as agriculture, small industry and health needed to implement

action plans). In the promotion of such skills, the attempt should be to assist the people to critically adapt and selectively absorb the knowledge from outside rather than a mechanical transfer of knowledge which alienates people. . . . Assistance to people's groups to develop contact with formal agencies, institutions and bureaucracies of relevance to their action programmes and to develop the skills to deal and negotiate with them. Supply of information to the people's groups about legislation, policies and programmes, formal procedures, channels of communication and allied matters would be of particular importance in this regard. (Tilakaratna, 1987: 35–7)

Financial assistance

It should be noted that direct financial assistance to the poor is not in the concept of animation–facilitation. Such assistance by external interveners is liable to give them an image of source of funds which may disorient their relation with the people; it also distorts the people's motivation for getting organised, particularly if the external funding is offered as a part of the 'project' for animation, in so far as the people might then look at the question of organising mainly as a means of getting external funds. PORP itself has learnt this lesson from failures of two of its own projects, one in India and one in Bangladesh, which took external finance to attract people to get together and engage in collective economic cooperation: not much cooperation could be stimulated, and whatever was achieved collapsed after the external assistance terminated. The relations and attitudes which are generated by such projects are contrary to the spirit of participation and self-reliance which animation work aims to stimulate. The 'ideology' in animation work is that solidarity among the poor, and their reflecting and working together to solve common problems, are desirable for their own sake, whether or not material help from outside is available. This solidarity is considered to be primary, so that 'participation' does not become contingent on the availability of external resources and hence dependent on such deliveries from outside. The task of animation is to generate such a sense of solidarity and collective initiative of the poor which (i.e. participation) may be sustained irrespective of the availability of external material help, which in any case is not available to help all the poor people in most countries with a problem of mass poverty on a wide scale. This is not to deny to the poor their rightful share of social and public resources, and the animator–facilitator assists the people in their struggle and negotiations for achieving this right. Experimentation with this approach in the work of PIDA in Sri Lanka and in the pilot project SARILAKAS of PORP mentioned above, and in a recent project, Planning Rural Development at the Village Level (PRDVL), in Tanzania in which PORP introduced its conception and methodology of animation work (Rahman, 1989a), have been very successful in animating the people to develop group solidarity and socio-economic cooperation without depending on external financial or material assistance, and the resulting grassroots formations are multiplying. These experiments confirm the validity of such animation work to promote participatory, self-reliant rural development in a way which, depending as it does on the mobilisation of internal resources and energy of the poor and the progressive involvement of the public resource system to provide them with supplementary resources rather than on external finance, is more widely replicable.

Phasing out of external animators
There is, finally, the question of the long-run relation between external animators and people's organisations. We have mentioned instances of external activists getting absorbed as a permanent organic element in people's initiatives so that there is no structural dichotomy between the two. Barring such cases, there are reasons to regard with some concern an indefinite continuance of animation–facilitation by external activists of people's groups *to whom they are not structurally accountable*. This would imply, in the first instance, that the people's organisation concerned is not becoming self-reliant in managing its own affairs, and continued dependence on external activists inhibits the free release of people's creativity. The people's processes also remain vulnerable to the possibility of sudden withdrawal of some external animators, which may happen for personal reasons; or in cases of sensitive work *vis-à-vis* vested interests and/or dominant structures including the state, such action may be stopped by the dominant structures if and when they feel seriously threatened. There is also always the possibility of distortion in the commitment of external activists as a result of pulls from the prevailing structures which have many ways of coopting such activism, apart from such distortions happening spontaneously since all human beings are susceptible to change in the course of the evolution of their lives in interaction with the evolution of the wider society. Such possibilities are of course also present for the internal leaders and cadres of a people's movement, but the dimensions of the question of accountability in the two cases, hence the question of self-reliance versus dependence, are fundamentally different.

At another level of consideration, a progressive 'phasing out' of external animators from any given location of work is considered to be desirable in order to assist people's initiatives over wider areas, and link them up with each other. Skill for external animation–facilitation work with standards as outlined above is scarce, and it is not easy for the people's own leaders to do such work with others in distant areas. Middle-class activists with their more privileged circumstances need, therefore, to move on to other areas for 'replication' of participatory processes. And when people's initiatives in different locations link with each other to form broader structures or coordinating mechanisms, the help of friends with such circumstantial advantages and skills, to assist in dealing with broader structures of the prevailing establishments and institutions (e.g. higher-level public agencies), is also in general needed, at least initially. This also requires that, when the people's processes thus move to higher levels, external animators reduce their involvement at base levels to be able to assist people's actions at higher levels.

For such a variety of 'ideological' (e.g. self-reliance and self-determination) as well as practical reasons, the need for progressive 'withdrawal' of the external animator from any give base location of work is increasingly being recognised. In turn, this question is also coming to be viewed as an ultimate test of the success of external animation work in promoting people's self-reliance and hence their authentic participation. A PORP Regional Workshop for Trainers in Participatory Rural Development held in the Philippines in August 1988 (PORP, 1988) underlined this as an important consideration in animation work; the question was also discussed in a parallel workshop for Francophone African countries held in Burkina Faso in July 1989 (PORP, 1989).

With the above in view, one of the important tasks of the external animator is considered to be to identify, jointly with the people, potential animators from within the ranks of the people, and to help them develop their own potential in this regard through 'training' processes and guidance so that, eventually, these 'internal animators' take over the roles that the external animators have been performing at the base level, releasing the external animators to work at higher levels or in new locations.

The training of external animators
The question of the training of external animators is, naturally, most crucial. Animation–facilitation work to promote people's initiatives is a task that not only requires a high degree of creative skill in relating with people in a special way, but also rests crucially on the personal motivation and sensitivity of the animator. Such creative skills, motivation and sensitivity cannot be given easily in structured, lecture-oriented training programmes. Most worthwhile training programmes for external animators combine an initial period of 'workshop'-style dialogical reflection, guided or, better, 'facilitated' by a 'trainer', with field action which is again reflected upon collectively by the trainees together and with the trainer (de Silva *et al.*, 1983; PORP, 1988).

A special methodology for the training of external animators has been tried with impressive results in two programmes with which PORP collaborated – the Change Agents Programme in Sri Lanka (Tilakaratna, 1984) and in the PRDVL programme in Tanzania mentioned earlier. In this approach, in which the trainees came from the cadre of field workers in rural development programmes of different government agencies, the initial dialogical session has been divided into two phases: the first phase invites the trainees to reflect upon their past work with the rural poor, and to ask and analyse the question as to whether they had been able to stimulate people's self-reliant initiatives. The answer being in the negative, the trainees are invited in the next phase to present and discuss self-critiques of why this did not happen, in terms of the conceptions and approach of their respective projects or programmes, the socio-economic realities of the villages in which they worked and their own personal styles of relating to the people. From out of this, a collective understanding of the inadequacies of the conventional project and programme approach to rural development in promoting self-reliant people's initiatives emerges. In a second phase, the trainees are invited to propose how, in the light of their present understanding in the workshop, they would want to approach the task of promoting self-reliant people's initiatives. Ideas are presented and debated, and from this emerges some consensus on how one might wish to try this task, taking it as their challenge now. The trainees are then sent to pilot villages to try out their ideas in practice – i.e. try animation work with the rural poor – and meet regularly among themselves once a month or so for several months to reflect together on the results of their efforts. Training and 'action research' thus merge into one process and continue as such.

The premise behind this approach to training – which has actually resulted in both the above cases in generating a high degree of motivation among the trainees taking on the challenge of promoting people's self-reliant collective initiatives, as well as in generating such people's initiatives without material deliveries from the various projects – is that the motivation and sensitivity needed for and in animation work are inner-directed and therefore best stimulated by critical self-inquiry and self-identification by the trainees when they attempt their task. In this approach there is also built in self-correction of wrong steps, and creative responses and self-adaptation to evolving situations and responses from action. Furthermore, the experience of self-inquiry untutored by any 'expert', and the fulfilment one derives from this, is also the best way to drive home the point that the animators, in their turn, must not tutor the people but must stimulate the people's self-reflection and self-deliberated action without reservation, to give the people in turn *their* fulfilment as creators of their own destiny which is the ultimate task of animation work. If, on the contrary, one is tutored, then one will in turn tend to tutor those whom one is supposed to help; and no amount of lecturing against such tutoring of the people may offset the experiential impact of being tutored, which is liable to be internalised in the tutored so that it may become their own inner-directed tendency in their relations with the people despite the wisdom they 'receive' otherwise.

Such and other approaches to the training of external animators were discussed in the Philippine workshop of trainers mentioned earlier, where the concept of 'liberating training' was elaborated (PORP, 1988; Rahman, 1989b). It was observed that the actual 'training period' for an external animator is a long one in the sense that it may take three to four years for an external animator of middle-class background to mature in his or her understanding and action in this task, and the initial training programme that the parent agency organises for him or her is, therefore, only a *starter* in this long learning process. This calls for some clarity in what the starter programme's function really is. It was observed that while most training programmes include a lot of *contents* by way of social analysis and principles to be followed in animation work, tools of such work, experiences of successes and failures, etc., much of such contents are liable to be forgotten over time, and even those that are 'remembered' may not spring up in the consciousness exactly when they might be useful. An animator has to respond creatively to field situations in which his/her general sensitivity and orientation are more valuable assets than stored knowledge. This sensitivity and orientation may not be promoted by 'educating' someone about the principles, tools and experiences in the art of animation; these are developed by prolonged practice and reflection upon practice. It is, therefore, necessary to look for a deeper purpose of a starter training programme. This purpose is embodied in the notion of 'liberating training', and the purpose must be *to liberate the trainees from the very need for a trainer*, so that they become, in effect, their own trainers for self-learning.

The starter programme's primary task in such liberating training is to put the trainees in processes of interaction in which they themselves take the initiative in raising questions and seeking answers to them, both in order to practise such self-inquiry and to gain confidence in doing so. Self-inquiry in this context includes, of course, discussion and reading so as to seek answers ultimately for oneself. Formal contents of a training programme may serve as exercise tools for the practice of such self-inquiry; but this *practice* is a more important part of the training programme than its technical *contents*. From this point of view it is immaterial how much of the contents in a training programme is covered and whether the 'module has been completed' – sometimes this is possible only by sacrificing the practice when it starts to become fulfilling so as to race against time, and ultimately by falling back on lecturing to complete the 'course'. Field observations reveal that such 'training' has helped little – the contents have at best been 'remembered' without much comprehension or stimulation and at worst forgotten, and dependence on guidance for further learning and tackling new situations has continued or has even been created.

A dilemma of self-reliance-promoting organisations (SPOs)

Intervention of the above nature, committed to the promotion of people's self-reliance, needs to be distinguished from interventions of a wide variety of types by a growing body of so-called non-governmental organisations (NGOs) as they are called in the development cooperation language. In the regional workshop of trainers in the Philippines, the term NGO was rejected as non-functional and misleading, and the term SPO (self-reliance-promoting organisation) was adopted instead to denote the challenge of self-reliance-promoting animation–facilitation work (PORP, 1988). It was also recognised that there is no reason to deny this challenge to government agencies as well, some of which in some countries may be contributing more to the promotion of people's self-reliance than many NGOs (SARILAKAS in the Philippines devoted purely to animation–facilitation work started as a pilot government project (Rahman, 1983), and PRDVL in Tanzania is also a government project).

Having thus rechristened themselves, participants in the above workshop faced the question: *are the SPOs self-reliant themselves*? The same question was also raised in a parallel workshop held in Zimbabwe for Anglophone African countries (August 1989), the third in a series of PORP regional workshops for trainers in participatory rural development.

Most SPOs are dependent for their own existence and operations on foreign donor funding. Self-reliance does not mean self-sufficiency, and external resources may be used if this is found to be advantageous. But the organisation in question must have the capability to survive and keep on with its work without external resources, so that it is not dependent on outside support to the extent that its *autonomy of action* is compromised. Not many SPOs can claim to meet this criterion, and for those who cannot, their lack of autonomy is liable to influence their grassroots work, and disorient it from its objective of promoting people's self-reliance if it does not get funding from donors with precisely the same objective.

There are, indeed, cases of SPOs facing constant pressure on their autonomy from some or other of their donors. An SPO in a South-East Asian country has experienced one of its donors sending foreign consultants to evaluate its work, with little understanding of the culture of the society and the kind of motivation with which dedicated animators live and work with the people for twenty-four hours a day under difficult conditions; these consultants are reported to have recommended that the animators should be given 'modern' terms of employment! There has also been an instance of a foreign-donor NGO putting pressure on an indigenous SPO in an African country not to develop relations of cooperation with an international organisation some of whose ideas on grassroots work it wanted to try. There are also examples of government control exercised on SPOs' work through the requirement of registering such organisations if they are to receive foreign funds: in one country in South Asia the government once formed an ad hoc committee to reorient the direction of an SPO's work away from pressure-group activities towards socio-economic programmes, and funds were not released to pay the salaries of its animators for three months.

Cases are also known of the corrupting influence of too much foreign funding on the personal orientation of SPO staff who are tempted to promote their salaries and privileges, thereby over-distancing themselves disfunctionally from the people with whom they have to integrate to discharge their tasks successfully. Finally, preaching self-reliance without the preacher organisation being self-reliant itself is not always very convincing, and the people are also prone to ask why they should not have a share of the cake the SPO is getting from the donors.

This remains an unresolved dilemma for SPOs, most of whom have not found an adequate answer to this question. Some SPOs are able to sufficiently diversify the sources of funding and are thus able to retain a significant measure of autonomy, but most SPOs are not in such a fortunate position. The idea of SPOs doing income-generating work themselves is considered: there are examples of SPOs running a printing press, a driving school, doing consultancies for other agencies and other income-generating activities. As reported in the above-mentioned Anglophone African Workshop of Trainers, the African Centre of Human and Cultural Development in Ghana seems to have been particularly successful in generating the needed funds locally by imaginative fund-raising drives and income-generating entrepreneurial activities. But this practice has not yet become common among SPOs. And as long as SPOs are unable to find an answer to this question, it remains perhaps the strongest reason why any SPO, which is structurally separate from people's organisations, should phase itself out from any given location after a reasonable period. It is also essential that this dilemma should be shared and discussed with the people, bringing home to them the vulnerabilities inherent in non-self-reliant SPO assistance, so that the people also see the need to become self-reliant *vis-à-vis* the intervening SPO as early as possible.

Expressions of people's initiatives

Successful animation work results in forward-moving people's processes according to the people's own priorities. These priorities vary according to circumstances. People's initiatives have ranged from economic undertakings to struggles for economic, social and human rights as observed in PORP studies and action research.

Collective means of action for economic improvement
In the economic sphere, people's initiatives show that means of action exist to promote the economic status of the poor which are not generally conceived or available in conventional externally designed projects and programmes (and in any case such projects and programmes reach only a fraction of poverty groups in most countries). Some of the more important means of action demonstrated by collective initiatives of the rural poor may be grouped into four broad categories:

Pressure-group action to gain access to resources
Through pressure-group action, organisations of the rural poor have in numerous instances achieved control over land for cultivation and water for irrigation or fishing, obtained modern agricultural inputs for increasing productivity, credit from the public credit system, and better wages and tenancy arrangements.

Internal resource mobilisation
Most people's initiatives are able to stimulate *personal savings* by the poorest groups who have hitherto not saved. The poor start saving from their current earnings however low they are, and from incremental earnings from economic endeavours when such endeavours are taken as a part of the popular mobilisation. The savings are usually put in a *collective fund*. One of the first benefits that accrues in many cases is weakening of the vicious circle of dependence on the village moneylender, as the collective fund grows into a size from which reasonable advances or grants to meet acute needs can be made. Experiencing the advantage of this *banking* as well as *social insurance* functions of the collective fund, participating groups often get stimulated to seek to augment this fund faster, by methods such as ploughing back a proportion of incremental incomes from collective economic projects to the fund, and charging interest to borrower members. The banking function can expand through innovative institutional development, for the poor to have their own bank under their own control (Musengimana, 1988).

The other way internal resources are mobilised is cooperative effort in economic and social activities. An organisation is by itself a *collective fund of human resources*, pooling human energy and talents otherwise available for individual pursuits only, and (for the poor by definition) inadequate to improve one's life, much of which tend to be wasted for lack of rewarding opportunities.

Changing the commodity market structure
Another way collective action of the rural poor has often improved their economic status is by developing alternatives to prevailing market structures in rural areas which are usually highly exploitative from the point

of view of small producers. Radical breakthroughs in this respect have been achieved by collective initiatives of small rural producers in several instances (Tilakaratna 1987).

Alternatives to dependence on oppressive market structures have been developed by such means as collective purchase of inputs, collective storage systems, collective marketing of inputs, collective groceries, and advances from the collective fund to enhance the staying power of small producers so that they need not be forced to sell low to meet immediate liquidity needs.

Skills promotion

Skills training, a critical prerequisite for more remunerative wage or self-employment in various occupations and for raising the productivity of labour, is beyond the means of most rural poor. The costs include both training and travel to training centres usually absent in villages. People's organisations are finding a solution to this problem as well. Such organisations have initiated skills training programmes of their own, mobilising internal as well as external resources. Selected members of the organisations are also sent to formal training programmes to come back and train the new skill to other members. Imaginative ways of spreading skills and knowledge from people to people are being devised, e.g. in the Six-S movement in Burkina Faso (Sawadogo and Ouedraogo, 1988), ways which are part of an overall spirit of collective identity and self-mobilisation not available to non-mobilisation.

This is not to say that all people's collective initiatives produce early tangible economic gains. No development strategy is, however, known which promises only 'success' in such terms. And people's self-initiatives have two unique advantages over externally designed strategies: first, in such initiatives the basic responsibility is assumed by the people themselves, including to that extent the responsibility for the outcome. Second, from successes as well as failures of people's initiatives, it is the people who learn, a learning that can be used in their subsequent efforts.

Holistic aspirations

Many people's initiatives, however, are revealing and assert that their aspirations and priorities are not necessarily confined to narrow material calculations but are often holistic, the total *human status* in society being an important parameter. This includes not only economic considerations but also considerations of human dignity and human rights, e.g. that the 'elite' has no right to physically or otherwise humiliate anybody no matter how low their economic status (de Silva *et al.*, 1979: Chapter 5; Rahman, 1986), or the men have no right to oppress and mistreat the women in so many ways. People's movements are known to have been sustained for prolonged periods with the unshaken loyalty of their participants and with unshaken solidarity, simply by raising the human status of the participants without necessarily improving their material status. And women's groups have stated that their life has changed dramatically ever since they formed their organisation not necessarily because of any material gains but because they can meet and talk their mind freely which they could not do before, and this gives them an altogether new experience of life which is immensely 'richer' than previously (Rahman, 1987b). Thus, quite apart from considerations of material improvement, solidarity and organised existence are being asserted as a higher form of social existence by the underprivileged.

In some recent studies and reports two other interrelated dimensions of some people's initiatives are being revealed. One is experimentation with *organic development* in harmony with nature rather than development by 'harnessing' nature, which has been the ethos of development thinking and effort of the 'modernisation' variety. The other is to root development effort in the *indigenous culture* of the people, which has also been more organically related with nature. In such initiatives, e.g. in Thailand (Tilakaratna, 1989), and in Hawaii (WCCADC, undated), the effort is to develop and use organic technologies of production seeking to preserve and enrich rather than progressively impoverish nature, this effort being an integral part of an effort also to develop a self-sufficient economic base free from critical dependence on the market, 'which would support the social, cultural and spiritual development of people and their families within the context of their communities' (WCCADC, undated).

Expressions of this nature of people's initiatives call for a serious rethinking of the very meaning of development and hence of the direction of development effort, towards a holistic view of the concept as distinct from the narrow economistic (consumerist) view that has pervaded conventional development thinking and effort. This question was most sharply, and poignantly, raised in the participatory research exercise of forest-based people's movements mentioned in the section 'In search of a research paradigm'. As this research concluded:

> We deliberated on writing a conclusion to our study. But we found it difficult to do so. Should we write our epitaph or should we dream and hope? We have not been able to resolve this dilemma. . . .
>
> We have . . . been able to assess what we have received from 'civilisation' in exchange of our habitat . . . it has been difficult for us to come to a conclusion. In fact, this study is the beginning of a process of systematisation of the process of our thinking and our struggles. It is therefore not possible to end this report with a set of recommendations, either for the government or for academicians, both of whom are victims of a vicious degrading cycle of false reasoning. . . . We have seen and we have tried to present the picture of degradation of our culture that we have seen throughout the country. It is often very difficult to share an

experience . . . with someone who has not experienced it personally. . . .

The life of a forest-dweller has many compensations which are not available to city-dwellers. Therefore, we do not envy city-dwellers. Through the path of 'development', when we arrive at cities, we arrive at its slums and not at its mansions. For 'development' we have to give up our lifestyle and our culture and through the process of monetisation we are gradually imbibing the culture and life of the slums.

We feel cheated, and the country as a whole has been cheated too. It is strange that what is good for us has been decided by those who have cheated us and the country. They have deprived us of our habitat and the country of her environment. . . .

Those who are interested in a new forest policy are not the forest-dwellers. Their major interest is the development of forest as a resource, rather than as a habitat of people. This basic difference distinguishes 'us' from 'them'. 'They' . . . believe that we (the forest-dwellers) should reap the dubious benefits of 'development'. Or, in other words, become like them or their serfs. We have tried in this report to show how we have lived for centuries – sheltered, protected and nurtured by the forest. This lifestyle is now fast disappearing along with the forest.

Our consensus is that we have to preserve what we have and develop a new perspective based on the flowering of our own eco-regions. Development to us does not mean a negation of nature and its forces, but being a part of it. To us, therefore, development of the environment means protecting it from destruction by men. (Dasgupta, 1986: Chapter 6)

Significance for social change

The question may be asked: what is the significance of such grassroots work for overall (macro level) social change, and for people's participation in national policy- and decision-making?

In general, work of this nature is of local rather than national dimensions, covering relatively small areas of any country. The largest grassroots mobilisation for participatory development is possibly in Burkina Faso, where the Six-S movement covers nearly two-thirds of the country's villages, besides having become a regional movement covering a number of other countries such as Senegal, Chad, Niger and Mali (Sawadogo and Ouedraogo, 1988). ORAP in Zimbabwe is a significant phenomenon in the Matabeleland region covering more than 600 villages. In some other countries the totality of grassroots work to promote participatory rural development may be considered significant in a national overview, e.g. in Bangladesh more than 10 per cent of the country's villages have organisations of the landless rural poor, men and women's groups and mixed groups engaged in different kinds of economic, social and human rights activities; and in India numerous movements, spontaneous as well as animated–facilitated by external groups, are known. There is no doubt that the growing interest in development thinking and in the development cooperation system in participatory development is not merely a theoretical concern today but is a part of, and is being further stimulated by, the advances grassroots work of this nature is making on the ground.

However, it cannot be said that such work and initiatives have come anywhere near influencing the overall (macro) direction of society in any country, in so far as such direction is controlled by centralised institutions and structures with specific social power over certain basic national policy, resource control and development strategy questions. This includes, specifically, questions of control over certain other strategic economic resources – such as land, forest, water, credit – to which the ordinary people have little access so that they are seriously handicapped in their effort to take initiatives to improve their own lives.

It is also to be recognised, as already mentioned, that interventions to promote people's initiatives coexist with a host of interventions to promote other kinds of 'development', e.g. government projects and programmes with a bureaucratic, top-down orientation, and NGO interventions of a wide variety, from charity and welfare-oriented to paternalist development delivery-oriented work, with only a few NGOs coming anywhere near the standards discussed above. The Grameen Bank kind of work which originated in Bangladesh (Egger, 1986) is also spreading, with its obvious appeal and benefit to the rural poor – an outstanding model of bringing credit to the rural poor; but its rigid rules designed from the top to ensure loan repayment go beyond designing financial discipline procedures and impose institutional forms upon the people, thus restricting their freedom to design their own institutions to promote their authentic participation for their self-development.

Thus, interventions to promote people's self-reliant collective initiatives are just one kind in a milieu of interventions of many kinds, and most interventions which are truly benefiting the poor have a *delivery* rather than *animation* orientation. This does not, *per se*, seriously restrict the *geographical* space for animation–facilitation work to promote people's participation, simply because there are not enough resources for delivery-oriented interventions to cover the bulk of the poor populace in most countries with a problem of mass poverty. In fact, this is, indeed, the *material* case for animation–facilitation work to stimulate and assist the rural poor to mobilise themselves and move forward with collective initiatives as far as possible, without waiting for deliveries from outside – the great bulk of the rural poor cannot be abandoned simply because there are not enough resources to be delivered to them, and development cooperation effort cannot be aimed simply at administering the very limited amount of resources which are available to be delivered in order to enable only a fraction of the masses to cross the 'threshold'. The constraints on more rapid spread of participatory initiatives arise from other sources. One is the supply of animators, a point which has already been touched upon (see section 'Promoting participation'). Another is the demonstration of delivery-oriented ('soft') programmes which raise false expectations among the masses in general and create or help strengthen a delivery-dependent mentality among the people, making animation for self-reliant initiatives to that extent more difficult. Animation work also requires resources for the animators' subsistence, travel and other operations and for the overheads of their parent organisations etc., and as discussed, most agencies dedicated to such work usually rely on foreign donor funding which also is scarce. At a structural level, such work is potentially particularly hazardous at both the micro and macro levels: at the micro level social awareness and organisation of the poor are immediate threats to vested interests who thrive by exploiting the poor and keeping them dependent upon them in a patron–client relationship; at the macro level, there is usually a basic suspicion on the part of dominant structures about such grassroots development spreading too widely, as this could then become a challenge to the continuity and power of such structures.

Finally, civil disorders may disrupt or overtake local-level participatory initiatives, e.g. the work of PIDA has become very difficult now with the current situation in Sri Lanka, and such work is not possible in some parts of the Philippines.

Ideologically, while the idea of people's collective initiatives is being supported by many 'liberal' quarters, its core philosophy has a parallel in the Marxist vision of the working people creating their own destiny, and many activists working with the people to promote participatory development have explicitly or implicitly taken inspiration from the socialist ideology. It is interesting to observe, however, that the formal left is hardly known to have been excited by the kind of people's initiatives that such grassroots work seeks to promote. Influenced by the Leninist concept of a vanguard party of intellectuals possessing 'advanced consciousness' *vis-à-vis* the working people who, therefore, must follow the dictatorship of such a party, the course of formal left-led revolutions got disoriented from the above Marxist vision of creative initiatives by the working people. Grassroots work to promote such initiatives, in many instances, has emerged out of, or was strengthened by, the resulting disillusionment of Marxist-oriented activists who could not accept such distortion of the premise of socialism. As discussed in a previous paper (Chapter 6 of this book; Rahman, 1982), the growth of such grassroots processes in recent years may be traced to the 'crisis of the left' as well as to the 'crisis of the right'. It has also been argued there that one reason for the re-emergence of elite domination over the people in post-revolutionary societies is the preoccupation of social revolutions with changing only the *material relations of production* while retaining the existing polarised *relations of knowledge* which give to the elites a source of social power independently of the relations of material production. The concern for restoring the status of popular knowledge and for systematic advancement of people's self-inquired knowledge is a basic point of departure of participation-promotional work from left-wing activism of the Leninist variety.

For some period, grassroots work to promote people's participation was debated hotly in terms of whether this could promote the cause of revolutionary social transformation ('socialism') or work counter to this cause (Sethi and Kothari, 1983). Today, after the collapse of the Leninist model of 'socialism' (to be constructed by a vanguard party of intellectuals unaccountable to the people) in Eastern Europe and the suggestion of military power rather than popular support as the main strength of the party in some other bastions of such 'socialism', this debate is no longer very pertinent. It may be suggested that more important today are four questions which have emerged in the agenda at this juncture of world development:

(a) the question of real *people's democracy* with political as well as economic rights permitting the people to take initiatives as creative human beings. One would suggest this as the question of the most fundamental *human right*, in so far as the fundamental distinction between human and other beings lies in the creative powers of humans which, therefore, deserve to be fulfilled as a matter of human right (Rahman, 1989d). The needed democracy is assured neither in the 'democracy' of the so-called 'free world' in which economic power concentrated in the hands of elites, often backed by military power, is a key determinant of the outcome of electoral processes which determine who 'represents' the people at macro levels; nor in the so-called 'socialist democracies' where elite rule is assured by dictatorship of a monolithic party unaccountable to the people;

(b) the question of subordination of and violence to *women*, i.e. to half the human race (this question has not been discussed in depth in this paper as there is another programme in the ILO addressing this question (Programme on Rural Women));

(c) the question of preserving a *plurality of cultures* and associated social institutions and their authentic evolution, including the cultural variations arising from ethnic diversities of people within nation states with a rich variety of modes of life which are threatened by the attempts of dominant structures to impose a singular concept of 'development' upon all peoples; and

(d) the question of *violence to nature* and, in turn, violence to the inherent popular sense of being an organic part of nature, and the associated technical question of *sustainability* of 'development'.

On all these questions, theoretical answers ahead of practical articulations would not have much value. History is showing repeatedly that the courses of society are not predetermined or predictable by theory. Today, with some of the great (macro) 'development' experiments of this century of both the right and the left varieties having run their full course and, having revealed their great inadequacies in fulfilling certain basic human urges, the primary need of the hour is to re-search for a direction for societies, in fact to start all over again in this search, with modest intellectual pretensions. Social movements to promote participatory people's development as well as those representing, simultaneously or separately, the other concerns mentioned above have started this search relatively early, and despite their still relatively small overall size, are at the frontier of this search.

Unfortunately, however, most societies are still controlled by structures and 'expertise' oriented to concepts of 'development' and 'modernisation' which have produced the human and ecological crises of the above nature. It is likely that such 'development' and 'modernisation' will continue to be pursued in most societies for a long time to come, and many newly 'developing' societies will be making the same mistakes in social leadership that their counterparts in the 'developed' world have done. But this will only heighten the crises, and make the above kind of social movements more and more the hope for mankind (cf. Frank and Fuentes, 1988).

Summary

Research on people's participation has been considered to require unconventional modes of inquiry which seek a research partnership with the people (participatory research). A participatory research study of the Bhoomi Sena movement in Maharastra, India, provided the first inspiration in such an inquiry. This was followed by participatory research exercises in Sri Lanka, in India with other popular movements, in the Philippines, and in Nicaragua, Mexico and Colombia. The research methodology varied from case to case according to local innovativeness and culture. The three Latin American exercises were systematised into a comprehensive methodological guide to participatory research. The epistemological premises of participatory research have been examined, to claim that such research generates knowledge that is both scientific (objective) and 'organic', i.e. an organic element of the very movement of life, unlike knowledge produced by observing life from a discreet distance.

Participation has been viewed as an organised activity of the people concerned (the underprivileged), who take self-deliberated initiatives and control the process of their action. This implies self-reliance in the sense of possessing a combination of mental and material reserves to assert autonomy of action. Participation thus conceived contains its internal tension as between formal power (organisation) which can be misused, and people's (countervailing) power which, therefore, needs to be conscious and vigilant.

PORP's research has been focused particularly on the problematic of promoting participation through external intervention. Such intervention has to be sensitive to the risk of creating dependence of the people on the intervener(s), both by the tendency of the people to lean on the intervener, as well as by a presumption of superior wisdom often seen in educated activists working with the underprivileged. Sensitive external intervention can generate self-reliant people's movements, of which examples have been cited from Sri Lanka, the Philippines and Thailand. Some African initiatives are observed in which external activists have merged organically with the popular movements which they have helped to create.

PORP's experience and reflections over the years have converged into a conception of 'animation' and 'facilitation' work by external interveners to promote participatory people's development, and of the methodology of training animators for such work. 'Animation' is conceived as stimulating the people to regard themselves as the principal actors in their lives, to develop a critical understanding of their situation, and take collective initiatives to meet life's challenges – through all these, to release the creative potentials of the people. The tasks and the style of work of the animator to play such a role are discussed. The task of facilitation which is also played by the animator in an initial phase is viewed as that of a resource person to assist the people in tasks which are facilitated by some formal education and institutional contacts. Direct financial assistance which is prone to disorient the people away from self-reliance, and is also not a widely replicable approach, is not considered to be an element of animation–facilitation work. A progressive 'phasing out' of external animators who are not structurally accountable to people's bodies is considered desirable for, and the ultimate test of, the promotion of people's self-reliance and hence the success of animation-facilitation work.

Successful methods of training of external animators have relied more on collective self-reflection by the trainees than on lectures, combined with field action which is again reflected upon collectively. The notion of 'liberating training' has been articulated, aimed at initiating processes of collective self-questioning and seeking answers whereby the trainees are liberated from the very need for a trainer, and experience a fulfilment which they may then be motivated to pass on to the people whose self-reliance they have the charge to promote.

Development agencies which seek to promote people's self-reliance are termed self-reliance promoting organisations or SPOs, a term more functionally focused than the negative and elusive term NGO. The fact of most SPOs not being self-reliant themselves presents a contradiction that needs to be faced.

Once stimulated, people's initiatives have ranged from collective economic undertakings to struggles for economic, social and human rights. In the economic sphere, such initiatives are showing that imaginative means of action exist to promote the economic status of the poor and underprivileged which are not generally conceived or available in conventional, externally designed projects and programmes. Examples of such means of action are given. Many people's initiatives, however, are revealing more holistic urges and aspirations in which one's total human status in society is a basic parameter. In some recently studied initiatives, experimentation with 'organic development' in harmony with nature, and the use of the people's indigenous culture as a developmental force, are being observed.

Finally, the significance of such grassroots movements for overall social change is discussed. While such movements are making advances on the ground, they have not come anywhere near influencing the overall (macro) direction of society in any country yet, and a host of interventions to promote other kinds of 'development' exist in most countries with which participatory development work has to compete. Ideologically, the premise of releasing the creativity of the people is parallel to the Marxist vision of the working people creating their own destiny, but 'socialism' in practice has retained elite domination over the people, with a presumption of superior wisdom of 'revolutionary intellectuals' who have not been accountable to the people. Recent efforts to promote participatory people's development in many countries are a response to the crisis of both the 'right' and the 'left'. These crises are expected to deepen, sharpening questions concerning real people's democracy, violation of women, preservation of a plurarity of cultures, violence to nature and the associated question of sustainability of development. The release of popular initiatives may more and more be seen as the hope of mankind.

References

ACC Task Force on Rural Development (1978) *Report of the Third Meeting of the Working Group on Programme Harmonisation*, Rome, 26 January 1978, UNIO/62(c) Ext.

Bhaduri, Amit and Rahman, Md. Anisur (1982) *Studies in Rural Participation*, New Delhi: Oxford and IBH.

Dasgupta, Subhachari (1986) *Forest, Ecology and the Oppressed (A Study from the Viewpoint of the Forest Dwellers)*, New Delhi: People's Institute for Development and Training.

de Montis, Malena (1987) *Participatory Research in Nicaragua*, New Delhi: PRAXIS.

de Silva, G. V. S., Mehta, N. C., Rahman, M. A. and Wignaraja, P. (1979) 'Bhoomi Sena: a struggle for people's power', *Development Dialogue*, No. 2, pp. 3–70.

de Silva, R. U. Ahmed, Dasgupta, S., Espiritu, R. and Tilakaratna, S. (1983) *Cadre Creation and Action Research in Self-reliant Rural Development*, Geneva: ILO, November 1983 (mimeo).

Egger, Philippe (1986) 'Banking for the rural poor: lessons from some innovative savings and credit schemes', *International Labour Review*, Vol. 125, No. 4, July–August 1986, pp. 447–62.

Egger, Philippe (1988) *Des initiatives paysannes de développement en Afrique: une auto-évaluation de trois expériences au Sénégal, au Burkina Faso et au Rwanda*, World Employment Programme Research Working Paper, WEP. 10/WEP. 47, Geneva: ILO.

Fals Borda, Orlando (1985) *Knowledge and People's Power, Lessons with Peasants in Nicaragua, Mexico and Colombia*, New Delhi: Indian Social Institute.

Fals Borda, Orlando (1985a) *The Challenge of Social Change*, London: Sage Publications.

Frank, André Gunder and Fuentes, Marta (1988) 'Nine theses on social movements', *IFDA Dossier* No. 63, January–February 1988.

Freire, Paulo (1972) *Cultural Action for Freedom*, Harmondsworth: Penguin.

Gajardo, Marcela (1987) 'La concientizacion en America Latina. Una revision critica', Report on a study for the ILO (unpublished).

Gramsci, Antonio (1971) *Selections from the Prison Notebooks*, London: Lawrence & Wishart.

Gregorio, Angelita Y (1985) 'Rural development animator – some experiences from the Philippines, a draft study', Geneva: ILO (unpublished).

Hall, Budd *et al.* (1981) 'Participatory research: development and issues', *Convergence*, Vol. XIV, No. 3.

Musengimana, Siméon (1988) 'La dynamique des organisations paysannes au Rwanda: le cas de l'intergroupement Tuzamuke Twese de Kabaya', in Egger (1988).

Oakley, Peter and Marsden, David (1984) *Approaches to Participation in Rural Development*, Geneva: ILO.

Paranjape, P. V. *et al.* (1984) 'Grass-roots self-reliance in Shramik Sanghatana, Dhulia District, India', in Rahman (1984).

PORP (1988) *Promoting People's Participation and Self-reliance, Proceedings of the Regional Workshop of Trainers in Participatory Rural Development, Tagaytay, the Philippines, August 15–28*, Geneva: ILO.

PORP (1989) *Autopromotion et participation populaire, compte rendu d'un atelier régional de formateurs pour le développement rurale participatif, Bobo-Dioulasso, 3–14 July 1989*, Geneva: ILO.

Rahman, Md. Anisur (1978) 'A methodology for participatory research with the rural poor', *Carnets de l'enfance*, Vol. 41, January–March 1978.

Rahman, Md. Anisur (1981) *Participation of the Rural Poor in Development. Development: Seeds of Change – From Village to Global Order*, Rome: SID.

Rahman, Md. Anisur (1982) 'The theory and practice of participatory action research', *IFDA Dossier*, No. 31, September–October 1982. Also in Fals Borda (1985a) and Shadish and Reichart (1987). (Chapter 6 of this book.)

Rahman, Md. Anisur (1983) *SARILAKAS, A Pilot Project for Stimulating Grass-roots Participation in the Philippines, Technical Cooperation Evaluation Report*, Geneva: ILO.

Rahman, Md. Anisur (ed.) (1984) *Grass-roots Participation and Self-reliance, Experiences in South and South-east Asia*, New Delhi: Oxford and IBH.

Rahman, Md. Anisur (1986) *Organising the Unorganised Rural Poor (Bangladesh Field Notes, October–November 1985)*, Geneva: ILO (mimeo).

Rahman, Md. Anisur (1987a) 'Participation of the rural poor in development (Bangladesh field notes)', *PRAXIS*, Vol. 1, No. 4, March 1987. (Chapter 5 of this book.)

Rahman, Md. Anisur (1987b) *Further Interaction with Grass-roots Organising Work*, Geneva: ILO (mimeo).

Rahman, Md. Anisur (1989a) *Glimpses of the 'Other Africa'*, World Employment Programme Research Working Paper, WE 10/WEP 48, Geneva: ILO. (Chapter 8 of this book.)

Rahman, Md. Anisur (1989b) *The Challenge of Promoting People's Self-reliance. Highlights of a Regional Workshop of Trainers in Participatory Rural Development*, Geneva: ILO (mimeo).

Rahman, Md. Anisur (1989c) 'People's self-development', National Professor Atwar Hussain Trust Fund Lecture, Asiatic Society of Bangladesh, Dhaka, 18 October 1989. (Chapter 10 of this book.)

Rahman, Md. Anisur (1989d) 'Qualitative dimensions of social development', Paper presented at the International Workshop on the Evaluation of Social Development Projects and Programmes in the Third World, Centre for Development Studies, Swansea, Wales, 19–22 September 1989.

Sawadogo, Antonio Raogo and Ouedraogo, Bernard Lédéa (1988) 'Auto-évaluation de Six-S: groupement Naam dans la province du Yatenga (Burkina Faso)', in Egger (1988).

Sethi, Harsh and Kithari, Smitu (eds.) (1983) *The Non-Party Political Process: Uncertain Alternatives*, UNRISD/Lokayan.

Shadish, William R. Jr. and Reichart, Charles S. (eds.) (1987) *Evaluation Studies Review Annual*, Vol. 12, London: Sage Publications.

Tilakaratna, S. (1984) 'Grass-roots self-reliance in Sri Lanka: organisations of betel and coir yarn producers', in Rahman (1984).

Tilakaratna, S. (1985) *The Animator in Participatory Rural Development: Some Experiences from Sri Lanka*, World Employment Programme Research Working Paper WEP 10/WP 37, Geneva: ILO.

Tilakaratna, S. (1987) *The Animator in Participatory Rural Development (Concept and Practice)*, Geneva: ILO.

Tilakaratna, S. (1989) *Retrieval of Roots for Self-reliant Development, Some Experiences from Thailand*, Geneva: ILO (mimeo).

WCCADC (Wai'anae Coast Community Alternative Development Corporation) (undated) *Short History of the Wai'anae Coast Community Alternative Development Corporation*, Wai'anae, Hawaii.

Women's Research Committee *et al.* (1984) 'The struggle toward self-reliance of organised resettled women in the Philippines', in Rahman (1984).

10.   People's self-development

Abstract

Against the culture of deficit and dependent planning at the top, there have been and are popular initiatives which demonstrate a spirit of self-reliance and imaginative self-development efforts by the people. This lecture discusses the perceptions and premises of the underlying urges and vision of development, and contrasts these with the 'liberal' and the 'socialist' trends in development thinking.

As distinct from conventional perceptions of professionals, popular perceptions of development emphasise the value of organic life with nature, standing up and moving forward in communal solidarity, in search for life and self-determination, and the primacy of human dignity.

Popular initiatives of self-development achieve economic betterment by taking imaginative economic initiatives to the extent that they have access to economic resources, and when domestic and external structures permit this. But reality is not always favourable for significant economic improvement early enough, and a creative engagement for collectively tackling life's challenges is the more universal aspect of popular initiatives. Fulfilling one's creative potential is also suggested to be the basic *human* need of people, and a creativist view of development is hence enunciated in terms of the development of human beings as creative beings, fulfilling their creative potential in ever newer ways. The creativist view of development is contrasted with the 'consumerist' view of the liberal trend in development thinking which seeks to eradicate poverty in material terms. The consumerist and 'have-not' orientation of such development discourse is

This chapter originally appeared in the *Journal of Asiatic Society of Bangladesh (Hum.)*, Vol. XXXIV, No. 2, December 1989. It was written in the speaker's private capacity, and does not necessarily reflect the views of the organisation in which he was working. Helpful comments on an earlier draft by Zafar Shaheed, Ajit Ghose, Monwarul Islam, Hameed Tabatabai and Andras Biro are gratefully acknowledged. They are not, of course, responsible for the views expressed herein.

suggested to have a negative motivational impact on the society.

The creativist view of development is traced to Karl Marx as far as scientific development discourse is concerned. But the Marxist view of the working class creating its own history got distorted in East European 'socialism' which followed the Leninist theory of a vanguard party of intellectuals leading the socialist revolution. Mao Tse-tung encouraged people's creative initiatives, to 'break paths unexplored and scale heights yet unclimbed', rather than talking of poverty as the problem to be solved, and this positive and challenging invocation resulted in a spectacularly sustained process of self-reliant development of China with hard work and shared austerity, in the course of which the material poverty of the people was also reduced significantly. But the question of a party unaccountable to the people remained, and remains, unresolved.

People's self-development as a practical expression of the creativist view of development rejects dogmatism about collectivism as the ultimate emancipation of labour, and leaves the question to the organic evolution of people's collective search for life. It also rejects the notion of macro structural change as a prerequisite of people's self-development, which can start immediately as a process of collective inquiry and action for solving problems with self-determined priorities. It is also suggested that a political leadership which is not involved in promoting people's self-development before a macro structural change will not have the competence for doing so after such a change.

People's self-development implies changing the relations of knowledge, to restore popular knowledge to a status of equality with professional knowledge and advancing 'organic knowledge' as a part of the very evolution of life and not distanced from it. This offers a new role for intellectuals, in initiating 'animation' work with the people to promote their collective self-inquiry and action.

Introduction

During the time I worked with the Bangladesh Planning Commission (1972–4) I learnt two great lessons. One was the utter inadequacy of our professional training as economists to suggest a viable path for the country's development. The other was that the best promise for development lay with the initiatives of the ordinary people.

Our failure as planners may perhaps be summed up as follows. The reasonings and calculations which we had learnt inevitably ended up with a huge resource deficit which could only be met, if at all, by massive foreign assistance. This implied some surrender, at least, of our autonomy as a sovereign nation; the country's economic structure also gets locked into a large import dependence; this, along with the debt burden, would perpetuate the overall continued dependence on foreign assistance; the country's indigenous knowledge, skills and culture would be humiliated in the hands of the alien knowledge and culture embodied in foreign expertise and resources coming in on such a scale; and a beggar mentality rather than a spirit of dignified hard work would dominate the psychology of the society. As economists we were trained mainly in this kind of deficit and dependent 'development' planning. We had not learnt how to plan the mobilisation of the human energy of the people, to plan to develop with what we have, not with what we do not have.

While going through the agonising process of applying the above logic and calculations in our task as 'development' planners, I was also fortunate to have had the opportunity to interact with a number of popular movements in the country in which the people's energy was being mobilised for development activities. I discussed some of these in my Farewell Address to the Planning Commission and elsewhere (Chapter 1 of this book; Rahman 1974a, b). Let me mention here two popular initiatives which had a profound educative effect on me.

One was the Rangpur Self-reliance Movement (Rahman 1974b, 1977). When in 1973 I first visited the Kunjipukur village where this movement started, the villagers proudly showed me the development initiatives they had launched in various fields, e.g. agriculture, health, literacy, cottage industry. And they said: 'We want persons like you to visit us, to give us your advice, your blessings, and the dust of your feet. But we do not want money from anybody.'

I was intrigued, and asked how they had reached this extraordinary consciousness. They replied: 'We have discussed this question. We have realised that ours is a country of villages, and if villages want money from the government, either the government has to take from us and give us back, or beg for us from other countries. So we decided not to ask anything from anybody.'

The other experience was a literacy movement in a few villages in Dinajpur (Rahman, 1986). Here, the village youth mobilised the villagers to wipe out illiteracy from their villages, and did so in two to three months of innovative campaigning. As a member of the Planning Commission I had education as one of my charges, and I had been supervising the calculations of my able colleagues as to how many new school buildings, teachers, literacy manuals, etc. were needed to promote literacy by a respectable percentage per annum. The input–output table was not very encouraging. The village youth, not yet trained in our kind of planning, found out how to solve this problem, and solved it without bothering us.

Unfortunately these two movements did not last long for reasons which I shall not discuss here. But initiatives like these have been taken in many

countries in recent years, either 'spontaneously' or by being 'animated' and
assisted by friendly quarters. *People's self-development* is emerging as a new
urge and vision of elements of the concerned intelligentsia, social activists
and the people's own ranks. In this lecture I propose to discuss the
perceptions and premises of this urge and vision, and contrast them with
two major trends in development thinking – one to be called the 'liberal'
trend, and the other 'socialist' trend – which have dominated the scene until
now.

Popular perceptions and initiatives

Deepest popular urges
Some years back the programme which I coordinate in the ILO[1] facilitated
the coming together of a number of forest-based people's movements in
India, to visit each other and reflect together in a series of workshops over a
period of one year, to articulate a common position on the question of
'forest, ecology and the oppressed'. The result was a revealing statement
(Dasgupta, 1983) in which, among other things, there was a poignant
commentary on the notion and actions of 'elites' in development. In essence,
the commentary was the following:

> We lived with the forest as one organic whole – there was no separation
> between us and the trees, physically, culturally, emotionally, in a daily
> living and growing together.[2] Then you came, with your notion of
> 'development', and separated us. To you the forest was a 'resource', and
> you could not even develop this resource as the forest is disappearing. We
> on the other hand did not count to you, and started becoming slum
> dwellers. We reject your notion of development and we want our life with
> the forest back. But we do not know how to achieve this. Your notion of
> development and your attempt to develop whatever it was, have
> destroyed even our hopes.

Where such elite efforts to promote 'development' have not yet matured
so that hope still exists, and the people have mobilised themselves for
self-development, one finds glimpses of the people's perceptions and urges
which embody what could be interpreted as their own vision of
development.

Reference has been made in chapter 8 to the self-identity of people's
groups in the ORAP movement in Zimbabwe, e.g.: Siwasivuka (we fall and
stand up), Siyaphambili (we go forward), Dingimpilo (search for life),
Sivamerzela (we're doing it ourselves), Vusanani (support each other and get
up).

In apparently simple-minded words these popular articulations of people's collective self-identity reflect deep conceptualisations of popular aspirations. We have seldom even been interested in a genuine dialogue with the people to make us understand what their deepest aspirations are, or in seeking *their* contribution to a social articulation of the notion of development in which the people themselves must be considered the most important actors.

What do the people do, when they get mobilised for self-initiated action? This depends, of course, on the situation in which the people find themselves.

The primacy of human dignity

The Bhoomi Sena movement of *adivasis* in Maharastra, India, which we studied in 1976–7 (Rahman *et al.*, 1979) gave primacy to liberation from bonded labour: a question of human dignity, achieving which was the first step in their self-development. The adivasis then fought for land rights and implementation of the minimum wage law. With an intense self-reliant spirit the movement since then has focused on cultural and political assertion of the adivasis, and assertion in particular of their autonomy of action in all spheres, i.e. their self-determination. The movement is avoiding getting into any kind of dependence on outsiders for 'development', even if this means a slower pace of *economic* development. To these adivasis development is, indeed, the very moving forward authentically, in the search for their own life.

In a different setting, human dignity has featured as a primary urge in some grassroots mobilisation in Bangladesh also. Organisations of landless men and women created by the intervention of Nijera Kori, a rural development agency which does not offer any financial assistance to the people and promotes their self-organisation, have not progressed much economically. But these landless groups consider their organisation to be a solid step forward in their lives. Among other results, as some of these landless groups told me when I visited them in 1984, 'The *jotdar* ('kulak'), the officials and the police can no longer humiliate us – they have to treat us with respect, because we are now organised' (Rahman, personal diary).

For some organised women's groups in the landless categories with utterly meagre economic resources, the perception is even more telling:

> We know that there is no easy and quick solution to our problem of food and clothing. But we as women did not even have the right to speak. In our organisation we can now meet and speak, and share and discuss our problems. We feel that we are now human beings. We look forward to our weekly meetings where we stand up and speak – we can thereby release ourselves as we have never been able to do before, and we now have the courage to speak the truth. (Rahman, personal diary)

Development philosophy

Economic self-development

Experiencing humanhood thus is a great leap forward, the first necessary step in anybody's development. But other mobilised people's groups have had better access to economic resources, some with small productive assets of their own, some acquiring rights to economic assets such as land or fishing water by collective struggle after getting mobilised, and some among them being also able to mobilise external resources like bank credit or donor finance. With these, they have taken initiatives to promote their socio-economic livelihood as well.

[The original paper contained illustrative accounts of the Change Agents Programme of Sri Lanka and the ORAP movement in Zimbabwe. These accounts have been presented in chapters 6 and 8 respectively in this volume and are therefore omitted here.]

Numerous cases that are known indicate that the mobilisation of the people's collective energy generates imaginative solutions to the economic problem alone – production, distribution, marketing, skills training, promoting social welfare and social security and, along with all these, the problem of *employment* – which are not conceived in or available to professionally designed and managed economic development projects and programmes. However, my point is not to highlight in particular the economic dimensions of people's self-development. Some of the popular efforts which have found ways of significant economic betterment within relatively short periods may be *the more fortunate ones*, and many countries may not have such possibilities for reducing economic poverty significantly in the short-to-medium run, as discussed below.

The problem of mass poverty

As a member of the Bangladesh Planning Commission I had made some calculations on the kind of improvement we could most optimistically expect in the incomes of the masses of the country's population over a medium-to-long term. I quote below from a submission I made in March 1972 to the then Prime Minister:

Bangladesh remains one of the world's poorest countries, and will take a long time to meet the aspirations of its people for a decent economic life. Under normal conditions, the income per head in Bangladesh would have been in the order of Rs 400 a year in 1972, or about Rs 33 a month. The devastation of the economy by the war has brought it down, perhaps somewhere between Rs 20 and 25 a month. If income per head grows at the rate of 5 per cent per year from now on, it will take close to 20 years for it to reach Rs 50 per month; for this, total income will have to grow at the rate of 8 per cent or so in view of a high rate of population growth, and such high growth rate in income would be an achievement by any standard. . . . But even Rs 50 a month would hardly be a tolerable level of income in absolute terms; in relative terms this would be even less so as international consumption standards would be rising all the time, and hence aspirations all over the world. . . . As long as some people's incomes remain above the average, rightly or wrongly, it will take longer for the average income of the masses to reach the figure of Rs 50 a month or whatever else may be postulated, than for the national average to reach the same. . . . In short, the possibility of meeting the aspirations of the people in the short run does not exist, and this is not the problem the government is facing today in any meaningful sense. The problem instead is how to carry the suffering people of Bangladesh through a long and extremely hard journey to the realization of their aspirations within the framework of a stable social order. (Rahman, 1972)

With such a perspective, I joined many other elements in the society – in particular from the ranks of the freedom fighters including the students – in advocating 'shared austerity' to prevent the society from falling apart as a result of a scramble for personal appropriation of undue shares of the tiny national 'cake', and to stimulate the society in a mobilisation for social reconstruction with positive values (Rahman, 1973). We failed in this regard, and this is where, in my assessment, we failed fundamentally.

The basic problem that we faced was not special to Bangladesh. For many countries in a state of mass economic 'poverty' and 'unemployment' there may not be an early enough 'cure', in terms of technological and/or social management possibilities with available resources, except for a specially small country which can be 'lifted' quickly by external assistance coupled with its own resources. And for any given country it should be difficult to predict or promise a significant reduction of mass poverty in the near future in view of many factors which are not within the control of the society no matter how mobilised its people are, including the internal and external resistances that are to be expected to the very effort to promote people's mobilisation and self-determined development. In this respect, the women's groups in Bangladesh referred to earlier may have shown a better perception of the problem than those development professionals who theorise about reduction of mass poverty, and the political forces who promise so generously. We have seen three 'decades of development' and for most of such countries the problem of mass 'poverty' and 'unemployment' has aggravated, or in any case appears to be intractable.[3]

In this sense, viewing the 'development' problem as many quarters do in terms of eradication of (economic) 'poverty', providing the population with ('entitlements' to) the 'basic needs', etc., is liable to raise aspirations more than can be fulfilled in any given generation. And this raises an operational question of social motivation to work constructively for the realisation of such a goal. As suggested above, the *first step* towards a possible solution of the problem requires constructive cooperation by those – the 'present generation' – who may hardly be significant material beneficiaries of the solution. But the operational development problem concerns this very generation, which has to be motivated to participate in a social endeavour towards what may be at best a gradual eradication of poverty from which they themselves may benefit very little. The theoretical economist's answer to this question – and I have myself been a party in this intellectual game-playing – is to conceive an 'inter-temporal social utility function' of 'infinite time horizon', and ask the present generation(s) to feel happy because their sacrifices would maximise this utility function. But we have not considered how precisely a mother will explain this utility function to her hungry and shivering child who is, furthermore, attracted by the toys of the elite's son. Failing this, the mother may have to steal, or try other devious ways of acquiring some privileges for her child *at the expense of others*. There go the social values, and the society gets into a race for private aggrandisement by depriving others, in which only a minority can win at the expense of the majority.[4] And as we see today in so many countries, the very concept of the nation state in the 'liberal' political philosophy as a guardian of society and trustee for its development (and for future generations) gives way to attempts by elements of the society to grab state power and transform the state also into a private enterprise for maximising personal aggrandisement as fast as possible, by depriving the masses of the present generation as well as by mortgaging the future of the society.

I suggest that a focus on economic needs and economic 'poverty', a culture of development discourse that becomes preoccupied with what the people *do not have*, gets trapped in the negative thinking and dependence orientation that this generates, rather than motivating the society to become constructively engaged in moving forward. With a constructive engagement, the people show imaginative ways of progressively fulfilling their needs and urges. This includes, naturally, their need and urge for economic betterment. However, in view of what has been said above, it is the constructive engagement, rather than economic achievement *per se*, which is the more universal aspect of popular initiatives – the fact that the people are mobilised, *engaged* in tasks set by themselves and going about them together, pooling resources and energy whereby they can do better than walking alone, drawing strength and sustaining power from a shared life and effort. Sometimes they succeed and sometimes they fail (in their own terms); but through all this they move forward in the evolution of (search for) their lives. It is such a positive evolution that is possible, and this is important in its own right, both for the people involved and for the future generations to whom they can pass on the heritage of constructive social engagement to move through life with all its odds, showing their creativity and a spirit of tackling challenges, developing thereby as a *human personality*.

Two views of development: the consumerist view

Philosophically speaking, there are two opposing views of development. One is a *consumerist* view, which regards the human being primarily as a consumer of goods and services. Basically, 'development' is seen in this view as an expansion of the flow of consumption. As a means to bring this about, an expansion of the productive capacity of the country is needed, but the primary logic of development remains a progressive increase in consumption. For a time, development was identified with aggregate economic growth to bring about a progressively higher flow of aggregate consumption irrespective of its distribution (the 'reactionary' view). Gradually, the interpersonal distribution question was raised, in terms of who *benefits* from such development *as consumers* (the 'liberal' view). The development debate then focused on questions such as growth first or distribution first, or whether we can have growth with distribution simultaneously, and how can 'entitlements' (command over goods and services) be truly ensured for all, etc. This debate continues to this date; but the basic consumerist view prevails,[5] concerned with who gets what as a consumer, and what is the intertemporal and interpersonal trade-off. But the question that this view does not ask is who in the society is able to take the needed initiative to produce the goods and services, and what happens to the different sections of the population as *creative beings*, i.e. *the distribution of the power and opportunity to fulfil themselves by creative acts*.[6]

The notion of 'poverty' follows the same viewpoint. The concern here is whether a person has the necessary income or access or 'entitlement' to the bundle of goods and services postulated to be the needs of human beings as consumers. 'Poverty' in terms of *lack of an 'entitlement' to develop as a creative being* is, again, not expressed as a concern. The problem of 'poverty' in this sense is a consumer's rather than a creator's problem, focused on the 'poor' not being able to consume the things desired (or biologically needed) rather than not having the opportunity to produce (or command) them through their creative acts.

It is worth reflecting on how the 'development' problem might have presented itself naturally to our forebears – let us say the earliest human communities. They *had to* create what they wanted, and, moreover, had no external standards to consider in deciding what they wanted. Given this situation, I should think, they could not have had any static set of 'wants' – their wants, to be meaningful, had to be defined and redefined continuously in the dynamic context of evolving possibilities of what they themselves could create. In this sense, a difference between wants and creative urges did not exist for them. They were not 'poor' – it was their life to move forward by applying their creative powers.

The two, however – wants and creative urges – got separated as a result of, first, class separation between people by which control over productive resources got polarised, giving the dominant class power over the lives of others. Second, the dominant class and its allies (together, the 'elites') developed certain consumption standards and were able to influence by their social power the culture and aspirations of society, so that to attain these standards came to be regarded widely as the purpose of life itself. This has resulted in *aspirations and urges dissociated from the immediate creative possibilities of the people.* In turn this is causing pointless frustration among the masses besides strengthening mass dependence on the elites, and submission to a view of development as the fulfilment of such aspirations, hence to submission of the initiative for development to the more 'successful', in the hope that such 'development' could possibly be 'delivered' by those who have attained it themselves. Many 'class struggles', local as well as on a wider scale, retain this consumer consciousness, with material aspirations which are way beyond the creative possibilities of the working class; implicitly, such struggles retain a dependency orientation, cherishing the hope that some other power (class) will deliver the kind of material development needed to satisfy such aspirations.

Basic *human* need: the creativist view
In recent times, the concept of satisfaction of the 'basic needs' of the population has emerged as a primary objective of development in liberal development thinking. Interestingly, the five 'basic needs' which have been identified – food, clothing, housing, medical care, education – are in some form or other the needs of *animals* as well, who typically do not create (materially, socially, culturally), except at a very elementary and static level (e.g. birds' nests). But the distinctive *humanness* in us is not in needing these elementary means of survival, but what the combination of our distinctive brain and limbs can do and, therefore, the urge we must have as human beings to fulfil this power. This urge is often for the sake of creation itself, but the process of satisfying this urge also creates the means of satisfying whatever other needs, 'basic' or 'non-basic', we wish to and can satisfy, *according to our own priorities.* Through such creation we evolve – *develop* – as creative beings. This is the basic *human* need – to fulfil our creative potential in ever newer ways – although it may not be expressed or asserted by all because of the conditioning resulting from structural social and cultural domination mentioned above.

As opposed to the consumerist view of the liberal school, there exists a *creativist* view of development which regards the human race primarily as creative beings. In recent times this view has been expressed by activist intellectuals working directly with the people to promote their self-development (Tilakaratna, 1987; Fernandez, 1986). But the underlying philosophy is not new. This is, of course, the central message in trends of some major religions.[7] At the level of scientific discourse this view was, perhaps, first suggested in the philosophy of Karl Marx.

The philosophy of Marx

Marx viewed human beings primarily as creators who because of their class situation either fulfil or become alienated from their creative power. Looking at the development of capitalism Marx was excited by its spectacular creativity: the central focus of his analysis of capitalism was the revolutionary development of *productive forces* in this phase of human history. Likewise, the central argument in his theory of revolution was the need for, and what he considered the inevitability of, the overthrow of capitalism as its creative phase comes to an end, and as further development of the productive forces would be possible only in the hands of the 'working class'. In tracing the development of capitalism Marx observed the phenomenon of 'exploitation' as the primary means by which the capitalist class appropriates the resources needed for the development of the productive forces in its hands; Marx's primary concern here was to explain the process of capitalist accumulation rather than to condemn it. In fact, he praised the capitalist class for the practice of *thrift* which he observed in them, as a necessary virtue to obtain *a high rate of investment* and hence development of the productive forces (see notes 11, 12).

While he was thus excited by the creativity of capitalism in its 'glorious' days, Marx saw the working class alienated from its own creative potentials and power, the free exercise of which alone could give it fulfilment as labour. The working class *as a producer* and not as a consumer must, therefore, revolt and take over the means of production, to fulfil itself as producer. The history of 'man' (as unalienated worker) would then truly begin. This implied that, through the revolutionary development of the productive forces in its hands, labour would eventually produce (and control) enough for everyone to have according to his 'need': but such (material) needs satisfaction would follow human creativity and does not appear in Marx as the primary motive force for human effort.

Experiments in socialism

Marx's writings, of course, shift from the philosophical to the political–economic to the polemical, and are separated by time and context, so that they may not necessarily always give the same message. However, the greatest followers of Marx have also been inspired by a creativist vision of the working people. Lenin had conceived of socialism as a social construction in which 'the majority of the working people engage in independent creative work as makers of history' (Lenin, 1918a: 646). But, unfortunately, Lenin's political theory of the party of professional revolutionaries led by intellectuals as the 'vanguard of the proletariat' with an 'advanced consciousness' contained the seeds of major distortions (Rahman, 1988). As it turned out, the Bolshevik Party increasingly centralised its own power *vis-à-vis* the workers' and peasants' soviets, and this could only strengthen the negative forces within the party seeking to impose elite and bureaucratic rule on the masses. In his last years Lenin became keenly aware of the degenerating tendencies in the party and struggled to his last day, unsuccessfully, to reverse this trend. But he did not see his own theory of the party, claiming that ultimate wisdom resided in 'revolutionary' intellectuals,[8] and the absolute power assumed by the party, to be the root of the problem.

What emerged in the Soviet bloc under the rule of such parties was far from the above Marxist vision of the working class as the principal architect of socialism. On the contrary, the notion of 'advanced consciousness' of the 'vanguards' was invoked to justify stifling dictatorship by the party over the working people.[9] This great distortion of socialism was accompanied by official interpretations and articulations of the ideology which had little relation with Marxism. Initiatives by the workers and peasants were hardly ever encouraged, and in glorifying the achievements of 'socialism' such initiatives and achievements, if they were taken at all, were hardly ever highlighted (after Lenin). Resistance to such distortion of socialism and dictatorial policies surfaced from time to time, coming from the Marxist intelligentsia as well as from the working class, only to be ruthlessly suppressed. Finally, the sheer incompetence in economic management, coupled with the corruption of elements in the party leadership, was challenged first in Poland by the working class (Solidarity) and subsequently in the citadel of the Soviet bloc by the very leader of the 'vanguards' (Gorbachev). Today, 'socialism' of this variety is being dismantled fast in Soviet Russia, Poland and Hungary, and the moral appeal of such models of socialism has all but eroded.[10]

The other great revolutionary leader of this century, Mao, encouraged people's initiatives more passionately, challenging the people to 'be fired with great, lofty proletarian aspirations and dare to break paths unexplored and scale heights yet unclimbed' (Han Suyin, 1976: 213). In this way Mao was able to keep the vast 'poor' Chinese masses engaged in a sustained process of development with considerable (shared) austerity,[11] building the economic base of a possible 'modern' China, in the process advancing significantly in meeting the material 'basic needs' of the population as well by a self-reliant mobilisation of the people which inspired progressive forces all over the world. I suggest that this, one of the two greatest developmental feats of this century,[12] could not have been achieved if instead of appealing to the creative spirit of the Chinese people Mao had highlighted their 'poverty' as the main problem to be solved. This is a basic question of what motivates the human spirit to move forward: one cannot move forward thinking of what one does not have; one can only move forward thinking of what one can accomplish with what one has.[13] However, Mao also was unable to solve the question of the party, a structure which was 'above' the people and susceptible to being taken over by elitist forces to rule over the people. The Cultural Revolution appears to have been Mao's own answer to such tendencies, but its strength rested heavily on his personal backing and it was no lasting, if any, solution to the problem.[14]

With the seizure of power by anti-Maoists as soon as Mao died, the Chinese revolution also started to unwind. Among the reversals on so many fronts it is pertinent to note that, while the people's creativity rather than their 'wants' were highlighted in Mao's time (something never highlighted in post-Lenin Russia or for that matter in the Soviet bloc), the new leadership in China started talking more of the 'poverty' and 'unemployment' of the masses than of their initiatives and innovativeness in taking on challenging tasks. Both undoubtedly existed and exist in both Mao's China and today's China; but from what one chooses to highlight one's basic philosophy (ideology) of social life and purpose is revealed. However, the shift in the ideology of China has been limited to the economic sphere and remains to be complemented by a parallel shift in the political sphere, thus creating a tension of the first order whose final resolution is still to be seen.

Many contemporary left parties seeking ways of coming to power in pre-revolutionary societies also show tendencies that contain the seeds of degeneration. The notion of 'advanced consciousness' of revolutionary intellectuals persists, and the revolutionary leaders go to the people 'as theoreticians, as propagandists, as agitators, and as organisers' in the Leninist tradition (Lenin, 1967a: 165), i.e. to indoctrinate and mobilise the people politically, but not to learn from them or to animate or work with them to promote their 'self-awareness' and self-development. I have argued elsewhere (Rahman, 1987, 1988) that the claim to 'advanced consciousness' is false: the consciousnesses of persons living very different lives (social existence) are not comparable within the same epistemological paradigm; and the fact that revolutionary intellectuals rather than the working people usually assume leadership of macro revolutionary movements is explained not by the former's intellectual superiority but by the constraints of the daily life's struggle and work obligations of the working people. This false claim of 'advanced consciousness' of intellectuals justifies and perpetuates the polarisation of the *relations of knowledge*, a major force in determining the power relations in a society irrespective of the *relations of material production* (Rahman, 1982). If ever the 'revolution' takes place under such leadership, it can only be expected to reconstruct the hierarchical relations between professionals – 'revolutionary intellectuals' as well as the general technocracy – and the people, a relation completely antithetical to the Marxist vision of the working people creating its own history. I shall return to this question in the 'Conclusion' of this lecture.

Two preoccupations of the left

Those who are working to promote people's self-development include activists who have had associations with formal left trends, but who got disillusioned by the dogmatism or totalitarian tendencies and other failures of such trends. Other activists have identified themselves with the objective of liberation of people's creativity without the mediation of a formal radical ideology (e.g. Marxism). They are a new breed of 'humanists', driven by the urge to see the human spirit truly liberated. Some of them – possibly many – would have ideological or intellectual differences with some or other of the 'Marxist' premises and assertions (whether these were enunciated by Marx himself or not). Among the issues that may be debated, the question of individualism *vis-à-vis* collectivism is a very important one.

Collectivism
Marxism has been identified with collectivism as one of its principal visions, and indeed this has been a major bone of contention in the great confrontation between the two rival ideologies of the present era. Marx himself saw in collectivism the final emancipation of labour from a state of alienation from one's supposedly true self – the collective man or woman.

It may be recalled that Marx was seeing collectivist production relations coming after capitalism in its advanced stage when all labour has become *associated* labour. The transition from associated labour to collectivism is a matter simply of such labour seizing the means of production and owning them together rather than dividing them up. This may be viewed as a natural step 'forward', and in predicting this Marx was expounding an *organic logic*. From this point of view Marx's vision of collectivism as the final emancipation of labour may be seen as a philosophical rationalisation of what he envisaged as the natural, organic evolution of the relations of production.

Actual socialist revolutions, however, have occurred and have been contemplated to occur, in societies at an early or pre-capitalist stage, in which associated labour has not become the dominant form of labour. In such societies the above organic logic to move to collectivism does not, in general, apply. There arises, then, the question of *organic* evolution of production relations in such societies where the people get mobilised for collective effort for their self-development, be it on a macro scale, where state power has changed into the hands of forces committed to the release of the people's creativity, or on a local scale.

Lenin, facing this question particularly for Soviet agriculture after the Bolshevik Revolution, desired the transition to collectivism to be indeed organic, and was against an attempt to collectivise agriculture by coercion. Stalin's forced collectivisation violated this organic logic, and the result was disastrous in terms of agricultural production itself (development of the productive forces in agriculture). The peasantry could hardly have been expected to feel 'liberated' by such a drastic coercive measure. What with the peasantry's response and Stalin's own view of 'socialism', what was conceived as 'collectivism' degenerated into a (disguised) capitalist form of production relations which Gorbachev recently has summed up poignantly: 'On state and collective farms, people have become divorced from the land and the means of production. . . . We have turned them from masters of their land into daily labourers' (Gorbachev, 1988). In China, Mao tried to promote collectivism (in agriculture) more organically, moving step by step from 'lower-order' to 'higher-order' cooperation, encouraging, highlighting and inspiring collectivist efforts, and finally completing the process by central policy when he assessed that the bulk of the peasantry might be ready for it. The result is part of the great accomplishment of Mao, as already discussed. However, it is noteworthy that the spirit of 'individualism' has not disappeared in China, notwithstanding Mao's vision and efforts, and seems to have been reasserting itself in response to the policies favouring private initiative which the present regime has been progressively taking.

Socialist experiments of this century do not demonstrate that human beings can transcend their individualism and become fully collectivist men or women. In this sense Marx's vision of collectivism as the final emancipation of labour remains questionable, independently of the organic logic of his specific model of transition from already associated labour to full collectivism.

Those who are working with the people to promote their self-development do not, by and large, have a dogmatic position on the question of collectivism. The people, when they are mobilised and deliberate themselves to set priorities and tasks, do a lot of pooling of resources and talents, and cooperation, and engage in a lot of collectivist initiatives (as several illustrations in this volume show). They do so as they see the objective advantage of doing so, and as they feel inspired from working together to identify and solve problems and develop greater trust in each other. The poorer and the more oppressed the people are, the more, other things being equal, are they likely to see the advantage of such cooperation and solidarity among themselves for material improvement as well as for resisting oppression and for emotional security. The development of such cooperation among the people may be enhanced by sensitive 'animation' work, but cannot be forced, without alienating them, by some ideological principle external to the organic evolution of their life, a principle to be applied mechanically (e.g. collective ownership of land or such other 'means of production'). And it may not be guaranteed that full collectivism may be attained some day, or even that there will be no shift back towards more individualism, in a possible permanent movement of dialectical tension between these two identities of the human species.[15] There cannot be people's self-development with any ideological dogmatism external to the people's evolving life and consciousness.

In any case, with the evolution of the great socialist experiments of the century towards greater individualism, the ideological debate over individualism and collectivism is weakening. At the same time it is being witnessed that rule in the name of the people and 'democracy' in the (so-called) free world, and in the name of 'dictatorship of the proletariat' and 'socialist democracy' in the (so-called) socialist world, actually represents rule of some category of elite over the people. This is clarifying the real ideological issue as the question of real social power: whether the working people could have the power to determine their own destiny within a framework of horizontal social interaction with other classes, as equals and not as inferiors. This, ultimately, is the question of real *democracy*, not the democracy merely of periodic elections and the freedom to express words on what should be done, but the freedom and opportunity of the people to take the initiative to do it themselves.

Structural change

As I have suggested, people's self-development can start even under conditions of extreme resource shortage – mobilising themselves for assertion of human dignity and self-determination, and to cooperate to accomplish collectively determined tasks, in the process developing in capabilities and in human personality. In fact, some conditions of the acutest resource shortage – e.g. under natural calamities – are known to have produced the most impressive popular mobilisations with such self-developmental elements. The possibilities and pace of self-development, however, are naturally constrained by the availability of physical resources to work with, and as observed before, people's self-mobilisations themselves have often been directed towards achieving greater access to such resources by collective negotiation and struggle. In countries where the bulk of physical resources are controlled by elites, a redistribution of the control over such resources in addition to redistribution of the social power to take development initiatives is necessary. *This* distribution question – rather than the question of distribution of 'incomes' *per se* or 'benefits from development', etc. – is the basic question of *equity* in the creativist view of development.

While thus calling for radical structural change in societies with polarised control over physical resources, this viewpoint questions the identification of *people's ownership* with *state ownership* which, as we have noted, may actually separate the people from the means of production (and thus inhibit rather than promote their self-development). The distribution question is, therefore, one of giving the people (individually and/or collectively) real control over resources to work with to develop their own potentials, not to be dictated by a state-appointed managerial technocracy. The concept of 'socialism' defined as 'social ownership' of the means of production which has often been identified with state ownership needs in this light a thorough re-examination.

There is need for rethinking also on the tasks *before* such structural change is accomplished, and on the prerequisite for such change to truly liberate and promote people's creativity rather than stifle it with new forms of domination. Most left quarters have been preoccupied with the *macro* question of capturing state power to initiate 'socialist' development before action is initiated to animate the people in self-developmental mobilisation. But micro level initiatives to promote people's self-development are showing that this need not await a redistribution of resources even for physical resource-poor communities who can start developing today at least in human personality, social values and social organisation, and *who themselves consider such advancement to be a positive gain*; on the other hand the question of macro structural change for most societies where this is desired remains uncertain and often intractable; it is not very convincing to suggest that generations should keep on waiting for the elusive 'revolution' before mobilising themselves to move forward with what they have and what they can acquire through local struggles. There is, furthermore, another profound need for working to promote micro level people's self-development right now, to enhance the very possibility that a macro level social change, if it does occur some day, may truly release and promote the people's creativity. I suggest that a *political leadership which is not involved in people's self-development now will not be able to promote this after coming into power, because it will not know what it means or how it can be animated.* This – what a leadership can do after coming into power – is also a question of organic logic resting on what it has done, and hence learnt, previously. As a corollary, the hope of a macro level structural change to promote people's self-development rather than even to suppress the popular initiatives we are witnessing today at a local scale, lies in the emergence of an 'organic vanguard' which is rooted in such popular movements and does not claim to be above (and unaccountable to) the people.[16]

Conclusion: breaking the monopoly of knowledge

Three years ago I had a four-hour dialogue with about one hundred leaders of landless workers' organisations in Bangladesh from about thirty contiguous villages.[17] This was one of the most stimulating 'seminars' I have had, surpassing in the intellectual quality of the discussions, in my judgement, many academic seminars I have attended. We discussed questions concerning their immediate environments as well as questions of national policy, politics and social change. On most of these questions the landless leaders – not a few, but many of them – had well thought-out positions: 'we have discussed this question for the last five years, and our thinking is this . . .' was a typical beginning of the answer to many of my questions.

The point is not whether their position was correct or not. The world's greatest social thinkers and scientists have made mistakes; sometimes the greater you are, the more profound is the mistake you make. The point is that the ordinary working people are capable of social inquiry and analysis, and that this capability can be enhanced by practice.

Anyone's self-development starts, as it must, with self-understanding to guide his or her own action, and is a process in which self-understanding develops as action is taken and reviewed. Formal efforts at social 'development' have, however, been in the hands of elites who have in general considered themselves wiser than the people, and instead of seeking to promote the people's self-inquiry and understanding have sought to impose their own ideas of 'development'. In doing this they have promoted their own self-'development' in some ways, while bringing the world to the dismal state in which we find it today. In any case this had to be at the cost of people's self-development, for one cannot develop with somebody else's ideas. This has been, I suggest, also the single most important intellectual error in many otherwise committed efforts towards social change for people's liberation which seek to *indoctrinate* the people in a vertical relation with them, and give priority to structural change over *liberation of the mind*. Only with a liberated mind (of the people), which is free to inquire and then conceive and plan what is to be created, can structural change release the creative potentials of the people. In this sense liberation of the mind is the primary task, both *before* and *after* structural change.

Organic knowledge and participatory research
This implies breaking the monopoly of knowledge in the hands of the elites, i.e. giving the people their right to assert their existing knowledge to start with; giving them the opportunity and assistance, if needed, to advance their self-knowledge through self-inquiry as the basis of their action, and to review themselves their experiences from action to further advance their

self-knowledge (Chapter 6 of this book; Rahman, 1982). In this reflection–action–reflection process of the people (people's praxis), professional knowledge can be useful only in a dialogue with people's knowledge on an equal footing through which both can be enriched, and not in the arrogance of assumed superior wisdom. Altering thus the relations of knowledge, to produce and advance 'organic knowledge'[18] as a part of the very evolution of life rather than abstract (synthetic) knowledge produced in academic laboratories to be imposed upon life, is a central commitment of what is being termed as 'participatory research' (Hall *et al.*, 1981). This is also the first and continuous task of 'animation' work to promote people's self-development.

Such animation work to promote organic knowledge offers a new role for intellectuals, distinct from their traditional role as 'uninvolved' social researchers, or involved social 'revolutionaries' in political structures separate from and 'above' the people. Professionally, and also circum-stantially as suggested before, intellectuals as a class remain in the more privileged position *vis-à-vis* the ordinary working people to take a leading role in social transformative work. The roles that they have been taking traditionally have contributed to keeping the people subordinate and dominated. A more humane and liberating role can be taken by the intelligentsia, and thereby the intellectuals can even satisfy their urge to provide leadership towards social change: a new kind of leadership that invites, stimulates and assists the people to collectively inquire and act for themselves.

Notes

1. Participatory Organisations of the Rural Poor (PORP).
2. Cf. 'My pain is entwined with the grass of the pathway which she treaded, and trembles with its breath' ('Ami Srabono akashey oi', a song of Rabindranath Tagore). By ignoring the organic relation with nature that we had, our 'development' efforts have not only brought about the ecological crisis which we are lamenting today, but we are also destroying a vital part of ourselves.
3. Much was expected of Vietnam, after this small, 'poor' nation humbled the world's mightiest war machine in an epic military struggle. One-and-a-half decades from then, the chairman of the State Planning Commission reported to the National Assembly, on 23–29 December 1987, that the socio-economic situation was 'continuously worsening'; unemployment was a growing problem and a cause of 'greater social instability'; the living conditions of the working people and the armed forces were 'very difficult' and even 'serious' in some areas; and 'social negativism' had developed (*Keesing's Record of World Events*, May 1988).
4. Such individualistic motivation has in some countries generated a dynamic entrepreneurial class which has taken a society 'forward'; but this has not

necessarily been a solution to the poverty problem.

5. Sen, who introduced the notion of 'entitlement', goes beyond entitlement at what he calls 'capabilities', converging with the creativist view of development:

> When we are concerned with such notions as the well-being of a person, or standard of living, or *freedom in the positive sense*, we need the concept of capabilities. We have to be concerned with *what a person can do*, and this is not the same thing as how much pleasure or desire fulfilment he gets from these activities ('utility') nor what commodity bundles he can command ('entitlements'). Ultimately, therefore, we have to go not merely beyond the calculus of national product and aggregate real income, but also that of entitlements over commodity bundles viewed on their own. (Sen, 1983; *italics added*)

The notion of 'desire fulfilment', of course, need not be limited to consumerist desire but could be extended to creativist desire which I have suggested as the basic *human* desire (see below).

6. The theoretical height of the consumerist view is the notion of maximising the 'intertemporal utility function' which is primarily concerned with the time-stream of consumption, considering *saving* as a necessary *sacrifice* to maximise this function, rather than being *a positive strategy to develop one's creative powers*. Likewise, labour is considered to have a disutility to be minimised, rather than being *the* expression of human creativity.

Tevoedjre (1978: 83) combines basic needs satisfaction with creativity in a framework of frugal living and solidarity: 'A regime of convivial frugality based on a self-sufficient collective development, which mobilises the energies of peoples involved in the creation of their own future and is aimed at satisfying the basic needs of a society united by a common feeling of solidarity – this I believe to be the foundation of a new kind of economy.' The reference to basic needs is redundant and may be misleading – a *self-reliant creative* people would naturally satisfy whatever needs, material as well as non-material (emotional, cultural), they prioritise themselves irrespective of what others may consider to be the 'basic needs' which they ought to satisfy.

7. E.g. 'I am the Creative Being' in Sufism, Islam; 'I am the Life' in Christianity; and 'I am the Ultimate Soul' in Hinduism.

8. ' . . . one very first and most pressing duty is to help train working class revolutionaries who will be on the same level *in regard to Party activity* as the revolutionaries from amongst the intellectuals (we emphasise the words 'in regard to Party activity', for although necessary, it is neither so easy nor so pressingly necessary to bring the workers up to the level of intellectuals in other respects). Attention, therefore, must be devoted principally to raising the workers to the level of revolutionaries; it is not at all our task to *descend* to the level of the working masses' (Lenin, 1902: 205). This is the key statement of Lenin implying that the intellectuals are ahead of (above) the workers, which got crystallised into a theory of 'advanced consciousness' of the vanguard intellectuals held by Leninist vanguards everywhere.

9. 'The free people's state has been transformed into the free state. Taken in its grammatical sense, a free state is one where the state is free in relation to its citizens, hence a state with a despotic government.' Ironically, this statement in

Engels' *Critique of the Gotha Programme* which Lenin quotes in his *State and Revolution* (Lenin, 1918B: 315) can be applied to what the party made of the state in the Soviet bloc.

10. In a recent visit (July 1989) to a Hungarian village to initiate participatory research, I was struck by the observation of a retired cooperative worker who said: 'What hurts most is the indignity of being *forced* to vote for the chairman who I know is corrupt.'

11. With an accumulation rate in the order of 30 per cent over 1951–78, the highest sustained rate any 'poor' country has shown in recent history (Ghose, 1984: 258, Table 83).

12. The other feat is Japan's, which has also shown exemplary *hard work* and *thrift* in order to become a leading economic power of the world.

13. One of the first well-known statements of Mao after the victory of the Chinese Revolution was: 'China has stood up.' Note the similarity with the names of the ORAP groups in Zimbabwe cited above.

14. The question here is the crucial one of creating people's power as *countervailing power*, and of keeping this power alive and effective. As I have stated elsewhere, 'Countervailing power is a living, collective consciousness and a vigilance of the people against the abuse of formal power, and a capability to resist such abuse and to assert people's will if formal power deviates' (Rahman, 1981: 45). This presupposes people's own critical awareness at all times, and hence a permanent process of people's collective review and analysis of what is happening. Mao had great respect for the wisdom of the people and asked the intellectuals to learn from them; but it appears that he considered the task of *synthesis* (even of people's own ideas) to belong to intellectuals. Mao Tse-tung's thought itself was claimed to be synthesised people's thought, not, however, called 'people's thought' but named instead after the 'great teacher'. This may have been one of Mao's great mistakes: the people waited upon the teacher to tell them what their thoughts were, and turned to new teachers after the old master died. The recent 'participatory (action) research' movement believes, and is demonstrating, that the people can synthesise their own thoughts, and a necessary and central task in developing people's countervailing power is to give the people the confidence in their ability to do so (see Conclusion).

15. Unless one wishes to believe the mystics, human beings are separated from each other by space and time, and to relate to each other entails, therefore, *a cost*. Rational individuals are expected to weigh this cost against the gain of any form of cooperation. At a certain state of existence – e.g. extreme scarcity of material resources to work with (material poverty) or conditions of natural calamity – the advantage of cooperation may be seen to outweigh its cost, and individuals then may join hands and pool resources to work together for *individual advancement* itself. This is the objective basis of human cooperation. The subjective (emotional) basis – e.g. a sense of collective identity – is more difficult to track down, and it appears that such identity may also cut across 'class relations' and express itself in family, kinship, ethnic or religious bonds which may either support or act counter to the objective basis for cooperation in a 'class' framework. We must not forget that even under conditions of associated labour in production, labour spends only a part of its time in the production process, and has an individual social life of its own outside this process. Thus the tension between individualism and collectivism may very well be permanent

notwithstanding the nature of relations of production.

16. In a different way, André Gunder Frank and Marta Fuentes are also looking at contemporary 'social movements' as the hope for a 'socialist' future:

> it is becoming increasingly clear that the road to a better 'socialist' future . . . does not lead via 'really existing socialism'. . . . The real transition to a 'socialist' alternative to the present world economy, society and polity . . . may be much more in the hands of the social movements . . . which can transform the world in new directions. (Frank and Fuentes, 1988)

17. In the programme of the Bangladesh Rural Advancement Committee (BRAC) which has a literacy-cum-awareness-raising (conscientisation) content of the Freirian type.

18. The term was first suggested, to the best of my knowledge, in a *Workshop on People's Initiative to Overcome Poverty* at the East–West Center, the University of Hawaii, Honolulu (March–April 1989), which I had the privilege to attend.

References

Chavunduka, Dexter M. *et al.* (1985) *Khuluma Usenza, the Story of ORAP in Zimbabwe's Rural Development*, Bulawayo: The Organisation of Rural Associations for Progress.

Dasgupta, Subhachari (1983) 'Forest, ecology and the oppressed, a study from the point of view of the forest dwellers', ILO Research Report (unpublished).

Draper, Hal (1977) *Karl Marx's Theory of Revolution, Vol. 1: State and Bureaucracy*, Monthly Review Press.

Fernandez, Maria E. (1986) *Participatory Action-Research and the Farming Systems Approach with Highland Peasants*, Columbia: Department of Rural Sociology, University of Missouri.

Frank, André Gunder and Fuentes, Marta (1988) 'Nine theses on social movements', *IFDA Dossier*, No. 63, January/February 1988.

Freire, Paulo (1972) *Cultural Action for Freedom*, Harmondsworth: Penguin.

Ghose, A. K. (1984) 'The industrial development strategy and rural reforms in post-Mao China', K. Griffin (ed.) *Institutional Reform and Economic Development in the Chinese Countryside*, London: Macmillan.

Gorbachev, M. (1988) Guidelines for the Central Party Meeting of 28 October.

Gramsci, Antonio (1971) *Selections from the Prison Notebooks*, edited and translated by Quintin Hoare and Geoffrey Nowell Smith, London: Lawrence & Wishart.

Hall, Budd *et al.* (1981) 'Participatory research: development and issues', *Convergence*, Vol. XIV, No. 3.

Han Suyin (1976) *Wind in the Tower, Mao Tsetung and the Chinese Revolution 1949–1975*, London: Jonathan Cape.

ILO (PORP) (1988) *Promoting People's Participation and Self-reliance, Proceedings of the Regional Workshop of Trainers in Participatory Rural Development, Tagaytay, the Philippines, August 15–28*, Geneva: ILO.

Kofi, Tetteh A. (1981) 'Problems and prospects of the transition from agrarianism to socialism: the case of Angola, Guinea Bissau and Mozambique', *World Development*, Vol. 9, No. 9/10, September/October 1981.

Lenin, V. I. [1902] (1967) 'What is to be done?', *Selected Works*, Vol. 1, Moscow: Progress Publishers.

Lenin, V. I. [1918a] (1967) 'The immediate tasks of the Soviet government', *Selected Works*, Vol. 2, Moscow: Progress Publishers.

Lenin, V. I. [1918b] (1967) 'The state and revolution', *Selected Works*, Vol. 2, Moscow: Progress Publishers.

Marx, Karl (1844) 'Critical notes on the king of Prussia and social reform', Marx and Engels, *Werke*, Vol. I.

Nyoni, Sithembiso (1989) 'People's power in Zimbabwe' in Rahman and Fals Borda (1990).

Participatory Research Group (1983) *Participatory Research, An Annotated Bibliography*, Toronto.

Rahman, Md. Anisur (1972) *The First Step*, 8 March 1972 (mimeo).

Rahman, Md. Anisur (1973) 'Priorities and methods for socialist development of Bangladesh', Paper presented at the International Economic Association Conference on the Development of Bangladesh within the Framework of a Socialist Economy, 7 January 1973.

Rahman, Md. Anisur (1974a) 'Planners and the society', *The Wave Weekly*, 3 November 1974.

Rahman, Md. Anisur (1974b) *The Famine*, University of Dhaka (mimeo).

Rahman, Md. Anisur (1977) 'Goodbye to gruel kitchens', *New Internationalist*, No. 49, March 1977.

Rahman, Md. Anisur with G. V. S. de Silva *et al.*(1979) 'Bhoomi Sena; a struggle for people's power', *Development Dialogue*, No. 2.

Rahman, Md. Anisur (1981) *Participation of the Rural Poor in Development, Development: Seeds of Change – From Village to Global Order*, Rome: Society for International Development.

Rahman Md. Anisur (1982) 'The theory and practice of Participatory Action Research', *IFDA Dossier*, No. 31, September/October 1982. (Chapter 6 of this book.)

Rahman, Md. Anisur (ed.) (1984) *Grass-roots Participation and Self-reliance, Experiences in South and South-east Asia*, New Delhi, Oxford and IBH.

Rahman, Md. Anisur (1987) 'The role and significance of participatory organisations of the rural poor in alternative strategies of rural development: theory and experience – an overview', *Third World Legal Studies*, International Third World Legal Studies Association, Valparaiso University School of Law.

Rahman, Md. Anisur (1988) 'Ganogabeshana o Shwamaj Paribartan', *Lokayat*, March 1983, pp. 41–52.

Rahman, Md. Anisur (1989a) *Glimpses of the 'Other Africa'*, World Employment Programme Research Working Paper, WEP 10/WEP 48, Geneva: ILO. (Chapter 8 of this book.)

Rahman, Md. Anisur (1989b) 'The challenge of promoting people's self-reliance: highlights of a regional workshop of trainers in participatory rural development', *Lokniti*, Vol. 6, No. 1.

Rahman, Md. Anisur with Fals Borda, Orlando, (ed.) (1990) *Action and Knowledge: Breaking the Monopoly with Participatory Action Research*, Apex Press.

Sen (1983) 'Development: which way now?' *The Economic Journal*, Vol. 93, No. 372, December, pp. 745–62.

Tevoedjre, Albert (1978) *Poverty, Wealth of Mankind*, Oxford: Pergamon, Systems Science and World Order Library.

Tilakaratna, S. (1984) 'Grass-roots self-reliance in Sri Lanka: organisations of betel and coir yarn producers', in Rahman (1984).

Tilakaratna, S. (1985) *The Animator in Participatory Rural Development: Some Experiences from Sri Lanka*, World Employment Programme Research Working Paper, WEP 10/WP 37, Geneva: ILO.

Tilakaratna, S. (1987) *The Animator in Participatory Rural Development (Concept and Practice)*, Geneva: ILO.

11. Qualitative dimensions of social development

Today
for the first time
the tribal labourers of this area
are going on strike
stopping work on their own initiative.
This may result in a wage rise of say Rs 100 per year
or Rs 50 per year.
What is important to us, however,
is that we
are asserting that we too are human beings.

Ambarsingh Suruwanti, a tribal labour leader in Maharastra, India, 1 May 1972

Distorted approach to development

Conventionally, social science and development cooperation have had an overwhelming bias towards quantitative indicators for assessing developmental progress. This has been unfortunate, and has generally given a distorted approach to development policy and action.

Imagine the development of a human child being assessed in terms only of indices such as his/her physical health, grades in school and, later, his/her financial earnings. A 'well-developed' person in such terms may very well be a social nuisance and/or a very miserable person even in a reasonably normal social environment. It is perfectly natural and valid for parents to want to see their child develop as a wholesome human personality, making a comfortable but not necessarily lavish living, able to handle life's tensions without cracking, develop creative faculties of social value and engaged in their application, emotionally content with life, loved by family and friends and held in broad respect by the wider society. Most such indicators of personal development are not quantitatively measurable but may

This chapter contains the text of a paper presented at the Workshop on the Evaluation of Social Development Projects and Programmes in the Third World, Swansea, Wales, UK, 19–22 September 1989. Responsibility for its contents rests with the author alone and not with the organisation in which the author was working.

nevertheless be at the core of enlightened human aspirations, for oneself as well as for one's near and dear ones. There is no reason why, for society or communities of people, the notion of development should be very different, and should take a narrower, predominantly quantitative, view, leaving out important, even vital, considerations which can be assessed by analytical reasoning if they cannot be measured by numbers.

Popular urges and priorities

One may ask whether for materially poor communities the question of access to the so-called basic needs – i.e. food, clothing, shelter, education, health care – are not of overriding importance, constituting the core indicators of progress which are quantifiable anyway. I have sought to test this question on various occasions, in dialogues with poverty groups who have become mobilised for collective struggle to improve their lives. Some have, indeed, indicated a predominantly basic needs-oriented bias in articulating their aspirations (although it has often appeared that they are only repeating what they have been told – I have also heard people say that they did not know that they were 'poor' before they were told they were). But there have been others who have responded, and revealed, differently. Some examples follow.

In a dialogue with leaders and cadres of the Bhoomi Sena movement in Maharastra, India (de Silva *et al.*, 1977), the question was asked as to why bonded labour was selected as the first issue to be tackled. The reply was that 'It was a question of human dignity. The reason was not only economic.' One could argue that the question of bonded labour itself, in any case, could be handled quantitatively. But human dignity is affronted in many other ways, by various modes of personal and social humiliation including physical humiliation, sexual abuse and outright assault backed by the social status and power of the offenders. There are numerous organised groups of disadvantaged people around the world who are struggling not only for economic but also for human rights. I had a most revealing experience in Bangladesh when an assembly of organised landless rural workers' groups who had been struggling for economic and other rights for about eight years without any significant gain in their economic status asserted that their lives nevertheless had changed, and that they would never give up their organisation, because 'the elites have to talk to us with respect now that we are organised' (Rahman, 1986). Similar groups in other places have said during flood disasters: 'If they cannot give us wheat, OK. But we shall not accept the abuses. They must treat us as human beings' (Rahman, 1987). And groups of very poor rural women who got organised have said that among the greatest gains to them have been the opportunity and ability just to talk in public, and that they try to attend every meeting to share their problems and seek solutions, sometimes simply to express their feelings and experience a sense of solidarity with other women – in an environment where customarily they stayed in and around their immediate families and did not have the right to speak in the presence of adult males except close relations; on the basis of this experience alone they consider that the development of their organisation has constituted a profound change in their lives (Rahman, 1987).

More poignant is the rejection of the elite's notion of 'development' by a number of forest-based poor people's movements in India, after a process of joint reflection on their status:

> We have seen and we have tried to present the picture of degradation of our culture. . . . The life of a forest-dweller has many compensations which are not available to city dwellers. . . . For 'development' we have to give up our life style and our culture and . . . we are gradually imbibing the culture and life of the slums. . . . We feel cheated. . . . It is strange that what is good for us has been decided by those who have cheated us and the country. They have deprived us of our habitat and the country of her environment. . . . Those who are interested in a new forest policy are not the forest-dwellers. Their major interest is the development of the forest as a resource, rather than as a habitat of the people. This basic difference distinguishes 'us' from 'them'. They believe that we [the forest-dwellers] should reap the dubious benefits of 'development'. Or, in other words, become like them or their serfs. We have tried in this report to show how we have lived for centuries – sheltered, protected and nurtured by the forest. This lifestyle is now fast disappearing along with the forest. (Dasgupta, 1986: Chapter 6)

A different dimension of people's self-assessment of progress was revealed in an evaluation exercise of the SARILAKAS project in the Philippines (described in Chapter 4) which provided animation work to promote organisations of various categories of rural workers in four villages (Rahman, 1983). The organisations were engaged in collective economic activities which brought different degrees of economic gains to their members. A random sample of the members of these organisations were interviewed and asked what was the most important benefit they had gained by organising. Without exception, every one of them replied 'education'. Gaining the knowledge, through actual experience, that they could improve their status by organising and working together was the single most important benefit they had obtained. No one, even out of those whose economic status had improved substantially, mentioned economic gain as the most important!

[In Chapter 8 I presented examples of people's collective self-identity of ORAP groups in Zimbabwe which reflect deep conceptualisations of popular aspirations and hence implicit popular notions of 'development'.]

Finally, in a recent visit to a relatively well-off village in Hungary, members of the community claimed that efforts to promote participatory development are no less needed for the 'rich', and that 'what hurts most is the indignity of being forced to vote for a chairman who I know is corrupt'. This indignity is a measure of one's poverty notwithstanding one's material well-being, and a measure, therefore, of social underdevelopment.

Who assesses development?

The above indicates that there are certain qualitative dimensions of life to which the ordinary disadvantaged or underprivileged people – whether materially poor or rich – give considerable importance, given their specific situations and life's evolution. In addition, the basic moral of the above examples is that these people, whose development concerns us in this workshop, have their own ideas about what they value in life. These ideas may or may not coincide with ours, rooted as we are in a very different life with a very different evolution which has shaped our perceptions about what is valuable in life. In this context, when we talk about indicators of social development, quantitative or qualitative, a basic question that has to be faced is the legitimacy of us – specifically, the kind of intellectuals and social development practitioners or promoters that we are – sitting in judgement over what constitutes social development, and how far we can go in articulating what should essentially be the prerogative of the people themselves to articulate.

Empowerment

There is, indeed, no escape from this question. Our legitimacy in this matter, today, may perhaps be rationalised in terms of the social power we possess, and have chosen to exercise, as we try to influence the process of social development of some societies towards a more participatory direction about whose dimensions we have some vision ourselves, our own as well as that derived from our interaction with people at the grassroots. However, given that the thinking of the people themselves may not necessarily coincide with ours, the absence of an authentic people's point of view remains a serious limitation on how we define the dimensions of social development. At best, our views must be considered tentative, subject to validation or modification by the people's own processes of reflection. In fact, a process of *empowering and enabling* the people to articulate and assert, by words and by deeds, their urges and thinking in this regard, must be one of the core dimensions of social development itself, for social development cannot have started if the people are unable to thus express and assert what social development means to them. This, then, is a fundamental indicator of social development in societies where such empowerment still remains a distant dream, and unfortunately this is the prevalent state of affairs in perhaps all nation states today.

Elements of empowerment

A quantitative element of empowerment is control over economic resources; but progress in this matter is by itself no indication of enhanced social power of the underprivileged to assert their developmental aspirations and their freedom to take initiatives for their self-development. The essential qualitative elements of empowerment are well suggested in many writings on participatory development, from which I would highlight three:

1. *Organisation* under the control of the disadvantaged and underprivileged people, with sufficient strength derived from direct numerical size and/or linking with other organisations of similarly situated people.
2. *Social awareness* of the disadvantaged, in terms of understanding derived from collective self-inquiry and reflection, of the social environment of their lives and the working of its processes. The knowledge itself, and the feeling of knowing from self-inquiry, are both important in giving the disadvantaged a sense of equality with the formally 'educated' classes of society, rather than a sense of intellectual inferiority which is often a powerful force inhibiting the generation of confidence in the disadvantaged to rely on and assert their own thinking and take their own initiatives for development.

   It is possible to acquire social knowledge without *literacy*, through methods of verbal inquiry and communication. But in many contexts not being literate amounts to surrendering power to literates to claim knowledge which the disadvantaged cannot verify, and sustain dependence on the literates for much information as well as for dealings with public and other agencies which require the use of written instruments. Such dependence, as well as the sense of helplessness *vis-à-vis* institutions and structures using the written language, is liable to have powerful adverse effects on self-confidence in situations where relations with such institutions and structures are an important element of people's normal life and development effort.

At the same time, the *mode of acquiring literacy* can have significant bearing on the development or otherwise of self-confidence of the disadvantaged. A vertical mode of learning from conventional teachers coming from the more privileged social classes can perpetuate a sense of inferiority *vis-à-vis* the teachers and their social classes, with a regard for them as the repository of knowledge and wisdom. As Freirian thinking has already well articulated, literacy, or for that matter education as an element of social development, must be viewed as an organic component of a process of 'awakening' or 'animation' (Tilakaratna, 1985). This implies not merely learning, knowing and understanding but also experiencing and grasping one's own intellectual powers in the same process, experiencing, in other words, self-discovery, including the discovery of oneself as a thinker and creator of knowledge. This is what makes literacy a qualitative rather than a quantitative process.

3. *Self-reliance*: people's power comes ultimately from self-reliance. Self-reliance is not autarky, but a combination of material and mental strength by which one can deal with others as an equal, and assert one's self-determination. Once more, any degree of control over material resources is by itself no indication of self-reliance, which is an attitudinal quality, inborn in some and acquired by others through social experience, social awareness and reflection. Self-reliance is strengthened by a collective identity, deriving not only material but also mental strength from solidarity, sharing and caring for each other and from thinking and acting together to move forward and to resist domination.

Elements of organic development

Once empowered with organisation, social awareness and a sense of self-reliance, the people develop as a collective personality. This development is an organic process, a question of the internal unfolding, progressive maturing, of the collective. External quarters may assist in this process of development; but a people cannot be developed by others.

Some of the elements of people's development are suggested below.

Development of *creativity*

What distinguishes the human from other species is that human creativity is dynamic, seeking ever newer forms of expression, fundamentally fulfilling a permanent creative urge, whereas other species at best create static structures (e.g. birds' nests) primarily for subsistence. The development of creative abilities and their fulfilment in economic, social and cultural spheres is perhaps the most basic element of human development.

Institutional development

As a people's collective develops, it creates institutions and progressively modifies or recreates them, in order to manage collective affairs. The quality of institutional development in the context of their respective functions is one measure of people's development. This quality may in particular be assessed from the point of view of three basic functions for which institutional development is necessary:

1. *Management of collective tasks*: a self-evident function.
2. *Mass participation* in collective deliberation and decision-making, implementation of collective tasks, in the taking of initiatives, in review and evaluation of collective activities and social progress. This is the question of internal democracy in collective development, to ensure both that activities are undertaken according to mass priorities and consensus, and that the wider body of people have sufficient opportunity to fulfil themselves by active participation in the activities of the collective.
3. *Solidarity*: this is the function perhaps most neglected in conventional thinking. For healthy development, a collective needs to have mechanisms: (a) to ensure that some elements of the body do not develop at the expense of other elements, so retarding their process of development or actually causing underdevelopment. Such a mechanism calls for an agreed concern to avoid such 'mal-development', a mechanism for collective deliberation if such mal-development occurs or threatens to occur, and procedures for correcting the course; (b) for handling internal conflicts and tensions of other natures without rupture; and (c) for caring for each other in distress (an internal social insurance function).

Women's development

This cannot be overemphasised in view of the almost universal experience of male 'development' at the expense of women's development. The question is complicated by culture and religious beliefs in many situations where exogenously conceived norms of gender equality may not be appropriate irrespective of the specific state of evolution of thinking and culture of the community concerned. However, progress towards women's articulation and assertion of their own points of view concerning gender relations in all spheres, and evolution of gender relations towards greater equality as assessed by the women themselves, may be suggested as an important indicator of social development. For most societies this implies independent forums (organisations) of women at least at the primary level.

Development of 'organic knowledge'

Development of a (collective) human personality involves not only doing things but also advancing, simultaneously, analytical understanding of the evolving situation in all its dimensions, social, technological, political, cultural, in order both to intellectually appreciate the unfolding experience and to take guidance from systematically experienced knowledge for future action. In most societies the task of systematically developing such knowledge has become separated from the actual evolution of social life, and has become concentrated in the hands of 'professionals' who by and large live a life very different from that of the ordinary people. This has created the question of the relevance for social development of much of the knowledge thus developed, which is not rooted in people's lives, and has also contributed to retarding the process of development of the people by undermining popular knowledge and their ability to create and advance knowledge. While professional knowledge of some kinds remains valuable for social development at certain levels of decision-making, the development of self-knowledge by the people as an organic part of their life's activities, i.e. 'organic knowledge', for developing knowledge more directly and immediately relevant for their self-development as well as for sustaining people's power to assert themselves *vis-à-vis* other social quarters, i.e. for self-determination, must be underlined as an important indicator of social development.

Social development of the wider society

The above concerns qualitative dimensions of social development at the grassroots, i.e. people's organisations. For the broader society (a development programme of macro dimension), social development means not only that grassroots people's organisations develop in the above senses, but also that society as a whole develops, revealing essentially the same kind of qualitative features at a broader scale of operation or relations, as for the development of grassroots people's organisations. Thus, concepts of self-reliance, social creativity, institutional development, capability for the management of broader social operations, democracy and solidarity are as much pertinent for assessment of social development for the wider society as for grassroots development. From the point of view of the status of the broad masses of people in overall social development, three desirable principles may be emphasised:

1. *Human dignity*. All people are entitled to human dignity, irrespective of economic status, ethnic origin, colour, caste, etc. A society has little claim to have developed if some sections of it can offend or abuse the human dignity of others and get away with it by virtue of their social power and position. (No one has developed as a person, I would suggest,

if he or she does not consider an offence to the human dignity of any person to be an offence to his or her own dignity: without this basic identification with the human race one is not human oneself.)

2. *Popular democracy.* At the level of institutional social discourse, an essential indicator of social development must be progress towards genuine popular democracy – a system whereby the broad masses of the people have an effective voice in the shaping of macro policy and in the conduct of public affairs. Neither the democracy of the so-called free world nor so-called socialist democracy has ensured this natural right of the people: the nature of effective political parties and the outcome of electoral processes to determine macro leaderships of society in the free world are critically determined by the distribution of economic power in a society, and the economically underprivileged masses may merely have the choice of influencing which set of privileged elites will rule over them. On the other hand, in 'socialist' countries, albeit with greater economic equality, the party remains typically unaccountable to the people. In one guise or another, in either type of society the real macro power remains in the hands of privileged elites. In this milieu of intra-societal political relations the entry of Solidarity of Poland, truly a workers' party, into the sanctum of macro power is a unique event that opens up the possibility in at least one modern society of a real sharing of macro power between privileged elites and the working people; it therefore deserves a mention in a discussion on popular democracy to give it substance. If it really becomes possible in a stable social order for the working people to acquire and maintain a real voice in the affairs of the state, then the standard of attainable democracy and macro social development will have reached a new height against which claims to democracy of other states, of both the 'free' and the 'socialist' world, could well be assessed.

3. *Cultural diversity*: finally, in recent years we have been witnessing an upsurge of assertions by popular sectors of their cultural identities, *vis-à-vis* attempts by dominant powers to impose a monolithic culture ('ideology') of development upon the people (and by superpowers upon the people of many societies). It is hardly even recognised today, e.g. in debates on individual *vis-à-vis* collective ownership of property, that many indigenous people do not have the concept of humans *owning* natural resources (e.g. land, water): many such communities have instead the concept of humans *relating* with nature as a partner in life. The implication of this concept (culture) of the preservation of nature for 'sustainable' development rather than the destruction of nature to satisfy the human lust for acquisition and conquest, may be noted. In any case, social development from the point of view of the broader society necessarily implies people's development at the grassroots, for otherwise only an abstract concept, e.g. the 'nation state', may be promoted in

some sense, but only structures for the manipulation and repression of society will result. People's development in its turn implies a people's authentic culture, which would develop at the same time, absorbing elements from other cultures with which it would interact but which cannot develop by the imposition of alien cultures. A healthy developing society would, therefore, be a society that encourages the authentic development of people's cultures, to interact with each other for mutual enrichment rather than for domination.

References

Chavunduka, Dexter M. *et al.* (1985) *Khuluma Usenza, the Story of ORAP in Zimbabwe's Rural Development*, Bulawayo: The Organisation of Rural Associations for Progress.

Dasgupta, Subhachari (1986) *Forest, Ecology and the Oppressed, People's Institute for Development and Training*, India: New Delhi.

de Silva, G. V. S. *et al.* (1979) 'Bhoomi Sena: a struggle for people's power', *Development Dialogue*, No. 2.

Rahman, Md. Anisur (1983) *SARILAKAS, A Pilot Project for Stimulating Grass-roots Participation in the Philippines*, Evaluation Report, Geneva: International Labour Office.

Rahman, Md. Anisur (1986) 'Personal field notes on visits to grass-roots work in Bangladesh'.

Rahman, Md. Anisur (1987) 'Personal field notes on visits to grass-roots work in Bangladesh'.

Rahman, Md. Anisur (1989) *Glimpses of the 'Other Africa'*, World Employment Programme Research Working Paper, WEP 10/WEP 48, Geneva: ILO. (Chapter 8 of this book.)

Tilakaratna, S. (1985) *The Animator in Participatory Rural Development (Concept and Practice)*, Geneva: ILO.

12.   Towards an alternative development paradigm

Introduction: do we want development?

> What economists need to do most urgently is re-evaluate the entire conceptual foundation and redesign their basic models and theories accordingly. The current economic crisis will be overcome only if economists are willing to participate in the paradigm shift that is now occurring in all fields.

Fritjof Capra, *The Turning Point* (1983, chapter on 'The impasse of economics')

It is a great privilege for me to have been invited to give the inaugural address to this biennial conference of the Bangladesh Economic Association. The privilege is all the greater because I left conventional economics about fifteen years ago and have been working since in a field in which economics is not necessarily considered to be the primary motivation. The fact that I am nevertheless addressing you today indicates an openness in the economics profession of the country which is truly healthy and encouraging.

In March 1990 I attended a seminar in Catigny, Geneva, entitled 'Towards the post-development age'.[1] In this seminar I listened to an all-out attack on the notion of development from a set of scholars and scholar-activists of both north and south. The attack included a vigorous plea for abandoning the word 'development' altogether. In starting my address I wish to share with you the substance of the discussion and debate in that seminar.

This chapter is an edited version of an inaugural address given to the biennial conference of the Bangladesh Economic Association, Dhaka, 4 January 1991. In developing these ideas the work of Gustavo Esteva (1990), Stig Lindholm (1977), Jean Robert (1990) and Wolfgang Sachs (1990) proved particularly useful. Philippe Egger and Ajit Ghose provided some useful comments on a previous draft; the responsibility for the views expressed here is, however, the author's alone.

It was observed that the idea of 'development' was born as part of the 'Truman design' of 1949 in response to the emerging cold war between the two great rival ideologies. The threat of the Bolshevik Revolution inspiring social revolutions in the so-called Third World was to be countered by a promise of 'development' and 'development assistance' to help 'under-developed' societies catch up with the 'developed'. Development was defined exclusively as 'economic development', reducing the degree of progress and maturity of a society to the level of its production. Development was considered possible only by emulating the ways of 'developed' nations, their aspirations, values, culture and technology. And financial and technical assistance were offered with a patronising assumption of superiority in the march to civilisation. The attraction of massive external finance and exciting technology generated client states in the 'underdeveloped' world where oligarchies able to capture the organ of the state could enrich and empower themselves as a class relative to the wider society to whom successive 'development plans' at the national level, and, subsequently, 'development decades' at the global level, were offered as a perpetual hope for prosperity.

The result: the economic benefits of such development have not even trickled down to the vast majority of the people in most countries honourably referred to as 'developing'. But the most fundamental problem as identified by the Cartigny seminar has been *the obstruction of the evolution of indigenous alternatives for societal self-expression and authentic progress.*

The vast majority of the people were classified as 'poor', and therefore as objects of sympathy, paternalistic intervention and assistance. Many of these peoples, under the blinding light of compassionate observation which was flashed upon them, have internalised this negative self-image. Perceiving themselves as 'inferior', they have sought to be 'developed' by the 'superiors', surrendering their own values, cultures and their own accumulated knowledge and wisdom. Others have been forced to do so by the sheer power of the 'development' effort which itself has concentrated power, privileges and wealth in a few hands with the ability to subjugate and exploit the broader masses and which has often uprooted vast masses of people from their traditional life to become inferior citizens in alien environments. Thus they have suffered not only economic impoverishment but also a loss of identity and ability to develop endogenously and authentically with their indigenous culture and capabilities: a *deeper human misery* which as economists we were not trained to recognise.

I had no problem in agreeing with this critique of 'development'. But I was struck by the intensity with which the very notion of 'development' was attacked. It was asserted that the notion of development is an 'opium for the people' which legitimises the exercise of power by dominating structures and creates dependence of people and societies upon them, and which destroys the vernacular domain in which the people could evolve authentically. (The term 'people' is used to refer to those sections of the population who have no economic or social status in society by the standards of the dominating structures – those whom Adam Smith referred to as workers and 'other inferior ranks of people'.) Granting this, I argued that we should have the right to give and assert our own conception of the term 'development'. I submitted that I found the word 'development' to be a very powerful means of expressing the conception of societal progress as the flowering of people's creativity. Must we abandon valuable words because they are abused? What do we do then with words like democracy, cooperation, socialism, all of which are being abused?

The debate was inconclusive. But it was a revealing indication to me that at least in some societies pro-people forces do not assess that they have the power to use the word 'development' to their advantage even by redefining it. This is perhaps not yet a universal phenomenon, and we know of authentic popular movements which are using the notion of 'development' as they conceive it, as a motive force in their initiatives and struggle. This throws us, social scientists, the challenge to understand and articulate what development might mean to people who have not lost their sense of identity and are expressing themselves through authentic collective endeavours, and also to understand how such a sense of identity and collective self-expression could be restored to others who may have lost them: in other words, to articulate an alternative development paradigm in which the evolution of popular life is not to be distorted and abused by paternalistic 'development' endeavours with alien conceptions but may be stimulated and assisted to find its highest self-expression which alone can make a society proud of itself.

Popular initiatives

In November 1990 I visited a number of organisations of landless workers in Sarail Upazilla in Bangladesh in the programme of a rural development agency. Every year that I visit such organisations in Bangladesh and elsewhere I learn a lot. Last November in Sarail in particular it was profoundly inspiring to see the kind of development some of these organisations of economically depressed classes are initiating.

The organisations of the landless in Sarail are managing, first, group-based saving-and-credit programmes, and the best of them compare well with the best such programme anywhere. Priority is given in these programmes to internal resource mobilisation over external credit. External credit is given only against an equal contribution from the base groups' own saving fund. The repayment schedule is tailored to the nature of the activity for which the loan is advanced, and unlike some other credit-to-the-poor programmes in the country there is no bias here against long-yielding projects by way of requiring repayment to commence immediately. Each credit application is endorsed by two members of the organisation concerned, who undertake to follow up the use of the credit and general financial condition of the debtor and to alert the organisation to any unforeseen problem that may arise which might affect repayment on time. The group discusses such situations with the debtor in its weekly meetings and seeks to assist the debtor to overcome the difficulty, sometimes extending the repayment period if the difficulty is considered to be genuine. The approach to the credit operation is thus *sociological, humane and self-educational*, unlike the approach of a credit bank with rigid procedural rules insensitive to specific human circumstances. The internal supervision procedure also reduces the overhead cost. All this, with a repayment record claimed to be nearly 99 per cent in recent years, is a worthy illustration of *people's self-management*.

What was also impressive was that a number of these organisations explicitly assumed responsibility for the welfare of not only their members but all the 'poor' in their villages. Cases of unusual distress among economically badly off families, whether they are members of an organisation or not, are brought to its weekly meetings and distress loans, grants and other kinds of assistance are extended. This is a service which some of the organisations that I visited were proud of and wanted to preserve: consequently candidates for membership are not taken in immediately but are asked to attend the weekly meetings of the organisation to be exposed to its issues and concerns, and are admitted only when the organisation assesses that the candidate wants to join not only for selfish interests but would also be concerned about the welfare of other poor in the village. Otherwise, they explained to me, 'our organisation would be disoriented'.

Some organisations have gone further and have initiated development work involving and benefiting the village community as a whole. They have convened meetings of all villagers and proposed large projects in irrigation or flood control to bring more land under cultivation extensively or intensively, or to protect land from flooding, with landowning farmers as well as agricultural labourers benefiting from greater production and employment. The groups have offered their own contributions from their savings fund and their labour to such projects and have invited other villagers, rich and poor, to contribute in cash, kind or labour. In a number of villages, such projects mobilising the resources of the whole community under the leadership of organisations of the landless are underway. In one village I had the privilege of witnessing a mass meeting to discuss a proposal for one such project: the construction of a dam which would save crop land from flood water as well as increase land for habitation; it was proposed that the extra land to be obtained from the earth work would be allocated in mass meetings to those who had no homestead at all. Such constructive and humane leadership in social development on the part of the downtrodden struck me as one of the most hopeful promises of social progress that I have seen anywhere.

In recent years such popular initiatives, spontaneous or 'animated' and 'facilitated' by social activists, have been increasing in many countries. Conventional development agencies have started recognising them in a 'participatory development' rhetoric without necessarily understanding their basic aspiration and message: such movements cannot be 'coopted' into the conventional development paradigm without being disoriented. Radical thinkers now disillusioned with the great experiments with 'socialism' are also looking at such movements with new hope.[2] However, these grassroots movements and associated animation and facilitation work have by now matured sufficiently and exhibit enough convergent thinking among significant trends through networking, exchanges, mutual co-operation and joint articulation in terms of their philosophical orientation, to provide the basis for outlining some key dimensions of their alternative development paradigm.

The conventional development paradigm

A development paradigm is an agreed school of thinking about how to view development and how to investigate and assess reality for development policy and action; in broader terms, how to generate knowledge relevant for development. The basic premise of the conventional development paradigm is a conception of a *hierarchical human spectrum* in which some quarters are 'superior' and are therefore qualified to guide, control, determine, the others' development. In this view, some nations are more developed than others; some classes within a nation are superior to others in terms of achievement, education, culture. These superior quarters create, or occupy and control already existing, structures to exercise organised domination over the 'inferiors' – globally, nationally, locally – and take responsibility for their development. A professional class of intellectuals serves these structures by assessing reality and constructing knowledge that are addressed to and supposed to guide their policy and action. Educational and training processes are developed to transfer this knowledge to members of the wider society through a hierarchical teacher–student, trainer–trainee relation. Such processes not only transfer the knowledge concerned but also deepen the hierarchy: the degree holders, the professionally or vocationally trained, are 'superior' to the non-graduate or the untrained, and are part of the structural 'cadres' of development.

The generation of knowledge in this paradigm is a specialised professional function that is discharged by prescribed methods which require *observation from a 'distance'* as opposed to getting 'involved'. The premise is that from one's 'superior' vantage point it is possible to look down and assess what an inferior life lacks and needs in order to formulate development policy and action to improve it.

This paradigm, finally, gives *primacy to economics* – the management of scarce resources – as a part of its ideology, reducing the notion of development to economic growth, now tempered with a concern for 'distributional equity'.

Needless to say, it is the development policy and action of the hierarchical structures dominating society which are responsible for the dismal state of so many individual nations and of the world as a whole: the ordinary people have not had responsibility for their own and society's development. In some of the most 'developed' societies we are witnessing social disease formations which are going beyond human control. On the whole, the economic, social, moral and ecological crises which we face today, coupled with the diversion of resources from productive uses to create means of mass destruction, are ample testimony to the inherent incapability of the dominating structures which have appropriated responsibility for social and world development to steer society and the world towards a course of healthy progress. Instead, these structures have lent themselves to malignant interests whose growth and power are now threatening the very survival of the human race.

Towards an alternative development paradigm

Endogeneity of development

The alternative view of development represented by converging trends in grassroots movements rejects the notion that development can be 'delivered' from 'above'. Development, meaning development of peoples and societies, is an organic process of healthy growth and application of the creative faculties. This process may be stimulated and facilitated by external elements, but any attempt to force it towards external standards can only result in maiming it. *Development is endogenous* – there are no 'front runners' to be followed. One can be impressed, inspired by others' achievements, but any attempt to emulate could at best produce a carbon copy in which the originality of a creative social life and evolution would be lost. In reality, even a carbon copy would not be attainable without its necessary historical preconditions, and an attempt to become such a copy can only yield gross distortions.

If development is endogenous, then in people's development *the people are the subject.* This has profound implications for the categorising of people as well as for the relations of knowledge in the society.

Non-hierarchical human relations
In the hierarchical scheme of the conventional development paradigm the broad masses of the people are the objects of development and most of them, with economic 'entitlements' below the standard defined by the dominant structures, are categorised as 'poor'. In fact, development is widely viewed today as meaning overcoming the problem of such poverty, thus reducing human aspirations to the attainment of a bundle of economic goods. But the problem of poverty has not been overcome and remains intractable for many nations after three 'decades of development'. In my lecture to the Asiatic Society of Bangladesh last year I elaborated the argument that poverty cannot be overcome by identifying it as the problem to be solved as this creates negative motivations. Subsequently, I was struck by the following story in a paper presented at the Cartigny seminar last March:

> I could have kicked myself afterwards. At the same time, my remark had seemed the most natural thing on earth. It was six months after the catastrophic earthquake in 1985, and we had spent the whole day walking around Tepito, a dilapidated quarter of Mexico City, inhabited by ordinary people but threatened by land speculators. We had expected ruins and resignation, decay and squalor, but our visit had made us think again: there was a proud neighbourly spirit, vigorous activity with small building co-operatives everywhere; we saw a flourishing shadow economy. But at the end of the day, indulging in a bit of stock-taking, the remark finally slipped out: 'It is all very well, but, when it comes down to it, these people are still terribly poor.' Promptly, one of our companions stiffened: 'No somos pobres, somos Tepitanos!' (We are not poor people, we are Tepitans.) What a reprimand! Why had I made such an offensive remark? I had to admit to myself in embarrassment that, quite involuntarily, the cliches of development philosophy had triggered my reaction. (Sachs, 1990: Essay 2, 1)

I have myself been a victim of this received culture of thinking and have called the people 'poor' in many of my writings. Not all people are able immediately to assert themselves as proudly as the Tepitans since many have internalised, as suggested before, the 'gaze' of the rich upon the poor.[3] *The development problem starts precisely here: there can be no development (which is endogenous) unless the people's pride in themselves as worthy human beings inferior to none is asserted or, if lost, restored.* The human quality of a people is independent of their economic condition; it can even shine and inspire under the most trying conditions. The people need this self-esteem to give their best, most creative and humane response to their situation, thereby to develop. They must, therefore, be invited and empowered to relate with anyone and with any structure horizontally, as equals, not vertically.

Generation and relations of knowledge

Together, the above two premises – the endogeneity of development and a non-hierarchical concept of human relations – lead to a third premise which concerns the vital arena of knowledge relations and the generation of knowledge relevant for development.

Development being endogenous, it is not possible with somebody else's thinking and knowledge. Nor is a relation of equality possible if one feels that knowledge essential for one's development rests with others.

I once visited a village in Bangladesh with an agency which went there to open a credit-for-the poor programme. I was introduced to the people as a very wise man: this immediately damaged the possibility of a dialogue between me and the villagers as equals. I tried to undo the damage by telling them that they had seen 'wise' persons like me before, and they knew that they had not benefited much from listening to them. If I were forced to make a living in their village, I would not be able to survive without their help. Maybe I knew something about international structures and linkages that they did not know, but they knew so much about their own environment that I did not know. Would they, therefore, let me learn from them? I did not have much success in changing the deep-rooted perception of vertical relations by a few minutes of such smart talk. (And after all, this 'wise' man had come with and had been introduced by agents of a programme proposing to give them money!)

Let us look at this claim to wisdom a bit more closely. We spend about twenty-five years of our early life in classrooms and studies shut off from active life, to become 'educated', wise. Life moves on meanwhile, struggling and moving through challenges and odds. Those who survive the odds must be very able and wise, including the ablest, wisest, most *resourceful*, even if 'resource'-less, and creative of all human beings. Yet we have the audacity after these twenty-five years of existence isolated from people's lives, to stand above them with our educational certificates in our hands, and tell them how they should move, not caring even to learn from them how they have come so far and what their own thinking on issues of concern to them is.

The 'educated' have not proved to be any more 'enlightened' or capable of wise and responsible decisions and conduct than the 'uneducated'. While we 'wise' persons have been responsible for the sad plight of the world today, there are numerous examples of ordinary, 'uneducated' people devising responses to problems confronting them which show great wisdom, sense of responsibility and morality. But the myth remains that it is professionals, and the 'educated' generally, who are the repository of the knowledge and wisdom necessary for development. And that it is they who are the only qualified agents to generate knowledge and construct reality for developmental action. The myth is not only factually false; by perpetuating a *vertical knowledge relation* it also vitally obstructs development.

Social reality does not exist 'out there' in an absolute sense, to be observed by standardised techniques. Reality is constructed by the observer, whose own perceptions, values and methods of observation determine what is seen, what is abstracted in distilling the observation and what is finally constructed. Reality, in other words, is constructed within a given paradigm, that of a particular epistemological school. Its validity therefore rests on the premise of designing policy and action within the given paradigm. The logical validity of educated professionals constructing social reality – knowledge – by standing apart from the life of the people and observing it from their own vantage point, for the purpose of prescribing policy and action addressed to hierarchical structures (and making great mistakes in doing so), is not in question. But the value of such knowledge stands or falls with the paradigm which premises structural subordination as the basis of development. If the people are the principal actors in the alternative development paradigm, *the relevant reality must be the people's own, constructed by them only*.

I was educated in this epistemological theory when in 1976 I visited a *shibir* for Lok Chetna Jagoron ('awakening of people's awareness') in the Bhoomi Sena movement in India. In that shibir attended by about forty acutely oppressed *adivasis* from a number of villages, the leaders of the movement and a few external 'animators' who were also there did not seek to transfer any knowledge external to the endogenous creativity of the people. Instead, they invited the people to create their own collective knowledge about their own social reality – their own social science. The central invocation in this 'animation' work was to invite the adivasis to assert their self-perceived life's experiences as *their 'truth'*, irrespective of the 'truth' being spread by the dominant structures or by the professionals (social scientists). This the participants were first invited to do individually, to assert their personal (subjective) truths; then to discuss the common elements in these personal truths and thereby to move to their collective (objective) truth. They were then invited to take collective action to promote their interests on the basis of the social knowledge they had generated, and engage thereafter in a systematic collective praxis – cycles of reflection – action–reflection – of their own, keeping on advancing their objective knowledge as well as their overall collective life, of which the generation and advancement of self-knowledge is an essential organic component; that is, to keep developing, endogenously.

Popular movements in many parts of the world are today using variants of this approach for the construction of social reality by the people themselves as a basis of and an organic part of their collective self-development. The Freirian movement of 'conscientisation', first started in Brazil and today found in many countries of the world, and the 'participatory research' movement pioneered by the International Council for Adult Education[4] and now also a global phenomenon, are overlapping movements with the same epistemological premise as Bhoomi Sena's Lok Chetna Jagoron. The ILO's programme on Participatory Organisations of the Rural Poor (PORP) has played some role in helping to sharpen both the theory and practice of this approach to social knowledge generation and people's own praxis. The central premise in this approach is social inquiry by collectives into the people themselves. A strategic task in such people's self-inquiry is the *recovery of history* by people's collectives for the rewriting of history with the people as the principal actors who take initiatives of their own, responding to action by external or hierarchical forces, and formulating and implementing collective policy and decisions which further their own interests. It is of critical importance for the people to take inspiration from history thus 'rewritten', to view and assert themselves as the subject of their destiny, reversing the negative self-image that we have given them. Another critical task is the recovery and reassertion of the core *values and cultural elements* of the people themselves which are being threatened or are eroding as a result of the operation of the development paradigm which the dominant structures have imposed upon them. Finally, the results of such popular inquiry are the property of the people and are to be documented and disseminated through means of communication of the people themselves in accordance with their level of literacy and cultural development.[5]

'Building' and 'sharpening' each other

In people's development, thus, reality will be constructed by grassroots social formations, not by 'top-down' professional investigation. This does not deny that professionals can contribute to the construction of specific aspects of reality, e.g. macro national or international aspects to which the popular forces may not have immediate access. Specific skills of professionals may also be of value to popular forces in assessing specific aspects of reality, and a constructive interaction between the two has the possibility of enriching popular construction of their reality, always granting, however, the right of popular forces to consider, adapt or reject any external input to their own effort at creating their own reality. Needless to say, from such a constructive interaction the professionals themselves have the opportunity to learn and be immensely enriched.

This brings us to the question of what is conventionally called 'education' and 'training', and to the idea of 'transfer of knowledge'.

There is need in every individual to improve his or her intellectual capacity, breadth of knowledge and specific skills. The conventional methods of 'teaching' and 'training' administered in a hierarchical relation and aimed at a 'transfer of knowledge' are a dull and depressing approach. The 'student' and 'trainee' go through the processes mainly because the dominating structures require them to do so for entry into the job market. The processes have very little to do with real learning, and actually invite the recipients of knowledge to seek ways of acquiring certificates without necessarily putting in even the prescribed efforts.

Knowledge cannot be transferred; it can be memorised for mechanical application, but learning is always an act of self-search and discovery. In this search and discovery one may be stimulated and assisted but one cannot be 'taught'. Nor can one be 'trained' to perform tasks which are not mechanical but creative. Institutions of teaching and training which seek to transfer knowledge and skills serve mainly to disorient the capacity that is in every healthy individual to search and discover knowledge creatively. It indoctrinates them, furthermore, in the value of hierarchy which they then tend to pursue with a vengeance, the humiliation of being subordinated is passed on to their subordinates.

For some time in recent years I have been looking for language to replace words like teaching and training. I got it in March this year from a workshop of African and Caribbean grassroots activists held in Zimbabwe on the training of field animators to promote participatory development. In this workshop I raised my question on the notion of training which, I said, is a hierarchical notion that creates hierarchy in both personal relations and institutions for 'training' with no organic relation with, and standing above, practical life. I asked the participants in the workshop to see whether in the vernacular language of the people with whom they had been working there was any word which expressed an alternative, non-hierarchical concept of learning.

The participants searched, and came up with two words in one of the southern African languages: *uakana* meaning 'building each other', and *uglolana* meaning 'sharpening each other'. I invite you all to reflect deeply on the power and richness these words have in expressing both the concept and practice of non-hierarchical learning in which no one teaches or trains anybody, but instead knowledge is sought and created through mutual dialogue and collective inquiry. I would also invite you to reflect upon the power and richness of such popular conceptualisation as an organic part of their urge for collective self-development in a non-hierarchical framework: a power and richness which we are trying to destroy by imposing upon them concepts of education and training derived from an altogether alien scheme of values, i.e. the values of structural domination.

Economics

I come, finally, to economics.

A distinction needs to be made between economics as an *ideology* and economics as *a tool for rational calculation*. As an ideology, as I have said before, economics puts economic development as the central concern for development within the conventional development paradigm in which the dominating structures and the professions serving them presume to decide what the people's aspirations and needs should be. As a tool for rational calculation, economics remains an important discipline, and the quantitative calculations with which economics is chiefly concerned are also very important in sizing up some major dimensions of the economy. However, it cannot be claimed that economic calculations are necessarily the prime considerations in the life and aspirations of individuals, communities and societies.

While most economically depressed communities would want to improve their economic condition, most would also have a finite trade-off between higher economic disposition and such treasures as human dignity, indigenous cultures and self-determination if this choice were starkly put.[6] At a more fundamental level, as I have stated in my Asiatic Society lecture (Chapter 10 of this book), since the distinctive human faculty is the faculty of *creativity*, every human being must have a fundamental urge to fulfil this faculty; hence the opportunity for creative self-expression – a synthetic representation of all the above treasures – must be the primary 'basic need' of human beings as distinct from animals. Whether this is quantifiable or not, economics cannot drop this primal human need from the desired 'bundle of goods' and yet claim to be talking of the development of humans rather than of animals. The development problem is, thus, not one of delivering a material bundle of goods to the people, but of facilitating the maximum scope for the people's creativity, enabling them to create their self-chosen bundle of goods including cultural and intellectual pursuits according to their own wishes.

The landless group in Sarail about whom I talked before, and innumerable other self-mobilised grassroots groups and communities all over the globe teach us more. They talk inevitably of *solidarity* among themselves, and many such groups talk of solidarity with other economically depressed or socially oppressed people in their neighbourhoods. The economics that we have learnt – the economics of private 'utility' or, to put it more crudely, *private greed* – reflects the value orientation of dominant structures of the West whose interests the mainstream of its economics has been serving. Another economics has been serving the interests of structures seeking to exercise domination over the people in the name of 'socialism', invoking the value of *bureaucratic collectivism*. Neither of these two economics recognises the concept of solidarity which self-mobilised grassroots groups are asserting – to share and care with and for others, to work together not just as a means of enhancing private fortunes but also to develop together, to extend a helping hand to others in distress or lagging behind, and to ensure that development of some does not take place by retarding the development of others. Talk to such mobilised grassroots groups and you will find these to be natural, spontaneous values which guide their collective efforts.[7]

It is unfortunate that economics has not recognised this *rationality of solidarity*, which is observed in popular behaviour, premised as it (economics) has been either on the rationality of private greed or on the rationality of bureaucratic, hierarchically managed, collectivism. The concern for distributional equity in modern economics which seeks to temper the rationality of private greed is not a response to the popular urge for solidarity which is a value concerned with daily relations among persons rather than with the distribution of social wealth for private pursuits. On the other hand such solidarity which existed in various measures in pre-socialist societies may actually have been suppressed, if not destroyed, in certain countries by the introduction of bureaucratic socialism, with accountability to hierarchical structures which was not conducive to the forging or retaining of independent bonds of solidarity among the people.[8] While solidarity as an authentic human value has been disregarded in the economics of both capitalism and socialism, both of which have been premised on hierarchical social relations, it is unfortunate that we too have allowed ourselves to be mesmerised by such economics of exploitative structures rather than rooting our economics in the authentic values of our own people.

People's behaviour is governed both by the rationality of individual interest and the rationality of solidarity with, let us say, 'social neighbourhoods' – family, kinship group, community, etc. This solidarity is not only a means of distribution of resources but is also a *resource itself* which 'augments' the totality of resources by putting individual resources, talents, ideas, at the service of a collective as well as by stimulating in a synergic way its creative energy. If grassroots groups are exhibiting this value, it is the responsibility of economics to redefine itself to recognise, and serve, this value.

There is evidence, further, that solidarity can be stimulated and strengthened by appropriate policy and action. The relation between individual interest and solidarity is dialectical, the two combining in a unity with its tensions, a unity which may show one face relatively more than the other under specific historical circumstances, and policy and action can and should be addressed to constructing a healthy synthesis between the two. (The argument extends to the question of inter-group or inter-community relations.) In the indigenous cultural evolution of the people such a synthesis is observable in the fabric of mutual support characteristic of traditional lifestyles. The economics of both capitalism and socialism have denied and sought to destroy this synthesis by championing the motivation of, respectively, private greed and bureaucratic collectivism.

Economics as the science of the administration of scarce resources has a potential value for serving human aspirations. But its presupposition of the devaluation of culturally determined behaviour has made it alien to popular efforts for authentic development. In order to serve authentic development, economics needs to know with what values people administer their scarce resources – in particular, when the people mobilise to assert their own consensual values and take collective initiatives to promote them as part of their own concept of development – and what implications this has for the very concept of resources and for assessment of the resources at the disposal of a society.

Finally, an economics that asks people to surrender their pride in themselves and queue up on the 'poverty line' is one which serves not the people but domination over them. People (as well as nations), like the Tepitans, must feel *proud* rather than *poor*, human spirits facing challenges; none can develop otherwise. The corresponding economics, of necessity, must be the economics of pride (creativity), not the economics of poverty (consumption).

In my Asiatic Society lecture I contrasted the creativist view of development with the consumerist view (see Chapter 10). The two corresponding economics will be radically different. In the creativist view the social optimisation calculus will not be the maximisation of the time stream of consumption but of *creatively engaged labour* – i.e. 'unalienated labour' in the Marxian philosophy, a concept which was grossly abused by bureaucratic socialism. The concept of employment will differ accordingly: employment to serve hierarchical structures saps one's creativity and is to be minimised. Saving and investment (in real terms, e.g. making a tool or constructing a dam) will not be considered a sacrifice of 'consumption' but a positive way of channelling one's creativity with a direct fulfilment or 'utility' of its own, in addition to increasing the scope for creativity in the future. Such fulfilment is the ultimate act of consumption, a concept which also, therefore, calls for a review.

To construct this economics of creativity which is implicit in so many popular initiatives for collective self-development is the challenge to economists if their profession is to serve the people rather than the structures which dominate them.

Concluding comments: the role of the state

I was asked by some colleagues in Dhaka last year what the macro counterpart of such thinking is: in essence, what the role of the state is in this paradigm. I responded that they should form a 'study circle' to examine this question in interaction with popular forces. Let me, to conclude this lecture, say a few more words on the question.

The machinery of the state is constituted by structures which have enormous power over the people; such power inevitably invites bids to take them over or control them in some way or other to promote private interests. This is the central lesson of the present century's experiments with social governance through the instrument of nation states: it has systematically undermined the people's own governing abilities and imposed social orders – e.g. capitalist, 'mixed', socialist – which have predominantly served the interests of minorities in the society.

It was thought that there was a persuasive case for 'guardianship' of society at least as a 'trustee for future generations'. Alas, what most nation states are bequeathing to their future generations is not very worthy, with massive destruction of nature to satisfy present greed, mortgaging the future of societies to the humiliating mercy of foreign creditors, malignant social diseases and a chilling sense of insecurity among our children about the future that they see before them.

The role of the state, in order to facilitate and coordinate popular initiatives rather than to dominate the people, therefore, needs indeed to be redefined. But I suggest that we should not put theory too much ahead of practice. For then, as in the case of democracy and socialism, theory would be abstract and would end up being used by forces with contrary commitments as a ploy to continue domination. The task of social science at the moment is to work with popular movements, and help them to articulate their own social visions and link with each other to develop broader popular forums for such articulation. The theory of the state, and a theory of how attempts might be made to bring about a desired form of state, should emerge from such processes rather than precede them or be developed independent of them.

Notes

1. Organised by the Christophe Eckenstein Foundation, Geneva.
2. E.g. Frank and Fuentes (1988).
3. Aptly expressed by Rahnema (1990: 4).
4. Based in Toronto, Canada.
5. As against the concept of 'copyright', as part of a culture of 'knowledge capitalism' of professional researchers who research upon the people using the

people's time and sell the product for private gains.

6. Examples of such popular urges are given in my Asiatic Society lecture (Rahman, 1989b), reproduced as Chapter 10 of this book.

7. One would have thought that socialism was premised upon such solidarity. Last July I visited a village in Hungary where animation work had been initiated under the ILO's PORP programme to stimulate the villagers to get together and collectively review their experience under socialism. The animator, a professional economist of the country, reported to me that he was finding it very difficult to make the villagers come together and talk about their problems. The culture of sharing personal problems had been destroyed by 'socialism' – the hierarchical control of society had generated mistrust in the villagers of each other and fear of offending the hierarchies by horizontal dialogue.

8. For many indigenous communities the idea of solidarity has extended to *nature* as well. The concept of 'owning' and 'harnessing' natural resources is relatively recent in many societies, imposed by alien elements after colonial conquests. I was told by colleagues in Hawaii in a workshop in Honolulu in March–April 1989 that they never had the concept of 'owning nature' (e.g. land, forests, the sea). To them nature was a living being to relate with and not to exploit. The same is true of many indigenous communities all over the world. From this we may begin to see the cultural root of the destruction of nature and the ecological crisis that 'development' is causing.

References

Capra, Fritjof (1983) *The Turning Point: Science, Society and the Rising Culture*, Bantam Books.

Ekins, Paul (1990) 'Economy, ecology, society, ethics: a framework for analysis – real life economics for a living economy', Paper for the Second Annual International Conference on Socio-Economics, George Washington University, Washington, DC, USA, 16–18 March, 1990.

Esteva, Gustavo (1990) 'Towards the post-development age?' Paper presented at the Fondation Christophe Eckenstein Seminar 'Towards the Post-Development Age', Geneva, Switzerland, 5–9 March 1990.

Frank, André Gunder and Fuentes, Marta (1988) 'Nine theses on social movements', *IFDA Dossier*, No. 63, January/February 1988.

Friedman, John (1979) 'Communalist society: some principles for a positive future', *IFDA Dossier*, No. 11, September 1979.

Lindholm, Stig (1977) 'Paradigms for science and paradigms for development', Paper presented at the second meeting of the phased seminar 'From Village to the Global Order', The Dag Hammarsköld Foundation, Uppsala, October 1977.

Rahman, Md. Anisur (1989a) 'Qualitative dimensions of social development', Paper presented at the Workshop on the Evaluation of Social Development Projects and Programmes in the Third World, Swansea, Wales, UK, 19–22 September 1989. (Chapter 11 of this book.)

Rahman, Md. Anisur (1989b) 'People's self-development', National Professor Atwar Hussain Memorial Lecture, Asiatic Society of Bangladesh, Dhaka, 16

October 1989; *Journal of the Asiatic Society of Bangladesh (Hum.)* Vol. XXXIV, No. 2, December 1989. (Chapter 10 of this book.)

Rahnema, Majid (1990) 'Poverty', Paper presented at the Fondation Christophe Eckenstein Seminar 'Towards the Post-Development Age', Geneva, Switzerland, 5–9 March 1990.

Robert, Jean (1990) 'After development: the threat of disvalue', Paper presented at the Fondation Christophe Eckenstein Seminar 'Towards the Post-Development Age', Geneva, Switzerland, 5–9 March 1990.

Sachs, Wolfgang (1990) 'On the archaeology of the development idea. Six essays', Paper presented at the Christophe Eckenstein Seminar 'Towards the Post-Development Age', Geneva, Switzerland, 5–9 March 1990.

Other relevant references are given in Rahman (1989b).

Index

230   *Index*

comprehension gap, 28
conscientisation, 5, 21, 23, 33, 38, 39, 42,
    62-3, 81, 83, 154, 221; camps, 36
consciousness gap, 3, 4, 7, 190
consumerist view of development, 178,
    186-7
cooperatives, 14
corruption, 104, 107, 164
cottage industries, 14
counter-consciousness, generation of, 75
creativist view of development, 187
creativity, 68, 113, 115, 116, 135, 156, 178,
    186, 187, 209, 225; development of,
    207-8
credit, 67, 69, 70, 124, 125, 126, 132, 169,
    214, 215, 219; availability of, 66; policy
    of, 72; right to, 69; soft, 70
crop seizures, 110
Cultural Revolution, 190
culture, 221; diversity of, 210; plurality of,
    171, 174; popular, use of, 147

dams, building of, 124
data gathering, 147
de Silva, G.V.S., 4, 6
debt, burden of, 180
decision-making, right to, 122
democracy, 193; people's, 171, 210;
    socialist, 210
dependence, creation of new forms of,
    152-4
development, 6; alternative, paradigm
    for, 212-28; and women, 208;
    assessment of, 205; authentic, 119;
    centres, creation of, 128; concept of,
    134-8, 212, 214; consumerist view of,
    186-7; conventional paradigm of,
    216-17; creativist view of, 187-8;
    critique of, 213; economic, 182, 213;
    endogeneity of, 217-18; experiments,
    172; human, 68; institutional, 208;
    meaning of, 167; mobilised, dynamics
    of, 26-9; participatory rural, 141-77;
    personal, 202; philosophy of, 183-91;
    social, 202-11; sustainable, 210
dialogical method, 142, 149
dictatorship of the proletariat, 115
dignity, human, 205, 209, 218, 225;
    importance of, 182, 203
Dinajpur, villages of, 180
distant observation, 217
division of labour, intellectual, 147
divorce, 103, 106
dowry, 103-4
drought, 118, 129
dry season, use of, 123

dual transformation, 83-4

earthquakes, 218
economic improvement, 165
economic rights, 59; achievement of,
    54-6, 68-9
economic self-development, 183
economic uplift, 67
economics, 223-5; as ideology, 223; as tool
    for calculation, 223; primacy of, 217;
    re-evaluation of, 212
education, 1, 38, 87, 124, 204, 216, 219,
    222; mass, 14
Egger, Philippe, 9
emotional stimulation of communities, 18
empowerment, 205-6; elements of, 206-7
energisation, 20
epistemology, 220
external aid, dependence on, 129
external funding, 113, 132, 163, 164, 213;
    rejection of, 180
external help, 85, 119, 124, 173;
    controlled from outside, 69;
    dependence on, 64, 67, 70, 118, 169,
    170, 179, 180; rejection of, 3, 19, 44,
    81, 123

facilitation, 155-8, 173
Fals Borda, Orlando, 5, 67, 75, 81, 147
family units, creation of, 130
fertiliser, 133; traditional, 129
feudalism, 18, 33
fishing industry, 56, 60, 106
Five-Year Plan
flooding, 112, 215, 216
Fondation Abbé Gervais Rutunganga
    (FAGR) (Rwanda), 127
Food for Work programmes, 102
forest peoples, 145, 181, 204
forests, 78, 120, 121, 169, 181, 204;
    control over, 104; rights, 57;
Freire, Paulo, 5, 62, 81, 87, 92, 154, 207,
    221
funds, group, 104, 105, 110, 111, 116, 132,
    136, 153, 165, 214

Ganamillan cooperative (Bangladesh), 13
gender question, 66
Ghai, Dharam, 9
gherao, 105, 106, 109, 110
Ghose, Ajit, 9
Gorbachev, Mikhail, 192
Grameen Bank, 106, 169
grass trade, 35
grassroots movement, 170, 209, 216, 221,
    223; meaning of, 168, 174